Economics & Property

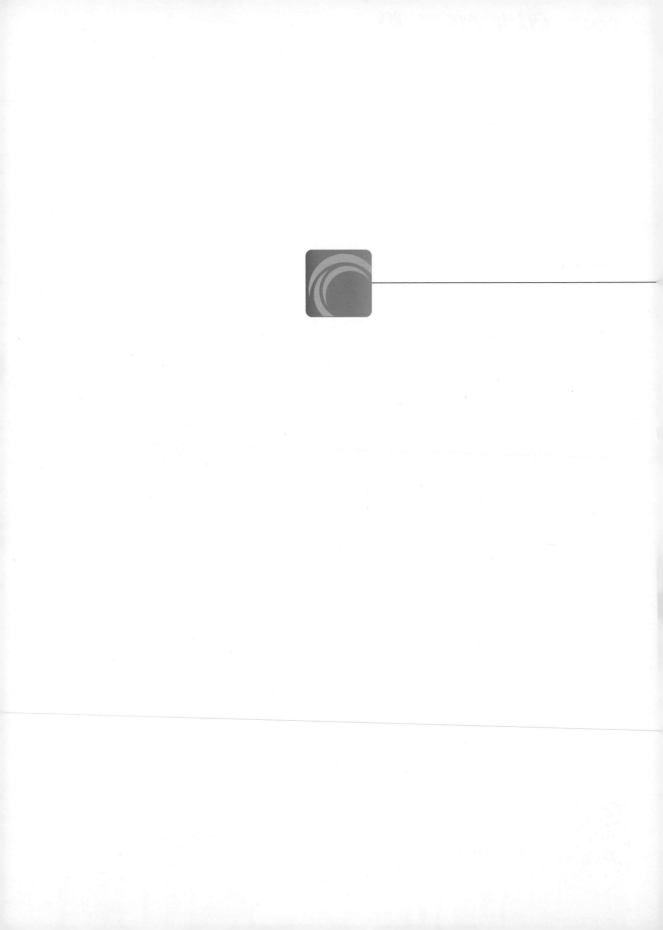

Third Edition

Economics & Property

Danny Myers

AMSTERDAM · BOSTON · HEIDELBERG · LONDON · NEW YORK · OXFORD
PARIS · SAN DIEGO · SAN FRANCISCO · SINGAPORE · SYDNEY · TOKYO
EG Books is an imprint of Elsevier

EG Books is an imprint of Elsevier
The Boulevard, Langford Lane, Kidlington, Oxford, OX5 1GB
30 Corporate Drive, Suite 400, Burlington, MA 01803, USA

First published 1994
Second edition 2006
Reprinted 2007
Third edition 2011

British Library Cataloguing-in-Publication Data
A catalogue record for this book is available from the British Library

Library of Congress Cataloging-in-Publication Data
A catalog record for this book is available from the Library of Congress

ISBN: 978-0-08-096994-7

Typeset by TNQ Books and Journals Pvt Ltd

Printed and bound in Italy

11 12 13 14 15   10 9 8 7 6 5 4 3 2 1

Contents

Preface

There have been many changes since the first edition of this text was published in 1994. For instance, the number of entry routes into the property industry has increased, as the range, and nature, of relevant three-year degree courses has broadened and one-year postgraduate conversion courses leading to a Masters qualification have been introduced. A unifying factor of these courses is the prerequisite of understanding some economics; indeed, the expectation is normally imposed by the RICS, and other professional institutions, as part of their accreditation.

The text is written to support those who come to the subject with no previous academic knowledge of economics. The key aim throughout is to explain economic concepts and make their relevance to property clear and understandable. For example, this edition commences by clarifying the role of property during the financial crisis that impacted on world-wide markets throughout the writing phase. In fact, Mervyn King (the Governor of the Bank of England) confirmed in October 2010 that the aftermath of this crisis would 'hangover' markets for many years to come. As a consequence the revisions that have been made to the text explain much about the current debate relating to the size and role of the state; and the policies that appear necessary to secure long term growth and sustainable development. Also in this new edition a greater emphasis is placed on the importance of understanding data, and the making of economic forecasts; as to fully master any subject you need to be able to use it. Therefore we strongly recommend an active approach and encourage you to take part in discussions and consider the questions that follow the readings and online resources by engaging with the language and ideas of economics between your tutors and peers.

As in previous editions several readings are provided to consolidate the content. Many of these extracts and the related resources available on the web are derived from the *Estates Gazette;* who fortunately continue to associate themselves with this title; and a specific acknowledgment should be made to Sarah Jackman, Professional and Legal Editor, who for a number of years has been a valuable support; allowing copyright permission and access to the *EGi* web material.

The list of organisations and people that contribute to developing a textbook of this nature is surprisingly lengthy and the team effort should not be taken for granted. In this instance it began with Eleanor Blow and Mike Travers, who set the project up on behalf of the publisher; next in the supply chain was the production team, managed by Renata Corbani, who organised the editing and proofing.

Alongside those working for Elsevier, I should also acknowledge the contributions made by Chris Wade who, as always, has been a great help in creating the Tables, Figures and PowerPoint slides that support this title. Thanks are also due to Dr. Melanie Dunster and Dr. Andrew Tallon for allowing me to draw on the ideas and resources that they use to support a module related to this title; their good work is explicitly evident in the *Topic Guides* that can be accessed from the web.

So although the cover might imply this is all my own work the book would clearly not have reached you without this team support, so thank you to all of them. Finally if you spot any errors or have questions then please encourage your tutor to get in contact through the book's companion site.

Danny Myers

An Introduction to Economics

Aims and Objectives

The aim of Chapter 1 is to introduce the central role of economics to understanding government policy, such as the current interest in achieving more with less; and analysing markets such as those involving property and the built environment. Specifically by the end of this chapter you should understand:

- The broad scale and nature of the subject matter
- That economics is about the allocation of scarce resources
- Property, as an asset, that makes a significant draw on these resources
- How to identify and retrieve the relevant data to support a study of property economics

---

The need for a new edition of *Economics and Property* gained momentum from the financial crisis that began in the American housing market during 2007 and took hold across Europe and beyond during 2008 to 2010. This period of instability and economic decline is thrown into sharp relief by the relative calm and continual economic growth that had set the backdrop for the previous two editions (dating back to 1994). Furthermore, a recovery from this low point would require a different regulatory approach to the risks involved in funding commercial property development and residential mortgages; as property assets represent around 75% of the loans made on behalf of the world's banks and financial institutions.

In a nutshell, what had happened in the run-up to the financial crisis was the relatively free flow of finance from banks to property owners had led to what some commentators called a credit bubble which, in turn, fuelled a bubble in property prices. The use of the term 'bubble' is interesting, and popular, because it captures the idea of something vulnerable, inflating and inflating, until it eventually bursts. Famous bubbles include the price of black tulips, which had been the subject of a bubble in Holland in the 17th century; and the value of British South Sea stock, whose bubble inflated and burst in 1720; and the more recent dotcom bubble in internet company shares that burst in 2001. The current bubble, however, represents the biggest of them all. Property prices and credit allowances had both inflated at unbelievable rates – from 2002 to 2007 – a good deal further and faster than any forecaster could imagine. Then the inevitable happened, the bubble burst. It had begun to leak here and there in 2007 and eventually burst across the world economies in 2008 – not with a pop but an all-mighty crash – as property (unlike black tulips) affects everybody.

Subsequently, thousands of customers of all major Banks and related organisations simultaneously defaulted on loans – to the tune of several trillion – and this led to the bursting of another bubble in which the people struggling to pay debts sold property assets which were rapidly falling in price. This incredulous breakdown in the financial system had serious worldwide implications for employment, productivity welfare and prices. As the press coverage at the time portrayed it: the credit crisis (and related asset bubble) had sucked the life out of the economy.

The lesson that can be learnt from this recent event is that, unless the assets of a business, a bank, an economy, or a household are sufficient to cover the liabilities of that business, bank, economy, or household, then the balance sheet is out of kilter; imbalanced, bankrupt, insolvent, *kaput* – whatever you want to call it. The reason for stressing the point is that the precise same fact applies to natural assets. But unfortunately the monetary value of ecosystems cannot be quantified as easily as the debts of financial institutions, and the imbalance is often overlooked. As environmental economists have consistently observed since the 1960s, the world should not be viewed as a gigantic economic production system, capable of supporting ever-increasing amounts of output without incurring worrying amounts of environmental debt. In short, just as a business can go through the sad experience of bankruptcy, so too can an ecosystem. Or to extend the analogy introduced above, just as the credit crisis can suck the life out of an economy, an environmental crisis could suffocate the ecosystem.

So this new edition is published during a time when financial stability and sustainability – in particular the greening of assets – are becoming increasingly important objectives of broad corporate strategy and government policy. Property economics, therefore, should not be considered as a narrow specialised entity, as it significantly contributes to these major concerns. Indeed, a case could be made to extend the title of this third edition to encompass more than just property. Retaining the ethos of the previous editions, however, property is still the 'key focus' and although more than 16 years have elapsed since the first edition, the prime objective is essentially the same: to provide a general introduction to economics for students of the built environment following courses leading to professions in surveying, planning and construction.

Obviously, new sections have been added to account for the impact of the financial crisis; and to review the progress of sustainable development in the property and construction sectors. The new edition has also provided the opportunity to revise all the data – which in economic terms, has generated many exceptional facts that need to be understood and discussed in a built environment context. In July 1999, the Urban Task Force reported to the UK government that there are four main forces responsible for transforming our towns and cities; namely technological, ecological, social and economic, and this text places economic factors squarely at the heart of these forces.

The text is structured around two basic principles:

1. Firstly, that property represents a major financial asset underpinning the wealth of every economy – Figure 1.1 highlights how the stock of built assets is distributed across the UK economy where it represents two thirds of all the wealth that society holds. This data emphasises the significance of the sector and the broad opportunities that it offers for employment in the management and development of property. (In Chapter 8, the distribution of wealth and income is discussed further.)

2. Secondly, that students using this book intend to become involved in one stage or other of a building's life cycle – as outlined in Table 1.1 (see page 4). Some may be studying for jobs that require an understanding of all stages, while others may become specialists concerned with one specific sector, such as the appraisal or marketing of new projects.

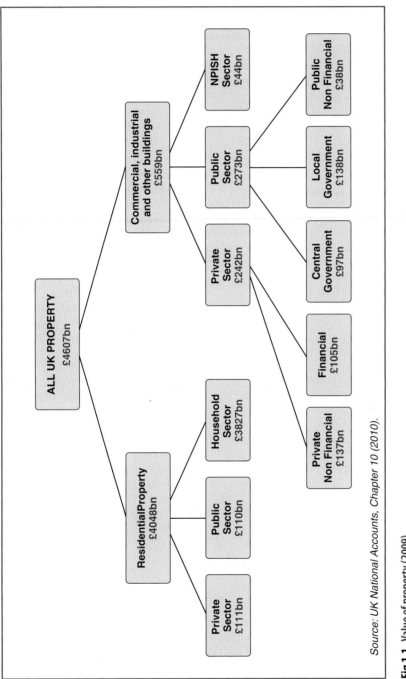

Fig 1.1 Value of property (2009)

Source: UK National Accounts, Chapter 10 (2010).

Note: NPISH – Non Profit Institutions Serving Households, such as charities, universities, churches or trade unions.

Table 1.1 The stages of a building's life cycle

Five stages	Examples of activities
Acquisition and Appraisal	Negotiate price of land; pay fees to solicitors, etc.; organise funding for land
Design and Construction	Estimate building costs; liaise with architects, quantity surveyors, engineers; funding building costs
Marketing	Organise advertising; liaise with letting agents; sale/rent of completed building
Repair and Maintenance	Monitor energy usage; facilities management; refurbishment at a later date
Redevelopment	May necessitate demolition; negotiate planning permission; satisfy building regulations

As a consequence, subsequent chapters examine the interrelationships that exist between various property markets and the broader economy. For example, Chapters 2 to 5 introduce an analysis of markets as, without some kind of market arrangement for the allocation of land, property, and construction, no modern economy could function properly. Chapters 6 to 9 look at the broader picture and the role of the government in managing a stable economy; as even though free markets, democracy and personal freedoms have gained worldwide appeal, the government still has a role to play as a regulator, policymaker, lender of last resort, and significant consumer of property services.

It is interesting to observe the relationships between property sectors and the rest of the economy as the property cycle seems to exaggerate what is happening in the economy generally. For instance, a powerful image of a booming economy is a town centre bustling with cranes and construction sites; while, at the other extreme, a strong symbol of a slump is large empty office blocks, plastered with 'to let' signs. Indeed, over the years it has been observed that property cycles show far greater amplitude than equivalent cycles in general business activity. In other words, periods of decline and expansion are far more rapid in the property and construction sectors than in the general economy. Consequently, many economists regard trends in property related sectors as a good forecasting indicator for the economy.

Clearly, a study of *Economics and Property* is more encompassing than the title might suggest; it certainly should not be regarded as a narrow discipline solely related to the study of costs or valuations. The subject matter is far wider, and one aim of the text is to demonstrate that economics affects the work of all professions within the built environment. The following section introduces the meaning and importance of some basic economic concepts. Further clarification of key terms, in bold in the text, can be found in the glossary at the back of the book.

Scarcity

Economics is about the allocation of scarce resources that have alternative uses. This is far more complex than it first appears. Many of the world's resources (factors of production) are finite, yet people have infinite wants. We are, therefore, faced with a two-pronged problem: at any point in time there is a fixed stock of resources, set against many wants. This problem is formally referred to as **scarcity**. In an attempt to reconcile this problem, economists emphasise that people must make careful choices – choices about what is made, how it is made, and for whom it is made; or in terms of property, choices about what investments are made, how they may be constructed, and whether they should be developed for rent or purchase. In fact, at its very simplest level, **economics** is 'the science of choice'.

Intriguingly, the challenges facing the surveying profession have been presented in a similar way. As the **Royal Institution of Chartered Surveyors (RICS)** point out in their publicity blurb: the world is already over populated (growing at a rate of about 240,000 people a day) and everyone needs to be fed and housed; yet the earth's resources are not infinite! According to the RICS, part of the solution to scarcity lies in the sustainable use of land and maximising the long-term value of all kinds of property. So they highlight that the choices we make affect not only how we live today, but how others will live in the future.

Resources (or Factors of Production)

Resources can be defined as the inputs used in the production of those things that we desire. Economists tend to refer to these resources as **factors of production** to emphasise that to produce any goods or services, various factors need to be combined. Therefore, the total quantity or stock of resources that an economy has determines what can be produced. To construct any property, for example, labour is required to develop a plot of land, and plant and equipment – which may be hired or purchased – is required to facilitate the process. Put in another way, land and labour are always combined with manufactured resources to produce the things demanded. These factors of production may be classified into three groups: natural, human, and manufactured resources.

Natural Resources

Land is the natural resource we think of most often as any property is dependent on the existence of a plot of land; and it is required in the production of all goods and services. To date, however, there has been a limited analysis of the supply of land, as in a purely theoretical sense it is ultimately fixed in supply and completely immobile (rural land cannot get up and move to seek better opportunities in urban areas). Land exists regardless of financial reward; its earnings are determined entirely by demand!

In the jargon of economics, the quantity of present and future available supply is completely inelastic with respect to price (this will be explained in Chapter 4). This has several economic implications; to take one current example, China is undergoing a period of unprecedented growth and the demands for property in cities such as Beijing and Shanghai are changing rapidly. In short, economic change has created new patterns of demand for land use and property in China – but the actual amount of Chinese land has not changed.

In the long run, which may be defined as the period of time firms need to adjust to price changes, it is the level of rent that signals changes to land use. In effect, rent (or price) allocates the use of land between buildings and other uses. It identifies what becomes used for transport infrastructure, for agriculture, for commercial and residential use and so on. As with every resource bought and sold in competitive markets, the highest reward determines its current use. In other words, the value of land is derived from its end use; the higher the value, the higher the rent. For example, some land is extremely fertile and commands its best value when used for agriculture, while other land is incapable of growing anything in its natural state and reaps far more value when it property is developed for sale or rent.

Human Resources

In order to produce anything, a human resource must be used. That human resource consists of the productive contributions of **labour** made by individuals who work, such as architects, estate agents, project managers, surveyors and construction workers. Whenever labour acquires training, the potential contribution to productive output increases; in other words, there is an improvement in **human capital**. Finally, there is another type of human resource; namely, entrepreneurial ability.

The **entrepreneur** is associated with the founding of new businesses, or the introduction of new products and techniques. But it means more than that. It also encompasses taking risks (possibly losing large sums of wealth on new ventures), inventing new methods of making existing goods, and generally experimenting with any type of new thinking that could lead to a monetary benefit. Without entrepreneurship, businesses would find it difficult to survive and property would not be developed. Entrepreneurship as a human resource is scarce: not everyone is willing to take risks or has the ability to make successful business decisions.

Interestingly, over the past 50 years there has been a significant number of government reports commissioned to encourage the construction industry towards a greater utilisation of its labour resource. A relevant example is the effect that good trained management can have on the efficiency of a construction project. Yet management expertise, throughout the world, seems to be one of the scarcest resources of the construction industry. The constraints imposed by inefficiencies in this sector will inadvertently affect the property developer, as cost overruns and time delays will impact on their budget and time horizon. (Property development as an example of entrepreneurial skill is explored further in Chapter 5.)

Manufactured Resources

When any form of labour or entrepreneurial skill is applied to land for agricultural or development purposes, something else is used. It may be a plough, tractor or cement mixer. In other words, land and labour are always combined with manufactured resources to produce the things that are in demand. Manufactured resources are often referred to as **capital**, and include things such as machines, buildings and tools.

A framework for classifying resources is shown in Table 1.2.

Table 1.2 Resource classification

Natural resources	Human resources	Manufactured resources
Land	Labour + entrepreneur	Capital

Economic Goods

Scarce resources produce what are called **economic goods**; and we face constant decisions about how best to use them. In direct contrast are **free goods** that do not depend upon scarce resources, as they are available from nature at a zero or free price. In short, if resources are not scarce there is no economic problem! In previous editions of this text there was a brief description of free goods and a short list of historic examples including: air for industrial uses, drinking water and even land for mining. However, as population and production has increased, the few 'free' goods that existed have become 'economic' goods; and nowadays all the previously stated, old examples come to market with a price attached; as resources become increasingly scarce. This comparison between 'economic' and 'free' goods helps to clarify the subject matter of economics and identify the essence of most formal definitions.

> **Definition**
>
> Economics is the study of how individuals and societies choose between the alternative uses of limited resources to satisfy unlimited wants.

Opportunity Cost

Analytically, it is necessary to consider carefully the definition(s) of economics as, by implication, every individual has competing wants but cannot satisfy all of them given limited resources. Therefore, choices must be made, and choosing just one thing inevitably means that another possible opportunity has been missed, lost or foregone. To highlight this dilemma, economists refer to the concept of **opportunity cost**.

> **Definition**
>
> Opportunity cost is the value of the alternative that is foregone when a particular activity is chosen.

In other words, economics emphasises how every want that ends up being satisfied results in some other want, or wants, remaining unsatisfied. Adam Smith, who wrote the first treatise of economics *The Wealth of Nations* (published in 1776) discussed opportunity cost in the context of whether a country should produce guns or butter. Today the choice is between more esoteric items and the alternatives have increased tenfold; for each decision made there is a trade-off between one use of a resource and several alternative uses.

Investment

In mainstream economic texts the property sector is not usually referred to. It does, however, represent a major form of investment; directly as residential or commercial property (as defined on page XXX) and indirectly via institutional funds and instruments.

From a purely economic perspective, **investment** refers to additions to productive capacity; activity that makes use of resources today in such a way that they allow for greater production in the future. For example, when a business puts funds into new equipment or develops a new factory, it is making an investment to increase its capacity in the future.

Two meanings of investment are usually distinguished: net and replacement. Replacement investment corresponds to depreciation and is determined by the rate at which capital wears out and net investment represents new additions to capital stock. The former is relatively constant as it is determined by time, but the latter is related to changes in economic activity.

In terms of property investment, these two categories can be associated with: the repair and maintenance of existing property assets, and new additions to property being let or sold for the first time. This distinction is useful as it serves to explain why the property sector is prone to fluctuate more than other sectors. Investment expenditure on maintenance and repairs will be fairly constant, whereas new additions will be one-offs to support expected changes to overall activity. For example, if a retail or manufacturing group manages £100 million pounds worth of property assets, they may spend a percentage of that (say 5%) each year on maintenance (£5,000,000). If economic activity in their sector rises, however, they will need to both maintain their existing property and increase their capacity for sales or manufacture by adding to the stock of property assets.

This example might be easier to understand from the converse position where economic activity decreases and, as a result, the firm releases or sells some of its property stock; in effect, it can meet the present level of demand with zero property investment. As a consequence, property investment tends to alter with greater amplitude than other sectors.

From a property perspective, however, it might be useful to broaden these traditional economic interpretations of investment to include the ownership of any asset that might enhance the flow of income in the future. This is because the relative returns made on other investments such as government bonds, company shares, or general business activities, might be more profitable. Investment in property must always be seen as an opportunity cost. In short, it is not possible to understand property in isolation; it is essential to recognise that it competes as an investment with other assets. Some of the interactions between property markets and the broader economy are discussed further in Chapter 7.

Chapter Summary 1.1

- The basis of economics emerges from the concepts of scarcity and opportunity costs. In very general terms, it is the study of how choices are made, and the subject matter relates to many stages of a building's life cycle.
- Scarce resources – such as land, labour, capital, and entrepreneurship – are required to produce any economic good or service.
- Scarcity is a two-sided concept; with competing wants on one side set against limited resources on the other.
- Economic goods are those demanded, but not directly obtainable from nature to the extent desired.
- The use of every resource involves an opportunity cost because an alternative use is sacrificed.
- Investment includes expenditure on repair and maintenance and new additions to stock. These are made primarily to generate income streams in the future.

Methodology

An important aim of this introductory chapter is to explain what economics of the built environment is about, so apart from identifying the basic concepts, the methods employed by economists also need to be reviewed; as the methodology of an academic discipline says a lot about the nature of the subject. In general terms, economics is a social science and it attempts to adopt the same kind of value-free approach as other sciences. In common with biology, physics and chemistry, therefore, economics uses **models** or theories; and empirical evidence is sought to validate the analysis.

Models can take on various forms such as verbal statements, numerical tables, and graphs and, at levels beyond this text, mathematical equations.

The type of assumptions made in economic models include generalised characteristics such as: all individuals behave in a rational manner; that information is freely available; that supply responds to demand; that prices adjust quickly; that investors seek to maximise profits, and so on. The model subsequently forms a reference point for asking 'what if' questions about the real world. The fact that the simplifying assumptions may not apply still throws light on to the central issues of the subject. For example, students may be expected to commence their course by completing an assignment based on

Definition

Economic models are simplified representations of the real world, based on generalised assumptions, to understand, explain and predict economic phenomena.

a theoretical economic model of competition in a specific marketplace. This provides a simple introduction to the economic framework and the opportunity to demonstrate how property markets deviate or reflect this reference point. In short, the model provides a starting point – it enables us to proceed.

Microeconomics and Macroeconomics

Textbooks of Economics are typically divided into two types of analysis: **microeconomics** and **macroeconomics**.

One way to understand the distinction between these two approaches is to consider some generalised examples. Microeconomics is concerned with determining how prices, values and rents emerge and change, and how firms respond. It involves the examination of the effects of new taxes and government incentives, the characteristics of demand, determination of a firm's profit, and so on. In other words, it tries to understand the economic motives of individuals – such as landowners, developers, builders, occupiers and investors. This diverse set of interests that represent the property market is fragmented and at times adversarial; but microeconomic analysis works on the basis that we can generalise about the behaviour of these parties. This type of analysis is introduced in Chapter 2 and we look at the theory of demand and the theory of supply in Chapters 3 and 4, respectively. The nature of specific markets for development, construction and occupation are then considered in greater detail in Chapter 5.

In contrast, macroeconomics is concerned with the outcome of *all* decisions made in the economy as a whole; taking account of the purchases made by all consumers, total capital investments made by businesses, the goods and services procured by central and local government and the balance of trade between imports and exports. In short, macroeconomics deals with aggregates or totals; analysing the overall level of prices, output and employment. Although at present there is a distinct lack of cohesive thinking about the overall role of property and how it could better serve the economic fabric of society, a broad understanding of the economy is central to anyone wishing to participate in the property world. Macroeconomics forms the basis of Chapters 7 and 8.

Making a distinction between micro and macroeconomics is arbitrary, and trying to identify the point in the analysis where the actions of a number of firms cease to be microeconomics and transfer over to macroeconomics is a futile exercise. For example, the total number of bankruptcies is important in describing the macroeconomic scene, but it does not provide a complete picture of every company in the economy. Even during the worst recession some firms will be performing well and increasing turnover; even though the aggregate bankruptcy data may suggest that most firms are doing badly. For example, during the run-up to Christmas 2009, high street retailers were said to suffer some historically poor results, yet Carphone Warehouse and Mothercare both bucked the trend and increased sales during the same period.

This is not stated to undermine the importance of either approach; the aim is quite the contrary. It demonstrates that an understanding of property sectors requires both micro and macroeconomic approaches, as effective property management necessitates an assessment of the current and future macroeconomic conditions and an insight into the related markets. For example, if interest rates rise sharply, consumer spending tends to decline and the demand for residential, retail and manufacturing property reduces and, in some instances, may even become surplus to requirements. Foreseeing these general cyclical turns is part of becoming a successful property entrepreneur; being able to recognise the exceptions to the rule is even more promising!

> **Definition**
>
> Microeconomics is the study of how individuals and firms allocate scarce resources.

> **Definition**
>
> Macroeconomics is the study of economy-wide phenomena resulting from all decision-making in an economy.

The Built Environment

The built environment is made up of various types of property (residential, commercial, industrial, etc.); linked by infrastructure (sewers, canals, roads, tunnels, etc.) and separated by spaces in between (parks, woods, playing fields, landscaped areas, squares, etc.). The professions shaping and creating this environment tend to be fragmented by function and culture. For example, there are approximately 100,000 registered surveyors in the UK and their professions are broken down into an array of specialist areas, such as building surveying, construction, facilities management, planning and development, project management, quantity surveying, valuation, and even, waste management. A recurring role with respect to economics is the surveyor's contribution to transactions; the buying and selling of property for occupation or investment; the giving of financial advice regarding the state of the market and/or the economy, and so on. In fact, much of their work can be broken down into technical or economic aspects; surveyors specialising in the latter are often referred to as 'agents'. Another form of categorisation may crudely divide the participants into different stages of the process and it is common to distinguish between those involved in development and those involved in the related stages of investment, construction and management.

Official economic statistics generally distinguish between construction and property activity: construction sector data tends to relate to the value-added activity of firms that construct buildings and infrastructure. Property sector data, on the other hand, specifically relates to the development, management, letting, buying and selling of commercial or residential property. The standard industrial classification (SIC) system, which historically forms the basis of most definitions, restricts the construction industry to include firms that are involved with building and civil engineering. This embraces a range of 'on-site' activities including those relating to infrastructure, new construction, repair, maintenance and (eventually) demolition. By comparison, a property industry is never clearly defined although 'real estate' is specified. This classifies a range of 'office based' business activities, dealing broadly with the development, management and marketing of commercial or residential property; rather oddly, this SIC classification also includes architecture and engineering! Furthermore, academics researching and writing within these specialist areas also tend to concentrate on either construction or property; the paradigms of each are kept separate. The implications of these fragmented and diverse sectors are discussed further in Chapters 5 and 9.

The Construction Sector

Table 1.3 indicates the type of work classified as construction activity and shows the associated monetary values in 2006 and 2008 for Great Britain. Repair and maintenance are clearly of major importance as they comprise nearly 50% of the total annual activity – this includes work carried out on houses, infrastructure and commercial buildings. On closer scrutiny, it is also evident that government departments and their agencies are significant clients of the construction industry. As Table 1.3 shows, official statistics draw a distinction between public and private sector activity. The public sector includes everything that is owned or funded by national or local governments such as: infrastructure, the National Health Service, schools, sports and leisure facilities, the police and fire services. The public sector accounts for at least 30% of construction industry turnover. Obviously this includes a range of contracts: varying in size from £10,000 for the maintenance of a small flood defence scheme to £500m to construct a new British Library. Private sector

Table 1.3 Value of construction output in Great Britain

Type of work	£ million 2006	£ million 2008
Infrastructure	6,532	7,735
Housing-Public	3,442	3,967
private	19,572	16,268
Public non-residential	9,939	12,287
Private industrial	4,888	4,124
Private commercial	20,138	23,448
Repair and maintenance	49,058	55,755
Total (of all work)	113,569	123,584

activity includes the construction of shops, garages, offices, houses and privately funded schools and hospitals.

The percentage of public sector work in the UK has fallen considerably since 1980, as many of the activities traditionally in the public domain have been privatised; see Chapter 2, especially Table 2.2. For example, in the UK, privately owned utilities and services such as gas, electricity, water supply, telecommunications and railways were previously state owned activities. More recently, the private sector has been given a greater role in the funding, building, maintenance and management of public facilities such as hospitals, schools, prisons and roads. In these **public private partnerships**, the private sector organises the funds and manages the risks, while the public sector specifies the level of service required and ultimately owns the assets – as they are commonly returned to public ownership after 10, 15 or 25 years. The important point for our purposes is that expenditure on the construction of public facilities – such as new schools and hospitals – is increasingly classified as private sector expenditure in the official data.

The Property Sector

Property can be classified into two broad sectors: commercial and residential. As a general rule of thumb, the commercial market is of interest to institutional investors seeking profit, and the residential market is the concern of individual investors seeking utility.

The Commercial Sector

Commercial property can be divided into four categories. The most obvious are office buildings and business parks. Less obvious are the industrial estates and traditional warehouses that formed an important part of the industrial age. Leisure outlets, such as hotels, pubs and cinemas, represent an increasing proportion of commercial property. And finally, but by no means least important, are retail properties, such as shopping centres, shops, supermarkets and department stores. These high street outlets represent the most significant proportion of the commercial sector.

The majority of commercial property development in the UK occurs for investment purposes insofar as more than 50% of these properties are built with no specific tenant in mind. In fact, much of the UK commercial property market is characterised by a separation of occupation and ownership. Commercial property is leased to occupiers (tenants) by investors (landlords). The freehold is owned by the investor who, in return for the capital outlay (purchase price), receives an income in the form of rent from the occupier. So, whereas the occupier is concerned with the property and its contribution to the business, the investor is concerned with the rate of return on the investment. Often requirements of the investor and occupier conflict so the developer acts as an arbiter, hopefully producing a property attractive to both parties. It is important to note that this situation will continue as long as occupiers in the commercial market prefer to rent rather than own property.

One of the key attributes of a commercial property developer is the ability to see things from both the occupier's and investor's point of view. These relationships are explored further in Chapter 5. (For a detailed analysis of the commercial market that takes into account the history of relationships between occupiers, developers and investors, the student might wish to read *Property and the Office Economy* by Rob Harris. See references to further reading for full details.)

The Residential Sector

Residential property can also be divided into four sub-categories. The majority of homes in the UK are of interest to the individual investor – more commonly referred to as the owner-occupier. A far less significant number (around 10% of the housing stock) represent investment property purchased to rent out to tenants. At present, more than 70% of this rented stock is run by small private landlords managing one or two properties. In the foreseeable future, the rental residential sector may expand as institutional funds via **Real Estate Investment Trusts (REITS)** are developed. (UK investment funds, however, traditionally favour commercial property.) Finally, there are two types of residential investment supported by the public sector: property rented from a local authority and property rented from **registered social landlords**. Together, this latter group provides social housing to about 20% of UK households. (More details on the residential sector are stated in Table 2.1, Chapter 3 and tutorial reading number 2.) For those that want a fuller account of the distribution of resources to housing in the UK they can refer to *Housing, Markets and Policy*, edited by Malpass and Rowlands. Their text draws on authoritative contributions from the main academics in UK housing studies over the last 40 years, and their combined analysis suggests that the housing system and policy that we have today can be traced back to the 1970s. For full bibliographical details, see references to further reading at the close of the text.

Property Sector Review

Table 1.4 summarises the way that commercial and residential sectors are typically divided, and the bottom line indicates the importance of each sector in terms of the number of transactions (the actual proportion allocated to each sector has been estimated by the author). Clearly, the number of transactions in the residential sector far exceeds the number for commercial property. In fact, the annual ratio is approximately 10:1; so in a typical year when one and a half million residential properties might exchange hands, there would be approximately 150,000 transactions in the commercial property market (but the actual numbers vary according to the state of the economy and, as a consequence, in 2009 there were relatively fewer transactions in all markets). In Table 1.4 the residential transactions represent a specific address bought or sold for any one of the forms of tenure, and the number is based on the **particulars delivered** to the land registry. A commercial transaction, however, may represent several properties as it could be a collection of buildings, such as a business park or shopping centre; the way the transactions are recorded are consequently somewhat *ad hoc*; the information presented here is based on returns relating to stamp duty land tax.

A further distinction between these two property sectors relates to the development process. Residential property is usually speculatively developed, in the sense that it is built ('on spec') without a specific purchaser (or tenant)

Table 1.4 Annual number of property transactions in the UK, 2009

Commercial property	Number of transactions	Residential property	Number of transactions
Office buildings	30,800	Owner-occupied	600,600
Retail properties	30,800	Private sector for rent	85,800
Leisure outlets	8,800	Local authority for rent	858,000
Industrial units (including warehouses)	17,600	Registered social landlord	85,800
Total	88,000	Total	858,000

being identified. Whereas, commercial property is increasingly developed for a named tenant, i.e. it is 'pre-let' (for sale or rent), to a specific occupier.

Sources of Data

Most of the key sources of economic data are published by the **Office for National Statistics (ONS)** and the website (*www.ons.gov.uk*) provides a comprehensive range of UK official statistics, including economic and social indicators. Census data can also be searched here by postcodes, but this will only be correct up until 2001, the date of the last census collection. The Bank of England (*www.bankofengland.co.uk*) and the Treasury (*www.hm-treasury.gov.uk*) also produce a wealth of statistical records relating to economic performance and property related issues.

For specific information relating to construction, the key source in the UK is the *Construction Statistics Annual.* This publication is compiled by the Department for Business Innovation and Skills (BIS), but since July 2007 has become the responsibility of the ONS. A new edition is published each year and it can be freely accessed from the BIS and ONS websites. The publication amalgamates all construction statistics produced by central and local government, trade associations and the private sector. It has an appendix that provides detailed notes on methodology and definitions to clarify the tables and figures. There is also a comprehensive subject index. Overall it manages to portray a broad picture of the UK construction industry through the last decade, together with some international comparisons. (The value of construction output shown in Table 1.3 was derived from the 2009 edition of the *Construction Statistics Annual*.) As with most economic data there is always a time lag, so the 2009 edition only presents data up until 2008. Consequently, data quoted in a textbook can easily appear out of date before it even goes to print. It is important therefore, that you develop the confidence to research data for yourself – and this is one of the reasons for citing websites across these pages.

The two government organisations with the most complete knowledge of property dealings in England and Wales are Her Majesty's Revenue and Customs Valuation Office (*www.voa.gov.uk*) and the Land Registry (*www.land registry.gov.uk*). Both of these agencies have recently broadened their services to provide comprehensive sets of data. For example, the Land Registry website reports on house prices and the number of transactions on a quarterly basis and postcode data enables specific sites to be investigated. Much of this information feeds through to official data on housing, which is available through the DCLG website (*www.communities.gov.uk*).

By comparison, the information relating to commercial property is not as comprehensive; and sample data make up the bulk of what is available. The leading real estate information business is the **Investment Property Databank (IPD)**. This organisation has the largest sample comprising more than 11,000 commercial properties, valued at £115 billion at the end of 2009; this represents approximately 75% of the total commercial property investment market. This is a privately run business but data is available from their website (*www.ipd.com*) or a University library. A limited amount of data comparing the value and number of transactions across the UK commercial property sector categorising different types of investors, including occupiers, is collated by an agent-sponsored information service called Property Data. Again, free access is relatively limited but it might be worth searching for past data, the web address is *www.propertydata.com*.

Comparisons are sometimes drawn between the information available on commercial property and the stock market. The latter has similarities as agents act on the client's behalf, but the market benefits from quick, reliable, comprehensive data as all transactions are recorded and made available via a computerised network. Not surprisingly, therefore, the quality of property data has caused a lack of confidence by fund managers and such like, who frequently regard real estate as the poor relation of other investment markets. For example, data relating to commercial property is often difficult to disaggregate. Also, data weaknesses are regarded as an obstacle to efficient management of the macroeconomy. Even if a miracle occurred, and comprehensive and complete sets of property data were freely available to all participants in the market, the evidence by its very nature will be retrospective. Indeed, the information service *Property Data* observes a time lag of up to six months between the completion of a transaction and its release into the public domain.

The real issue is market expectations. This requires the development of forecasting techniques and, in this regard, surveyors will always be dependent on their own value judgments, personal data records and overall experience. Students, however, have to rely on anecdotal data gleaned from the *Estates Gazette* where much of the commercial property and land coming to the market is advertised and property related news is reviewed in the editorial pages. In terms of data, there is a weekly feature that tracks the financial performance of market sectors (including stocks and shares). These financial comparisons are drawn together from various sources, including several of those referred to above.

Finally, before closing Chapter 1, we should reiterate the importance of acquiring confidence in data retrieval, as being able to access comprehensive, up-to-date, reliable and relevant data, is really a complimentary aspect of studying property economics.

Chapter Summary **1.2**

- Microeconomics involves the study of individual economic decision-making.
- Macroeconomics involves the broader study of economic activity as a whole.
- Modern economic analysis involves blending micro and macro approaches together. Both depend on data to make the approach scientific (empirical).
- Sectors of the built environment may be classified in many ways. Ranging from construction through to commercial and residential property.
- Commercial markets tend to be of interest to a broad range of institutional investors supplying property for profit and the residential market is more the concern of individual investors seeking shelter from the elements.
- To understand property economics the availability of comprehensive and reliable information is most beneficial. There are many sets of data that can be used to help complete the picture, namely: official government data (including statistics collated on construction) and specialised data relating to commercial property and housing.

Economic Systems of Resource Allocation

2

Summaries to Review

Scarcity (1.1)
Scarce Resources (1.2)

Aims and Objectives

This chapter explains the development of the economic system used by most of the world's economies; and discusses the current preference for reducing the scale of the state. To support the analysis we introduce aspects of markets for housing and infrastructure. Specifically by the end of this chapter you should understand:

- Three main approaches to allocating resources and their respective characteristics
- How the process of transition towards a market economy is supported by deregulation and privatisation
- The importance of achieving efficiency and equity
- How to express market forces using a basic supply and demand diagram
- The possibility of market failure

The problem of **resource allocation** is universal as every nation has to tackle the issue of determining *what* is produced, *how* it's produced and *for whom* goods and services are produced. In short, the economist studies: who gets what (when) and how. The answers they discover vary around the world according to the **economic system** in use. In Figure 2.1 we begin the explanation by introducing two idealised systems: the **free market model** and the **centrally planned model**.

Fig 2.1 A spectrum of economic systems

On the extreme right-hand side of the diagram is the free market model, and on the extreme left-hand side, the centrally planned model. Cuba is a country whose system closely resembles the centrally planned model. At the other extreme is the USA, which comes close to the free market model. In between are the mixed economies of the remaining nations of the world.

The Free Market Model

The free market system is typified by limited government involvement in the economy, coupled with private ownership of the means of production. In effect, the system is decentralised as individuals pursue their own self-interest without government intervention. (The system may also be described as a market or capitalist economy.)

An important feature of such a system is **free enterprise**. This exists when private individuals are allowed to obtain resources, to organise those resources, and to sell the resulting product in any way they choose. Neither the government nor other producers can create obstacles or restrictions to block those in business from seeking profit by purchasing inputs and selling outputs.

Additionally, all members of the economy are free to choose what to do. Workers may enter any line of work for which they are qualified and consumers may buy the goods and services that they feel are best for them. The ultimate voter in a free market, capitalist system is the consumer, who votes with pounds and decides which product 'candidates' will survive. Economists refer to this as **consumer sovereignty** as the final purchaser of products and services determines what is produced – and, therefore, 'rules' the market.

Another central feature of the free market economy is the **price mechanism**. Prices are used to signal the value of individual resources, acting as a kind of guidepost which resource owners (producers and consumers) refer to when they make choices. The flowchart in Figure 2.2 suggests how the price mechanism works. For example, when supply exceeds demand, a price change occurs which brings the producers and consumers into harmony. This is precisely what happens during the January sales; the price of stock that has not been previously sold is reduced to the point where demand is sufficient to clear the market. Conversely, when demand exceeds supply, the price of the goods in question will rise until the market is in balance. This may be seen at a property auction where, to begin with, several buyers compete for a specific property. Together they bid the price up, until finally there is only one interested party prepared to pay the final purchase price to the **vendor**.

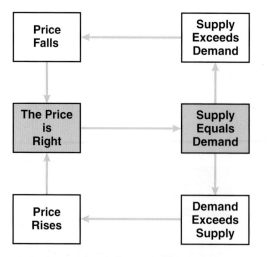

Fig 2.2 Flowchart of the price mechanism

For the price mechanism to function properly it is essential that all resources are owned privately, so they can move freely between competing uses.

Prices, therefore, are seen to generate signals in all markets (including factor markets). They provide information, they affect incentives and they enable buyers and sellers to express opinions. And, provided that prices are allowed to change freely, markets will always tend towards equilibrium, where there is neither excess demand nor excess supply.

The What? How? For Whom? In the Free Market Model

What   In a free market economy, consumers ultimately determine what will be produced by their pattern of spending (their voting in the marketplace). As far as producers are concerned, their decisions about what goods to produce are determined by the search for profits.

How   Since resources can substitute for one another in the production process, the free market system must decide how to produce a commodity once society votes for it. Producers will be guided (by the discipline of the marketplace) to combine resources in the cheapest possible way to achieve a particular standard or quality. Those firms that combine resources in the most efficient manner will earn the highest profits and force losses on their competitors. Competitors will be driven out of business or forced to combine resources in the same way as the profit-makers.

For whom   The 'for whom' question is concerned with the distribution of goods after production. How is the pie divided? In a free market economy, production and distribution are closely linked, because incomes are generated as goods are produced. People get paid according to their productivity; that is, a person's income reflects the value that the market system places on that person's resources. Since income largely determines one's share of the output 'pie', what people get out of the free market economy is based on what they put into it.

The Centrally Planned Model

A centrally planned system (also referred to as a command economy) is typically characterised by a dominant government sector, coupled with the common ownership of resources. In other words, there is a central planning authority that takes the place of the price mechanism in allocating resources. The precise nature of a central planning authority depends upon the political system governing the economy. Indeed, it is worth noting that the terms 'socialist' and 'communist' properly refer to political systems and not economic systems. In fact, a right-wing dictatorship could operate a centrally planned economic system as effectively as a left-wing commune.

The common motivation for having a centrally planned system is the conviction that government commands are more likely to produce the 'right' mix of output; because state planners have the opportunity to direct resources to society's most pressing needs. As the respected American economist J.K. Galbraith once observed, one of the few saving graces of the disintegrating communist economies is that nearly everyone has some kind of home, whereas many capitalist economies have not yet resolved the problem of providing affordable housing for the poor.

The flow diagram in Figure 2.3 outlines what a centrally planned system might involve. The three-stage process shown is a simplification of a bureaucratic reality. For instance, at stage one, various planning committees would exist to consider specific economic sectors and/or geographic areas. Similarly, at stage two, production targets and wages would be 'negotiated' with factory officials, workers, management and others involved in the chain

Stage 1

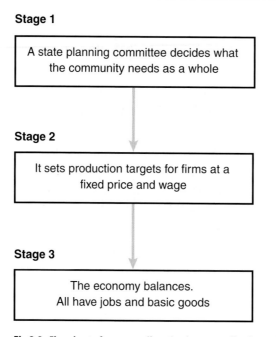

Stage 2

Stage 3

Fig 2.3 Flowchart of resource allocation in a centrally planned (model) economy

In a pure command economy the resources need to be centrally owned and controlled.

of production. Finally, by stage three, the plans often become fraught with many difficulties, to the extent that there may be shortages and/or surpluses.

In today's market driven, global culture, such a system may seem hard to imagine, but it was used for more than 60 years from 1928 onwards when Stalin introduced Russia's first Five-Year Plan. It was also the system of resource allocation adopted in the People's Republic of China, after its revolution in 1949. Following the death of the revolutionary leader Mao Tsetung, the economic reforms of 1978 began the process of opening up trade links and allowing competition to operate. China is now fast becoming the workshop of the world and the Chinese clearly embrace the market system – although they still regard themselves as socialist.

As a consequence, most of the large, previously centrally planned, nation state economies are now involved in a transition towards market-oriented systems. Transition, however, is not without its problems; much is still influenced by the old regime of the centrally controlled plan. Anecdotal evidence suggests that there is in fact some kind of culture shock (including corrupt responses) as the 'visible hand' of the command economy is replaced by the subtle signals of the 'invisible hand' of the free market.

The What? How? For Whom? In the Centrally Planned Model

What   In a centrally planned economy, the collective preference and wisdom of the central planners ultimately determines what is produced.

How   The central planners decide on the methods of production. This means that they need to know how many resources to allocate to each industry, many of which interrelate.

For whom   The relative rewards that people receive are set by the central planners rather than the market, and as a result there is a greater opportunity to achieve equality between people.

The Mixed Economy

The two economic systems introduced in this chapter do not exist in a pure form. The economic models used are simplified representations of the real world. In practice, most economic systems are far more complex; countries are neither purely free market nor purely planned. In the complex setting of everyday life, all nations have a **mixed economy**. Economists do not, therefore, study systems in which the activities of consumers and producers interact freely through a market or simply according to government plans. They study systems that contain mixtures of private decision-making and central organisation; the private decisions, made in response to market forces, exist alongside the centralised controls of state legislation and economic plans.

One way of comparing the range of economic systems that exist in the world is to imagine them located on a wide spectrum – similar to that in Figure 2.1. In theory, each nation could be positioned according to the proportion of resources owned by the public and private sectors. Nations that have a high proportion of government-owned resources would be located close to the centrally planned model, and those dominated by privately owned resources would be located at the other extreme near to the free market model. Such an exercise illustrates that all economies of the real world are mixed economies; some may come close to one or other of the economic models, but no nation fits precisely into the pure planned or pure free market category. During the last three decades there has been considerable movement along the spectrum. Indeed, we cannot confidently pinpoint the position of any country in Figure 2.1, because as soon as economies are located, their position becomes out-of-date.

In general terms the **transition economies**, such as China and the eastern European states of the former Soviet Union, have slowly shifted away from the pure centrally planned model, while many other economies have moved closer towards the free market model under the influence of **privatisation** and **deregulation**. In other words, the mix of public sector and private sector activity has varied over time as the main political parties have adopted differing philosophies towards state intervention.

In the UK there have been two distinct periods of transition towards the market. The first followed the 1979 UK election when the Conservatives, under the leadership of Margaret Thatcher, made a determined effort to encourage the market to become the dominant means of allocating resources. The second period of transition followed the 2010 election when the Conservatives and Liberal Democrats formed a coalition government, under the leadership of David Cameron, and on taking office made significant cuts to public spending, to encourage efficiency and private enterprise. In both instances the political rhetoric employed supported a shrinking of the state; based on sharp distinctions between the inefficiency of a centralised and bureaucratic welfare state and the market efficiency of private enterprise. In other words, the thrust of the argument was based on the virtues of a free market system that promoted freedom, choice, and individual incentives to make a profit and generally increase efficiency.

From Shrinking State to Expanding Market

A common aim of contemporary periods of economic transition has been to move society away from a reliance on centralised state control, towards systems that favour private market-based incentives; and in many instances the justification is simply because it costs the state far less money! Several historic and relevant examples can be drawn from policy questions relating to the allocation of resources across the built environment; and to exemplify the process we look at the transition in housing policy and infrastructure funding that has occurred since 1979.

Housing Policy (1979 to 2009)

A specific objective of the government that took office more than thirty years ago, in 1979, was to make sure that there was a far greater emphasis on the market to allocate housing resources by widening owner occupation and extending the opportunity to rent from the private sector. Indeed, Margaret Thatcher (the incoming Prime Minister at the time) is renowned for her belief that a 'property owning democracy' lay at the heart of a market economy. To support these beliefs, the 1980 Housing Act gave council tenants the **right to buy** their flats and houses; and the 1986 Housing and Planning Act permitted local authorities to transfer their housing stock to private landlords. To promote these Acts of Parliament, various discount schemes were introduced to provide a financial incentive to private ownership. For example, the average price for a discounted council property purchased between 1970 and 1986 was £15,000 – which accounted for a total government discount (subsidy) of £6 billion. Alongside these generous discounts were the tax benefits that used to support those with a mortgage, namely **Mortgage Interest Tax Relief (MITR)**. This scheme was gradually reduced from 1990 onwards until it was phased out in 2000, but the subsidy it provided had added a definite incentive to encourage people into the housing market throughout the period in question.

As a consequence, the current allocation of housing resources is now largely market determined. As Table 2.1 indicates, the owner-occupied and private rented sectors now represent more than 80% of the housing stock; while **social housing**, supported by government subsidy, has decreased to less than 20%. This shift is quite phenomenal when one acknowledges the total numbers these proportions represent. For instance, in 1979 there were slightly more than 6.5 million dwellings provided by local authorities, but by 2007 only 2.5 million remained. The previous local authority tenants had

Table 2.1 Stock of dwellings in UK by tenure

Tenure	1979		2007	
	Thousands	(%)	Thousands	(%)
Owner-occupied	11,638	54.8	18,527	69.5
Rented privately	2,915	13.7	3,303	12.4
Rented from local authorities	6,700	31.5	2,585	9.7
Rented from registered social landlords			2,238	8.4
Total dwellings	21.253	100	26,653	100

Source: Adapted from DCLG, Housing Statistics.

transferred to the private sector (about 2 million had become owner-occupiers and about 2 million had been involved in block transfers to **registered social landlords**).

The origins of social housing lie in the idea that governments should pay a subsidy towards housing to make up for the shortage of accommodation available to low-income families. However, as our example makes clear, in the UK from 1979 onwards both Conservative and Labour governments favoured free market policies. As a consequence, much of the local authority housing stock has either been transferred to housing associations to allocate, manage and maintain, or sold to tenants, thereby transferring stock to the owner-occupied sector. A similar process has occurred in Australia, Cuba, Italy, Holland and the United States where privatisation of the social housing stock has also been a key feature favouring the market.

Infrastructure Policy (1979 to 2009)

During the Conservative's second and third term of office, the privatisation programme really took off. Alongside the sale of council houses, other state assets were transferred from the public sector to the market sector. In fact, more than 50 state corporations were sold off between 1984 and 1996; examples of the 'key' industries that were privatised are listed in Table 2.2. This large-scale UK privatisation programme prompted similar schemes in more than 100 other countries.

Table 2.2 UK privatisation programme

The list identifies the sales of the 'commanding heights' of the economy such as gas, water, electricity and telecommunication.

Date	Company
1984	British Telecom
1986	British Gas
1987	British Airways
	British Airport Authority
1988	British Steel
1989	Water Companies
1990	Electricity Companies
1991	Generating Companies
1994	Coal Board
1996	British Rail

Source: HM Treasury.

In fact, worldwide the private sector share of investment in infrastructures has significantly increased with more than US$1.5 trillion being raised through the privatisation of utilities, such as power supply, transport, telecommunications and oil facilities. A related trend, which has witnessed the transfer of even more private funds to traditional government areas, is the emergence of **public–private partnerships**. These relatively new business models offer opportunities for private capital and expertise to be used to support public service goals. There are literally hundreds of examples worldwide including many large-scale projects ranging from major road building schemes, bridges and metro systems to public sector real estate such as schools, hospitals and government offices. These partnerships are explored further in Chapter 5.

Obviously the transfer of economic resources from the public sector to the market sector changes the character of an economy; as competition and private ownership are considered to be powerful drivers of economic efficiency, innovation and choice. To consider the effect just in the UK, more than six million people now own shares in privatised companies, more than one million jobs have been transferred out of the public sector, more than £100 billion has poured into Treasury funds, and 1995 to 2007 represented a period of continuous economic growth.

At present, it appears that all the major political parties in Britain are strongly in favour of extending the principles of the market and the political divide has blurred. In fact, there is an economic consensus based on market forces emerging across the globe and this has changed the political climate both at home and abroad. For the foreseeable future, therefore, there will be an increasing reliance on unregulated private actions by individuals and companies to resolve the difficult questions of allocating resources.

Chapter Summary 2.2

- In reality all economies are mixed economies, since elements of private markets and state coexist in all nations.
- It is the degree of market orientation, or of state intervention, that distinguishes one economic system from another.
- Economies of the world are in a state of flux and political views will continue to bring change. The current preference is for the market system to lead on questions of resource allocation.

Equity and Efficiency

One of the downsides of market reforms relate to the issue of social justice. There are certainly many social inequalities spawned by the market mechanism; as those with the greatest wealth have most 'votes' about what is produced, while those with no incomes, if left to fend for themselves, get nothing. On the other hand, the market mechanism does provide an efficient system of communication between producers and consumers that effectively signals 'what' to produce and 'how'.

Equity

Equity does not, in its economic sense, simply mean equality. In this discipline, equity relates to fairness and social justice. From an economist's point of view, therefore, discussions of equity become closely related to considerations of sustainability such as respecting and treating stakeholders fairly – the 'for whom' question. Equity may also be broken down into two parts, **horizontal equity** and **vertical equity**, both of which depend upon government intervention.

Horizontal Equity

This concept involves treating people identically. For example, a government policy of horizontal equity would support and promote equal opportunities between people of identical qualifications and experience, regardless of race or gender.

Vertical Equity

This concept is more contentious since it is concerned with being 'fair'. Vertical equity is about reducing the gap between the 'haves' and the 'have-nots'. It can involve governments providing targeted support to specific categories of people. For example, it may involve taxing the rich more heavily to provide services to support the poor.

Efficiency

In economics, efficiency is mainly concerned with resolving the questions of 'what' to produce and 'how'. The concept is accordingly often divided into two parts – **productive efficiency** and **allocative efficiency**, both of which are satisfied in a pure free market economy.

Productive Efficiency

Productive efficiency means using production techniques that do not waste inputs. Expressed in the language of policy documents concerning sustainability, it means increasing growth rates while reducing the use of resources. In any free market economy, businesses will never waste inputs. A business will not use 10 units of capital, 10 units of labour and 10 units of land when it could produce the same amount of output with only 8 units of capital, 7 units of labour and 9 units of land. Productive efficiency, therefore, refers to output that is produced at the lowest possible cost. During the last decade, for example, the increasing use of prefabricated components on site has enabled improvements in construction productivity – as this has encouraged greater levels of output with fewer workers. These developments depend upon managers responding correctly to the various input prices facing them. The more expensive the inputs, the more incentive managers have to economise. Market prices, therefore, signal 'how' production should technically occur.

Allocative Efficiency

This concept relates to maximising the total value (sometimes called utility) of the available resources. That means that resources are moved to their highest-valued uses, as evidenced by consumers' willingness to pay for the final products. The process of demand and supply guides resources to their most efficient uses. Individuals, as business people looking after their own self-interest, end up – consciously or subconsciously – generating maximum economic value for society. 'What' is produced, therefore, should involve no welfare losses; the utility of all groups in society should have been considered.

Equity versus Efficiency

It should be clear from the explanations above that equity and efficiency do not easily complement one another, and they can be imagined as polar extremes – as far apart as the two economic models shown in Figure 2.1. In this case, the centrally planned model economy, based on government intervention, is seen as more closely akin to the concept of equity; whereas the free market model economy is more suited to supporting the concept of efficiency. The implication is that, in order to foster efficiency, society is encouraged to take over as many state functions as possible. Yet to confidently maintain equity still requires a degree of state intervention. The trade-off between these two qualities accounts for many of the changes that nations experience as they shift between economic systems; and it certainly accounts for the fact that most nations have chosen some type of mixed economy.

The conflict of objectives can be exemplified by considering some of the debates relating to the provision of social housing. The **Right to Buy (RTB)** policy discussed above has considerably reduced many of the government opportunities to directly subsidise housing to those in need. As Julian Le Grand, a welfare economist, has pointed out, housing subsidies (such as RTB and MITR) provided by the British government during the 1980s and 1990s were inefficient and inequitable as they favoured the rich seven times more than the poor. The subsequent drive for **affordable housing** that involves a range of shared ownership and other government initiatives to help people on to the housing ladder is not much better (*see* Tutorial 2 on pages 61–63 for further details).

A problem with all state-provided welfare is cost. To continue with the housing example, in July 2010 it was stated that the housing benefit allowance budget had ballooned to £21 billion per year. Apart from the possible disincentives of such benefit it is unbelievably difficult to fund. The average taxpayer only contributes £6,250 to government revenue so it requires 16 taxpayers to generate £100,000 – therefore, scaled up it requires more than 3 million taxpayers to provide a revenue stream sufficient to just support housing benefit!

This basic calculation puts into perspective the careful balance that governments seeking efficiency and equity have to achieve. Indeed, these two concepts lie at the heart of the debate about the scale of state welfare provision. They also help in understanding the challenges facing a sustainable society and the notions of equity and efficiency will be reviewed several times in this text.

Chapter Summary **2.3**

- There are two concepts of efficiency: productive efficiency – when inputs are not wasted; and allocative efficiency – when resources are employed in their highest-valued uses.
- There are two concepts of equity (or fairness): horizontal equity – equality of opportunity; and vertical equity – actions to achieve social justice or fairness.
- A free market system encourages 'efficiency' and a centrally planned system promotes 'equity'. To blend the two requires a carefully balanced mixed economy.

The Market Mechanism

Respect of the **market mechanism** dates back to the classical economists. They emphasised how prices and wages continually adjust to keep the general levels of supply and demand in balance. According to Adam Smith, a founding father of economics, a market-based economy could be regarded as a product of natural order; since market prices act as signals that guide human endeavour. In his terms, the management of an economy could simply follow a *laissez-faire* approach. In other words, the need for government intervention is minimal – as governments are only needed to provide a forum for determining the rules of the game and to act as an umpire to assure the rules are enforced. Without intervention, high prices encourage enterprise and factors of production to be channelled into particular economic activities. Conversely, falling prices suggest a decline in the interest of the product, or an increase in competition, and ultimately there will come a low point when factors of production begin to exit the activity. Consequently, price signals can be seen to serve the greater good. Indeed, a belief in free markets, democracy and personal freedoms has now spread to all corners of the globe.

Price Signals

For a market economy to function effectively, it is important that every individual is free to pursue 'self interest'. Consumers express their choice of goods or service through the price they are prepared to pay for them – in their attempts to maximise satisfaction. Producers, and owners of resources (and for most people this is their own labour power), seek to obtain as large a reward as possible in an attempt to maximise profit.

If consumers want more of a good than is being supplied at the current price, this is indicated by their willingness to pay more to acquire the good – the price is 'bid up'. This, in turn, increases the profits of those firms producing and supplying the good – and the incomes paid to the factors producing that good increase. As a result, resources are attracted into the industry, and supply expands.

On the other hand, if consumers do not want a particular product, its price will fall, producers will lose money, and resources will leave the industry. This is precisely what happened in the 'new build' market during the recession that followed the financial crisis in 2007/2008. The demand for new houses declined and prices fell; producers either concentrated on other construction work or went bankrupt. As a result, between 2008 and 2010, the completion of new homes fell by more than 30%; reaching the lowest level since 1924.

In simple terms, the **price system** indicates the wishes of consumers and allocates the productive resources accordingly. Or, in the terms we used above, the price mechanism determines *what* is produced, *how* it is produced and *for whom*. To take a specific example, there are more than three million private firms in the European construction industry; indeed, there are approximately 200,000 private firms in the UK construction sector alone. This makes the markets for construction relatively competitive and very distinct from manufacturing. In the manufacturing sector there are usually a few national firms producing a specific product that can be freely examined and easily priced before purchase. In construction the opposite seems to apply, as a construction project usually involves many small local firms combining their skills on site to produce a 'unique' product that will not stand up to close scrutiny or examination until it is actually finished. In fact, the terms of the contract will probably cover the possibility of work being handed over late, over price, or failing to meet the specified performance standards.

The reason individuals and businesses turn to markets to conduct economic activities is that markets tend to reduce the costs of trading. These costs are called **transaction costs** because they are part of the process of making a sale or purchase. They include the cost of being informed about the qualities of a particular product, such as its availability, its durability record, its servicing facilities, its degree of safety, and so on.

Definition

Transaction costs are the costs that enable exchange to take place.

Table 2.3 The transaction costs on a property of £200,000

Item	Cost
Buying	
Commission a survey of property – a valuation report	300
Instruct removal firm	400
Processing searches (local authority and land registry)	430
Solicitor's fees	750
Stamp duty @ 1% of purchase price	2,000
Transaction costs for purchaser before moving	**3,880**
Selling	
Single Estate Agency fee @ 2% (including VAT)	4,700
Energy Performance certificate	100
Additional legal work	700
Total transaction costs prior to moving	**9,380**

Consider, for example, the transaction costs in the property market. Buyers of property have to search the market for information about prices and availability. Indeed, in the commercial property market both buyers and sellers employ agents to negotiate and/or search on their behalf. The agent is relied upon to know about comparable price and rents, and the availability of certain types of property. For their expertise regarding sales value and advertising, a commission has to be paid. This can range from 1 or 2% in Britain to 6% in the USA. The commission costs cover arrangements to: view the property, provide information about the local market, explain contractual requirements and features relating to the property, and last but by no means least, advise on price and value. Ultimately, the agent negotiates a sale or purchase on behalf of the client paying the commission. In a purely theoretical or highly organised market these costs do not exist, as it is assumed that everybody has access to the knowledge they need for exchange to take place. However, this is not usually the case in the property market where transactions, in relative terms, are infrequent and both buyers and sellers have to make significant financial commitments and meet associated legal costs. The main transaction costs incurred in buying a house are listed in Table 2.3. If these costs did not exist people would move far more frequently.

Some economists argue that the increased use of electronic communication will reduce transaction costs both between businesses and between businesses and consumers. In fact, there is an ongoing academic debate about the significance of the **new economy** and its implications for B2B (business-to-business) and B2C (business-to-consumers) transactions. A relevant example is a new service provided by the Land Registry which enables you to find all the prices that a specific house has traded at throughout its history (see *www.net houseprice.com*).

The Marshallian Cross

Analysis of the price (market) mechanism has played a significant role within the history of economics. As far back as 1776, Adam Smith wrote in *The Wealth of Nations* about the 'hidden hands' of supply and demand determining market prices. It was not until 1890, however, when Alfred Marshall published the first edition of *Principles of Economics,* that these two concepts were brought together in one graph. Since then a standard part of any introductory economics

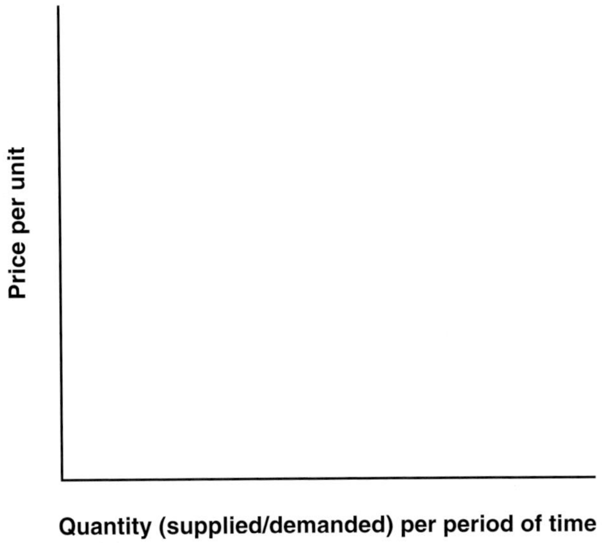

Fig 2.4 The axes of a supply and demand graph

On the vertical axis we plot the price per unit. On the horizontal axis we plot the quantity demanded and/or supplied per period of time.

course has involved the study of supply and demand graphs. This is probably because it is easier to communicate an idea visually – as the saying goes 'a picture is worth a thousand words'. A supply and demand graph enables the relationship between price and quantity to be explored from the consumers' (demand) perspective and the producers' (supply) perspective. The standard layout of each axis is shown in Figure 2.4.

Using the labelled axis in Figure 2.4, can you determine what the pattern of demand in relation to the price would look like? To put the question in more formal terms, can you plot a **demand schedule**? Clearly, as the price of a commodity rises, the quantity demanded will decrease and as the price falls, the quantity demanded will increase. That is, from the demand side there is an inverse relationship between the price per unit and the quantity purchased. This is because consumers seek to maximise their satisfaction and get best value for money.

Using the labelled axis in Figure 2.4 can you determine what the pattern of supply in relation to price would look like? To rephrase the question in more formal terms, can you plot the **supply schedule**? Clearly, as the price of a commodity rises, the quantity supplied will increase and as the price falls, the quantity supplied will decrease. That is, from the supply-side there is a **direct relationship** between the price per unit and quantity sold: an increase in price usually leads to an increase in the quantity supplied and vice versa. This is because suppliers seek to maximise their profit and get the biggest possible return for their efforts.

As suggested, these basic principles seem easier to appreciate when plotted on a graph. See if you agree by considering Figure 2.5.

Three Methodological Remarks

Economists have devised various procedures to add rigour and academic value to their analysis. Three of these small but important techniques need to be highlighted, especially as textbooks often fail to constantly enforce them.

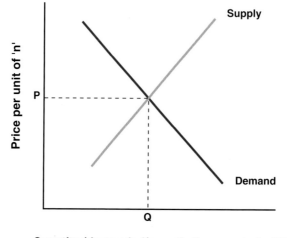

Quantity (demanded/supplied) per period of time

Fig 2.5 A simple supply and demand diagram

The demand curve displays the fact that the quantity demanded falls as the price rises, while the supply curve displays the converse; the quantity supplied rises as the price rises.

Per Period of Time

On the horizontal axis of Figures 2.4 and 2.5 we ended the statement with the qualification *per period of time*. This is to highlight that supply or demand is a flow that takes place during a certain time period and it is quite common to assume that the market period refers to a time when there can be no adjustments. Ideally, however, the time period should be specified as a month, year, week, or whatever. Without a time dimension, the statements relating to quantity lack accuracy.

Ceteris Paribus

The second qualifying remark relates to the Latin phrase **ceteris paribus**, which means other things being equal or constant. This is an important assumption to make when dealing with a graph showing two variables. For example, price is not the only factor that affects supply and demand. There are many other market conditions that also affect supply and demand and we cover these in Chapters 3 and 4. In the exercise above, constructing Figures 2.4 and 2.5, we assumed *ceteris paribus*. We did not complicate the analysis by allowing, for example, consumers' income to change when discussing changes to the price of a good. If we did, we would never know whether the change in the quantity demanded or supplied was due to a change in the price or due to a change in income. Therefore, we employed the *ceteris paribus* technique and assumed that all the other factors that might affect the market were held constant. This assumption enables economists to be more rigorous in their work, studying each significant variable in turn. The *ceteris paribus* assumption approximates to the scientific method of a controlled experiment.

Supply and Demand Curves

When using supply and demand curves to illustrate our analysis, they will frequently be drawn as straight lines. Although this is irritating from a linguistic point of view, it is easier for the artist constructing the illustrations and acceptable to economists, since the 'curves' rarely refer to the plotting of empirical data. It is worth noting, therefore, that so-called supply and demand 'curves' are usually illustrated as straight lines that highlight basic principles.

The Concept of Equilibrium

Look again at Figure 2.5 – inevitably there is a point at which the two curves must cross. This point represents the market price. The market price in Figure 2.5 is P and this reflects the point where the quantity supplied and demanded is equal, namely point Q. At price P the market clears. There is neither excess supply nor excess demand. Consumers and producers are both happy. Price P is called the **equilibrium price**: the price at which the quantity demanded and the quantity supplied are equal.

Most markets tend towards an equilibrium price, including the housing market, construction market, the market for rented commercial property, the market for student accommodation, the market for paving slabs, or whatever. All markets have an inherent balancing mechanism. When there is excess demand, price rises; and when there is excess supply, prices fall. Eventually a price is found at which there is no tendency for change. Consumers are able to get all they want at that price, and suppliers are able to sell the amount that they want at that price. This special market concept is illustrated in Figure 2.6. The concept of **equilibrium** is important in economics and we will be referring to it in different markets and in different contexts as we study the economy.

In other words, equilibrium prevails when opposing forces are in balance. If the price drifts away from the equilibrium point – for whatever reason – forces come into play to find a new equilibrium price. If these forces tend to re-establish prices at the original equilibrium point, we say the situation is one of **stable equilibrium**. An unstable equilibrium is one in which, if there is a movement away from the equilibrium, there are forces that push price and/or quantity even further away from this equilibrium (or at least do not push price and quantity back towards the original equilibrium level). In these terms, property markets can be characterised as unstable, especially as once they move away from a period of equilibrium they tend to take a relatively long time to adjust to new conditions of demand and supply.

The difference between a stable and an unstable equilibrium can be illustrated with two balls: one made of hard rubber, the other made of soft putty. If you squeeze the rubber ball out of shape, it bounces back to its original form. But if you squeeze the ball made of putty, it remains out of shape. The former illustrates a stable equilibrium and the latter an unstable equilibrium.

Definition

Equilibrium is a situation in which the plans of buyers and the plans of sellers exactly mesh.

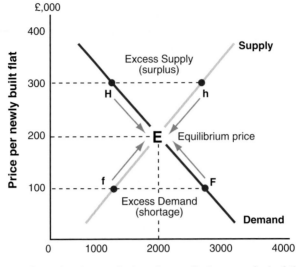

Quantity demanded and supplied per period of time

Fig 2.6 The equilibrium price

The equilibrium price for each new house is £200,000 and the equilibrium quantity is 2,000 units. At higher prices there would be a surplus: houses would be in excess supply and may remain empty. For example, at £300,000 the market would not clear; there needs to be a movement along the demand curve from H to E and a movement along the supply curve from h to E. These movements necessitate the price to fall. At prices below the equilibrium, there would be a shortage: flats would be in excess demand and there may be a waiting list. For example, at £100,000 the price would rise, reducing the demand from F to E and supply from f to E. The market will settle at a price of £200,000.

Now consider a shock to the system. The shock can be shown either by a shift in the supply curve, or a shift in the demand curve, or a shift in both curves. Any shock to the system will produce a new set of supply and demand relationships and a new equilibrium. Forces will come into play to move the system from the old price–quantity equilibrium to a new one. Now let us consider a specific example in the housing market.

A Change in Market Conditions

To illustrate the dynamics of the market imagine what might happen if mortgage interest rates rise, while other things remain constant. This will reduce the demand for owner-occupied property at each and every price. This decrease in demand is shown in Figure 2.7, by shifting the demand curve to the left from D_1 to D_2. If property prices now stay at P, consumers will only demand Q_a while suppliers (sellers) will continue providing Q. Consequently there will be an excess amount of supply in the marketplace equal to $Q-Q_a$. However, providing prices are allowed to move to make the amounts supplied and demanded equal again, suppliers will be able to offload vacant properties by reducing their prices. As the price falls consumers will become interested in buying and demand will increase. Consequently, a new equilibrium price will be arrived at. This new price is P_1 in Figure 2.7 and the new quantity demanded and supplied will now be equal at Q_1.

The demand curve only shifts (as in Figure 2.7) when the *ceteris paribus* assumption is violated. In other words, demand and/or supply curves only shift to a new position when the market conditions change. We explore these 'shifts' in more detail in the next two chapters.

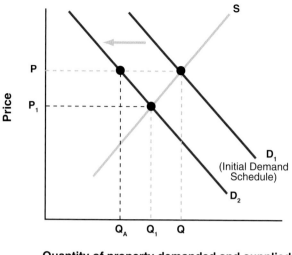

Quantity of property demanded and supplied
for owner occupation per year

Fig 2.7 Changing market conditions lead to a new equilibrium price

The leftward shift of the demand curve indicates that consumers are less willing to buy properties in any price range due to the increase in mortgage rates. The excess supply of properties on the market at the old price P causes a new equilibrium to be found at the lower price P, at this point the quantity demanded and quantity supplied are once again found to be equal.

Market Failure

Finally, to complete our introductory overview of resource allocation, we need to recognise the existence of **market failure**. So far we have implied that the market provides the best means of allocating resources and any market distortions have been overlooked. For example, we have assumed that labour moves freely to wherever work is most profitable and consumers buy whatever they desire in freely determined markets. Yet, in reality, monopolies, oligopolies, upward only rent reviews, immobility, subsidies, trade unions, externalities, high transaction costs and other market imperfections distort the situation. We shall examine these issues in more detail in Chapter 6. But they are worth bearing in mind throughout the text, as *Economics and Property* intends to raise questions about the capacity of a modern market economy to develop in ways that are efficient, equitable and sustainable.

Chapter Summary **2.5**

- When we combine demand and supply curves, we find the equilibrium price at the intersection of the two curves. At the equilibrium price there is no tendency to change; the market clears (see Figure 2.6).
- Equilibrium exists whenever the separate plans of buyers mesh exactly with the separate plans of the sellers. Price points the buyers and sellers in the right direction. If conditions in the market change, the relevant curve shifts and a new equilibrium position is established (see Figure 2.7).
- Market failures exist, and these form an important consideration when setting an agenda aimed at achieving equity, efficiency and sustainability.

Tutorial 1

Tutorial **1**

☑ CHECK POINT

By this point in the text you should be able to:

- ✓ Understand that most economic issues boil down to questions relating to the allocation of scarce resources.
- ✓ Appreciate that a central tenet of any modern economic system is based on a strong belief in market forces.
- ✓ Recognise the close relationship between the development of property assets and the scale of an economy.
- ✓ Compare and contrast the different characteristics of economic systems.
- ✓ Begin to appreciate that the study of economics will help you to analyse markets.
- ✓ Understand that economic principles inform government policy, such as the current debate about the size of the welfare state.

Introduction to Tutorial 1

Chapters 1 and 2 have highlighted that a central concern of economics relate to problems of resource allocation; as outlined resources are scarce, relative to the numerous demands made upon them. If resources were not scarce there would be no economic problem. Likewise, if there was only one objective to satisfy there would also be no problem. These economic concepts are too important to be simply learnt by rote; they need to be used and understood in a specific context. To help achieve this there are five sets of tutorial readings. Studied in their entirety they will help you to think like an economist and appreciate the value of property economics; therefore these sections form an essential part of the text.

The first tutorial exercise is based upon four edited extracts from the *Estates Gazette* of 10 April 2010 when Milton Keynes, Bristol and Bath were in 'Focus'. Commentary, of this type, represents a regular feature of the magazine as each week the *Estates Gazette* reviews property development in a specific geographical area of the UK. You should take time to read each of the extracts carefully, before answering the associated questions.

Tutorial Reading

Extract 1: Hatching a plan in Milton Keynes

Milton Keynes has hit middle age. To celebrate the 40th anniversary of the publication of architect Llewelyn Davies' original new-town masterplan, the city is doing what it does best – making a plan for the next 40 years.

The latest bit of strategising is called *MK2050* and it aims to work out where the ultimate postmodern city should go from here...

'We've gone plan bloody mad', says an exasperated David Louch, director at local surveying firm Douglas Duff. 'I've got totally tired of it all. We have a problem in Milton Keynes, because we are better at writing down what we are seeking to achieve and publishing it in glossy brochures than we are at achieving it in the flesh'.

MK2050 is the brainchild of Liberal Democrat council leader Sam Crooks, who counters that there is a need to consult widely on the direction of the city in the period between now and 2050.

'Regeneration is a key issue', he says. 'Part of the city from the 1970s is showing signs of wear and tear, and we don't want a two-speed city developing. We need to work out what our new unique selling points will be to attract investors'.

One of those USPs is likely to be based around establishing the infrastructure for electric cars, as part of low-carbon plans for the future Milton Keynes.

'We thought car use might decline because of the energy crisis', Crooks says. 'But the rise of electric cars means there will still be cars. They will be CO_2 free and more socially acceptable, but we will still need them'.

Changing housing

Crooks's other big idea revolves around digital infrastructure, including 'ultra-fast broadband delivered directly into the home, at speeds that are unheard of'.

Changing housing and demographic trends – such as what types of suburban housing people want, and how Milton Keynes manages significant levels of ethnic diversity – are other key issues identified by the council leader. Crooks stresses that he is keen to invite ideas from as wide a cross section of residents as possible.

'We are hoping to establish a different kind of participation to the way these things are usually done', he says. 'We want an informal debate first, then we will look at things more formally in the autumn'.

One of the methods for facilitating this informal debate is the creation of a Facebook group. In answer to the question of how Milton Keynes should develop by 2050, much of the response from group members revolves around sticking with the urban design principles that made the city successful in the first place.

[For example] Pete Winkelman, chairman of Milton Keynes Dons Football Club and developer of a proposed casino says: 'I believe in the original vision of Milton Keynes – easy access, low density and with large green spaces. There are big lessons to be learned from the past and a high threshold of quality to aim at…'.

Extract 2: Agents in Milton Keynes are confident of a swift recovery across two retail centres

The battle is on to win a slice of the spending power of Milton Keynes' expanding population. Two major retail developments are slugging it out in the town, with Legal & General's *Midsummer Place* squaring up to PRUPIM and Hermes' *thecentre:mk*.

'Yes, *centre:mk* is definitely our main rival', says Rob Williams of Strutt & Parker, *Midsummer Place*'s main agent, 'but we are feeling very positive indeed. We are holding zone A rents at £200 to £220 per sq ft, and we don't have a single vacant unit on the books right now'.

Williams maintains that it was the decision three years ago to target *Midsummer Place* at young, aspirational fashion retailers that has made the difference. 'This policy has stood us in good stead', he says. 'It has allowed us to get through the downturn without any major signs of deterioration'.

Abercrombie & Fitch's laid-back Californian fashion label Hollister moved into a 7,700 sq ft space just before Christmas on a 10-year lease, and H&M recently upsized its unit from 20,000 to 25,000 sq ft.

But *thecentre:mk* will not be outdone easily, and Hermes and PRUPIM are developing a £10m 'Destination Dining', which will create a new restaurant quarter for the shopping centre with four restaurant units, each of them around 5,000 sq ft.

Café Rouge and Nando's signed up last autumn, and Carluccio's and Yo Sushi! Both said yes at the end of February.

Robert Goodman, director of *thecentre:mk*, says: 'Although market conditions remain tough, the success in preletting the restaurant quarter demonstrates encouraging levels of interest'.

Tutorial 1

Another facet of broadening the mix has been *thecentre:mk*'s desire to move more upmarket with its 'Premium Retail Quarter'.

Even though it has traditionally had mass-market tenants, it is actively targeting quality brands such as Kurt Geiger, Phase8 and Jaeger, all of which took units – totalling 5,200 sq ft – on Silbury Arcade in *thecentre:mk* last summer.

Anthony Ross, asset manager at Cushman & Wakefield Investors, says this shift into upmarket brands is all about positioning. 'The reconfiguration of the units on Silbury Arcade to create a premium retail quarter for the centre is part of the £20m package of enhancements announced last year,' he says. He points out that the plan is to group these premium retailers around the new restaurant quarter and 'opposite House of Fraser, Patisserie Valerie and Gap Kids'.

Extract 3: A tale of three retail centres in Bath and Bristol

SouthGate Centre in Bath

Opening a shopping centre this year is unusual and probably a little fraught. But Aviva and Multi Development, developers of Bath's £360m SouthGate centre, will throw open the doors on its second phase in just a few weeks' time.

Momentum is growing and a number of occupiers are due to make their debut in the city.

The 400,000 sq ft scheme, which has attracted, among others, New Look, H&M, All Saints and Cult into its first phase, is now gearing up for the phase two launch in May, including three main space users (MSUs), and a third phase – a Debenhams department store – which opens in September.

Top Shop has signed up for nearly 17,000 sq ft. River Island is taking 9,000 sq ft, and Urban Outfitters 15,000 sq ft. It is known that there has been competition for units, with TK Maxx and Next also in the frame.

The promise of a new, revamped SouthGate has helped other parts of the town. Mike McElhinney, partner in charge of King Sturge in Bath, says the marketing of the centre has 'done something fantastic for Bath'.

'Multi has probably knocked on the doors of everybody in fashion. Lots of those designer names have come to Bath, looked at SouthGate, said "very nice" and have then looked around the rest of the town as well'.

For example, Bath's upmarket Milsom Street has been crowned the best fashion shopping street in the country. The gong, awarded recently in a Google Street View poll, saw it beat, among others, London's King's Road.

Ken Elliott, director of L&R Group, is particularly pleased by that achievement because his company's Milsom Place development has for some time been nurturing a strong fashion line-up – Traffic People, for example, has just opened its first boutique outside London in the street. He is sure that SouthGate has been instrumental in raising Bath's status 'right up to where it should be'.

Elliott is not the only one eyeing boutique operators. Marketing is also under way for Little SouthGate, a parade of boutique units targeted at niche operators.

Stuart Harris, leasing director with Multi Development, says demand for the scheme has been strong: 'We have been turning down more deals than we have been accepting'.

He also says terms have improved, with rent-frees coming down. Headline rents, although far short of original ambitions of £295 per sq ft, are getting close to the city's normal prime tone of £250 per sq ft.

Cabot Circus and Broadmead in Bristol

Eighteen months after it opened, Bristol's Cabot Circus appears to be living up to its promises.

Jerry White, director at DTZ, one of the scheme's letting agents, says the city has long endured a poor reputation but is now being seen by more and more retailers as a credible location for expansion.

US brand Hollister joined the Cabot line-up earlier this year in an 8,000 sq ft unit and the store is said to be outperforming those in longer-established UK malls.

Agents are also poised to make what they describe as a 'significant' letting on a 10,000 sq ft MSU that has been void since Cabot opened.

However, the picture in the wider Broadmead shopping area is variable. The second-largest Primark in the UK now anchors the western end, and other gaps are being filled. Stephen Jones, director of Western Retail, says it is a 'testimony' to Cabot Circus that DSG, for example, was persuaded to open an in-town format of PC World in the former Zavvi unit. But, more generally, the western end continues to suffer from higher vacancy rates as occupiers are lost to the new centre.

Broadmead project manager Jo Hawkins confirms that fashion-led Cabot Circus has proved a challenge for that part of Broadmead – but says Primark is now driving extra footfall there and vacant units are being marketed to new retailers. She stresses that only 15 stores moved from Broadmead into Cabot – much fewer than experts had predicted.

Extract 4: The start of a new office building in Bristol

Developer HDG Mansur ended years of speculation two weeks ago when it erected cranes over the site where its 110,000 sq ft speculative office building, Bridgewater House, is now under construction.

Despite the ribbing HDG has received from those in the local market for failing to deliver on its previous assurances that construction would start, there are many who will now say it is a courageous move. Equally, there are those who admit the delay could be fortunate.

At the start of the recession, Bristol was faced with the prospect of a huge oversupply of new city-centre office stock. But the brakes were put on development and, after extremely tough letting conditions in 2009 – according to King Sturge, take-up was 49% below the 10-year average at 327,480 sq ft – the new decade has started off with more promise.

Vacancy rates remain in double digits. However, the agent says that, by the end of the first quarter, more than 300,000 sq ft had been taken in the city…

HDG Mansur plans to complete Bridgewater House in May 2011, and now that agents no longer have to speculate on when construction will start, their thoughts are turning to what rents the building might achieve.

City centre office rents have held up reasonably well during the recession, albeit with some generous incentives. A rent of £27 per sq ft was achieved at *Templeback* when NFU took its initial tranche of space in the building, but this was negotiated back in 2008. According to King Sturge, the best rent achieved on a deal negotiated last year was £26 per sq ft at Portwall Place.

Jeremy Richards, partner in charge at King Sturge, is putting his marker in the sand by predicting that the quoting rent on Bridgewater House will be £29 per sq ft, and it will probably achieve between £27–28 per sq ft.

HDG was bullish when Bridgewater was first proposed, and predicted that it would set a new headline for Bristol. It even suggested it would

Tutorial 1

break the £30 per sq ft barrier before the recession nipped such ambitions in the bud.

Tony Nicholas, head of department at Knight Frank, which is joint agent on the scheme with BNP Paribas RE and Strutt & Parker, says: 'Next year, when we haven't got the competition [from other new buildings], it will be a landlords' market, and rents on Bridgewater won't be less than £27.50 per sq ft...'.

Source: adapted from The *Estates Gazette* of 10 April 2010 (pp 66–68, 71, 78–80). 'Focus section on Milton Keynes, Bristol and Bath'.

Tutorial Questions

1. From the above extracts, select examples that can be used to fully explain any two of the economic concepts introduced so far.
2. Using economic ideas summarise the recurrent themes of all four extracts.

The Theory of Demand  3

Aims and Objectives

This chapter introduces the demand-side of property market, taking a detailed look at the demand for housing and commercial property. It introduces the theoretical background to understanding markets in practice. Specifically by the end of this chapter you should understand:

- What economists mean when they discuss demand
- The basic determinants of demand, and how to discuss them in relation to the markets for commercial and residential property
- The application of a generalised demand model
- The ways that the basic tools of markets analysis work

As suggested in Chapter 2, the concepts of demand and supply are the basic building blocks of economics. In this chapter we focus specifically on demand, and in the next chapter we deal with supply.

When economists speak of demand they refer to **effective demand**. Effective demand is money-backed desire. It does not refer to the demands of a crying baby or of a spoilt child wanting and grabbing at everything it sees. Demand analysis focuses on how much is being spent on specific items and how that demand may alter if its price changed. In other words, demand from an economist's point of view is real, 'genuine' demand backed by the ability to make a purchase. It is distinct from need. For example, in 2010 the total number of households needing accommodation exceeded the total number of homes in the housing market. Only those who had sufficient means to 'demand' accommodation – that is, they could afford to buy or rent at market prices – were confident of securing somewhere to live. This anomaly explains the hundred thousand homeless people living in bed and breakfast hostels at a cost to the UK government.

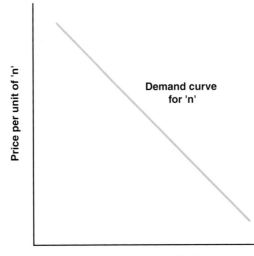

Fig 3.1 A market demand curve

The demand curve for most goods and services slopes down from left to right, as the higher the price, the lower the level of demand (other things being equal).

The Basic Law of Demand

As established in Chapter 2, a demand curve has a negative slope; it moves downward from left to right. This is illustrated in Figure 3.1. The shape of the demand curve for most goods or services is not surprising when we consider the basic **law of demand**.

The law of demand, therefore, tells us that the quantity demanded of a product is inversely related to that product's price, other things being equal. To continue with this analysis, we must consider the 'other things being equal' phrase more carefully. Clearly, demand is not only affected by price. As implied in Chapter 2, it is easy to see that other factors may also affect demand. Conditions in the relevant market may change significantly enough to cause consumers to change the quantity demanded at each and every price. For instance, imagine that Figure 3.1 represents the demand curve for property. What events may cause more or less demand for that product at every price?

The determination of demand for property is a complicated process; due to the size, cost, longevity and investment nature of buildings. The level of complexity will become clearer as we consider factors affecting demand for housing and commercial property.

Demand for Housing

As suggested by Table 2.1 (page 21), there are more than 26 million households in the UK. The majority can afford to demand a home. It is important to remember, however, that at any point in time there is always a minority that cannot afford a home. As the introductory point about effective demand emphasised, a distinction should be made between 'need' and 'demand'. Each household requires a: flat, bungalow, terraced house, maisonette,

Definition

The law of demand states that: at a high price, a lower quantity will be demanded than at a low price (and vice versa), other things being equal.

semi-detached house, or at the very least some kind of shelter. The related resources are allocated through the market mechanism and the public sector, or through a mix of the two. It is difficult to envisage just one housing market; the simplest of divides is between those who own outright or via a mortgage and those who rent from the private or public sector or some hybrid of the two. However, when statisticians discuss the housing market it is usual to define four sectors (or submarkets).

Definitions

1. The owner-occupied sector – made up of households that ultimately own their properties, once they have paid off a related mortgage.

2. The local authority rented sector – made up of housing stock made available by the local authority (council) at a subsidised rate from public funds.

3. The private rented sector – comprising private property that is let at a market rent; deemed 'fair' to tenants and landlords.

4. The registered social landlord sector – made up of property that is managed by non-profit making organisations, that combine public and private funds, to provide housing for those in need.

These four sectors have been listed chronologically in order of size. In general terms, however, it is sufficient to understand that housing demand may be either for owner occupation, or rent, or for some combination of the two, via shared equity organised by a housing association or similar organisation. We now consider the main factors determining demand for housing within these markets.

Demand for Owner-Occupied Housing

Most households in Ireland, Scandinavia, Australasia and much of Europe want homes to own and occupy. Some 70% of the households in the UK currently reside in this form of tenure, and the relative size of the owner-occupied sector in Spain (80%), Ireland (76%) and Finland (78%) is even larger. This form of ownership is generally supported by government initiatives that encourage demand by making the process of home buying as fast, transparent and as consumer friendly as possible. In fact, across Europe there is a strong tradition of tax incentives for owner occupation, usually paid in the form of a subsidy on mortgage repayments. **Mortgage interest tax relief**, as it is universally known, continues to support markets in Ireland, Netherlands and Spain. However, it has been abolished in the UK since 2000; regardless of this, home ownership has not suffered as a result, and house prices have continued to rise.

The logic behind government's providing incentives and benefits to support owner occupation is that if people own the property that they occupy, they will maintain it better. The feel-good factor derived from ownership makes the transaction costs of choosing and funding worthwhile, especially as a house provides an investment as well as a shelter.

As you can imagine, there are several factors that determine the demand for privately owned housing, and in Table 3.1 we identify the main ones.

Demand for Privately Rented Housing

Since the Second World War there has been only a small market demand in the UK for privately rented accommodation. At present, no more than 10% of UK households demand this type of accommodation. This is in direct contrast

Table 3.1 Demand factors for owner-occupied housing

The current price of housing
The price of other forms of housing
Income and expectations of change
Cost of borrowing money and expectations of change
Government measures, such as tax benefits and stamp duty
Demographic factors, such as the number of households
Price of associated goods and services, such as maintenance, furniture, council tax, insurance, etc.

to some European economies, where as many as 40% of households are living in private rented accommodation. However, there has been a strong change in the pattern of housing demand in the UK. At the beginning of the 20th century, people from all income levels routinely rented from private landlords. In 1915, for example, 90% of UK families lived in the private rented sector. The change in the pattern of demand is closely associated with the supply drying up. This happened following the introduction of rent controls by government – as these imposed a ceiling on rents, and created a big disincentive for landlords. As a result, current demand is mainly met by small-scale individual landlords who maintain and manage properties in their spare time. In an attempt to reverse this trend, the private rented sector in the UK has been largely deregulated in recent years.

In general, the market in private housing to rent varies greatly from country to country for a number of cultural and economic reasons. The main economic factors affecting the demand in this sector are listed in Table 3.2.

Table 3.2 Demand factors for privately rented housing

Current rent levels and expectations of change
The price of owner occupation
Income distribution, which determines affordability
The cost of borrowing and expectations of change
The law on rents and security of tenure
Demographic factors, such as household formation

Demand for Social Housing

Housing rented from local authorities and registered social landlords, such as housing associations, is generally referred to as social housing. The origins of social housing stems from the idea that governments should pay a subsidy towards housing to make up for the shortage of accommodation available to low-income families. In the UK during the 1980s and 1990s – with both Conservative and Labour governments favouring free market policies – much of the local authority housing stock was either transferred to housing associations to allocate, manage and maintain, or sold to tenants, thereby transferring stock to the owner-occupied sector. As noted in Chapter 2, a similar process has been experienced in other countries such as Russia, China, Czechoslovakia and Poland, where privatisation of the housing stock has been a key feature of the transition process from a centralised command economy towards a free market.

Regardless, the local authority and registered social landlord sectors still represent 'home' for around 4.8 million households as tenants (i.e. slightly less than 20% of all households). The more significant problem, however, is the fact that demand for property in this sector far exceeds the supply with a similar number (4.5 million in 2010) on waiting lists. The factors that determine the demand for this type of housing are quite different from those driving demand for owner-occupied and privately rented housing. The main factors of demand for social housing are listed in Table 3.3.

Table 3.3 Demand factors for social housing

The current price (rent) of social housing
The price level of other forms of tenure
Availability of finance, such as income support and mortgages
Levels of government subsidy

A Demand Model for Housing

The factors affecting demand in the various sectors of the housing market set out in Tables 3.1 to 3.3 suggest some general themes. For example, it seems that the recurring determinants of demand are the price (rent) of a property, the price of other forms of tenure, the level of income, and government policy. Economists can, therefore, state a generalised model for the analysis of housing markets. The model is set up in such a way that it can equally apply to any sector of the housing market. The model is typically presented in the form of a general equation as follows:

$$Qd = f(P_n, P_n - 1, Y, G, Z)$$

This model is formally referred to as a **demand function**. It may look complicated but it is only a form of shorthand notation. The demand function represents, in symbols, everything we have discussed above.

It states that Q_d the quantity demanded (in our example a specific type of housing) is f, a function of all the things listed inside the bracket: P_n the price, or rent, of a property; P_n-1 the price of other forms of tenure; Y income, G government policy, and Z a host of other things. Remember this type of equation may be adapted and extended as necessary to analyse the demand of any specific good, service or asset.

Demand for Commercial Property

There are approximately 2 million commercial buildings in the UK and the majority of these are rented. As an example, Table 3.4 shows the distribution of the six classifications of commercial property, as designated by the Valuation Office Agency (VOA) of England and Wales in 2009.

Table 3.4 Stock of commercial property in England and Wales, 2008

Valuation office classifications	Floorspace (000's m²)	Number of units (hereditaments)
Retail premises	106,299	547,870
Offices	101,456	350,202
Factories	208,171	261,009
Warehouses	158,942	205,954
Miscellaneous	20,681	59,839
Non-bulk	13,394	369,718
Total	608,943	1,794,592

Source: Adapted from Commercial & Industrial Floorspace & Rateable Value, 2009.

A close look reveals that retail premises absorb marginally more floorspace than offices but account for significantly more units (formally referred to as **hereditaments**). Buildings classified as miscellaneous include many 'community' type establishments, such as social clubs, garden centres, gymnasia and fitness centres and some unusual properties, including cold stores, abattoirs, miniature railways, bird sanctuaries and war game courses. Finally, those units categorised as 'non-bulk' (as they often lack physical presence) are often not buildings in the strictest sense as they consist either of land parcels (with limited floorspace) or unconventional premises that are not valued on floorspace criteria. Examples of hereditaments classed as 'non-bulk' are radio masts, advertising hoardings, open-air car parks, sports grounds, and some public facilities.

The important point to note is that none of these buildings, or special purpose structures, are required for their own sake, but for the services they provide. Consequently, demand for commercial property is based on factors related to the specific sector in which the building will be used. Demand of this type is known as **derived demand**.

Derived demand emphasises that commercial property is rented or purchased not because it gives satisfaction, but because the property can be used to produce goods or services that can be sold at a profit. This is different from the factors affecting the demand to buy a house. For example, in the months following the September 2001 terrorist attack on the World Trade Centre in New York, global business confidence was dented and the demand for commercial property in the UK declined considerably (but during the same period the demand for housing was experiencing a boom).

Investments in commercial property, therefore, depend on the expectation that the users – the occupiers – will make profits in the future. If business confidence is low, investment will not take place; even if there is current demand for an increase in production or sales. The factors affecting demand for commercial buildings are largely dependent on the state of the economy, and business expectations concerning output and profit. In other words, because demand is derived, it is dependent on many things other than price. Some of the general factors of demand for commercial property are shown in Table 3.5.

Table 3.5 Factors affecting demand for commercial property

The rent or price level
Location, nature and size of property
The state of the economy and government policy
Business expectations regarding profits and turnover
Level of technology

The final item in Table 3.5 is of current interest, as the developments of online marketplaces have had a significant impact on the demand for commercial space. As described in Chapter 2, the **new economy** based on IT has implications for the ways businesses communicate with one another, their workforce and their customers. For example, it is estimated that in 2006 about 30% of the world's top companies employ 35% of their workforce outside the boundaries of the formal workspace. In other words 'hot-desking', working from home and shopping on the internet reduce the amount of desk space required per employee and the floorspace needed per shopper.

A Demand Model for Commercial Property

Adopting a similar approach to the analysis of the demand for housing, a model can be derived for commercial property. It would seem from the above analysis that the quantity demanded of commercial property can be generalised as follows: the quantity demanded Q_d is a function of rent (price) R; the state of the economy, E; expectations regarding output, E_o; and the amount of space required per employee, shopper or service user, S_{req}. Expressed in the form of an equation, the demand function for commercial property could be stated as follows:

$$Q_d = f(R, E, E_0, S_{req})$$

Demand for Government Property

The demand for government projects such as power stations, rail, roads, tunnels, bridges, hospitals, schools, prisons, museums, police and fire stations cannot be excluded, as the government has overall responsibility for approximately 40% of the annual spending on property. These goods and services are explicitly or implicitly through regulated sectors controlled by government departments who need to assess and prioritise the demands that will be met. This is difficult as the demands are created by society at large in the sense that, left to their own devices, individuals may not be able or willing to pay the market price for the desired facility. Or the goods or service are regulated because of its market structure, in which case the government decides the level of demand that should be available. This does not mean that the public sector inevitably finance all of these projects. In many countries public policy, or a lack of public funds, means that the provision of some of these facilities is provided in partnership with the private sector. Examples of public–private sector partnership include power supplies and distribution, rail networks, and air traffic. The private finance initiative (discussed in Chapter 5) ensures that some of the facilities previously provided by the public sector are now financed by the private sector.

The demand for community-oriented facilities can be judged on a similar basis to commercial buildings: price (rent), state of public finance and space requirements, etc. However, assessing the demand for these products is more complex as the associated floorspace may not generate a sufficient income flow to justify the investment; the value placed on public (collective) goods is largely subjective. The demand decision, therefore, depends on the assessment of need and the funds available. Some of the main factors of demand for this broad area of public goods that provide the essential physical and social fabric on which modern society relies are summarised in Table 3.6. In considering these factors, one can understand the political difficulties of choosing which of society's needs should be transferred into effective demand.

Table 3.6 Factors affecting demand for government property

Assessment of need, present and future
Availability of finance and levels of government subsidy
Government policy
The age and condition of existing stock
Civic pride
Changes in technology

> **Chapter Summary 3.1**
> - The basic law of demand is that as price rises, lower quantities are demanded; and as price falls, higher quantities are demanded. There is an inverse relationship between the price and the quantity demanded; other things being equal (see Figure 3.1).
> - In the housing market there appear to be many determinants that affect demand, including the price (rent) of the property, the price of other forms of tenure, current levels of income and government policy.
> - Much of the demand for commercial and government property is of a derived nature, in as much as the property is not demanded in its own right but for what it can add to the final good or service being produced.
> - In the case of government property, assessing demand is subjective as the decision depends on what it can contribute to society as a whole.
> - The relationship between the quantity demanded and the various determinants of demand can be expressed in the form of a model or demand function.

Changing Market Conditions

There are many non-price determinants of demand, such as the cost of financing (interest rates), technological developments, demographic make-up, the season of the year, fashion, and so on. For illustrative purposes, we will consider just four generalised categories – income, price of other goods, expectations and government – taking each in turn and assuming *ceteris paribus* in each case.

Income

For most goods, an increased income will lead to an increase in demand. The phrase increase in demand correctly implies that more is being demanded at each and every price. For most goods, therefore, an increase in income will lead to a rightward shift in the position of the demand curve.

Goods for which the demand increases when income increases are called **normal goods**. Most goods are 'normal' in this sense. There are a small number of goods for which demand decreases as incomes increase: these are called **inferior goods**. For example, the demand for private rented accommodation falls as more people can afford to buy their own homes. (It is important to recognise that the terms normal and inferior in this context are part of an economist's formal language, and no value judgments should be inferred when the terms are used.)

Price of Other Goods

Demand curves are always plotted on the assumption that the prices of all other commodities are held constant. For example, when we draw the demand curve for lead guttering, we assume the price of plastic guttering is held constant; when we draw the demand curve for carpets, we assume the price of housing is held constant. However, the prices of the other goods that are assumed constant may affect the pattern of demand for the specific good under analysis. This is particularly the case if the other good is a **substitute good** (as in the example of guttering) or a **complementary good** (as in the carpet and housing example). Economists consider how a change in the price of an interdependent good, such as a substitute or complementary good, affects the demand for the related commodity.

Let us consider the guttering example a little more fully. Assume that both plastic and lead guttering originally cost £10 per metre. If the price of lead guttering remains at £10 per metre but the price of plastic guttering falls by 50% to £5 per metre, builders will use more plastic and less lead guttering. The demand curve for lead guttering, at each and every price, will shift leftwards. If, on the other hand, the price of plastic guttering rises, the demand curve for lead guttering will shift to the right, reflecting the fact that builders will buy more of this product at its present price. Therefore, a price change in the substitute good will cause an inverse change in the pattern of demand for the other alternative.

The same type of analysis also applies for complementary goods. However, here the situation is reversed: a fall in the price of one product may cause an increase in the demand for both products, and a rise in the price of one product may cause a fall in the demand for both.

Expectations

Consumers' views on the future trends of incomes, interest rates and product availability may affect demand – and prompt them to buy more or less of a particular good even if its current price does not change. This is particularly evident when we consider the demand for property (see Tables 3.1–3.3 and 3.5). For example, potential house purchasers who believe that mortgage rates are likely to rise may buy less property at current prices. The demand curve for houses will shift to the left, reflecting the fact that the quantity of properties demanded for purchase at each and every price has reduced due to consumer expectations that mortgage rates will increase.

Government

Legislation can affect the demand for a commodity in a variety of ways. For example, changes in building regulations may increase the demand for double-glazed window units, regardless of their present price. The demand curve for double-glazed windows will shift to the right, reflecting the fact that greater quantities of these units are being demanded at each and every price.

The government can also influence the level of demand by changing taxes or creating a subsidy. An interesting example in this context is the Climate Change Levy that began in 2001, as it imposed a tax on the use of energy in commercial and industrial property. The levy is incurred in relation to the amount of fossil fuel-based kilowatts used in a commercial building. In effect, therefore, the government is creating an incentive for those that demand commercial property to acquire buildings that use environmentally friendly energy sources, as these are exempt from the levy. The extent that this has shifted the demand curve to the right for commercial property using renewable energy sources is arguable and will be discussed further in Chapter 9, where we consider the debate about the **sustainable development** agenda.

Revisiting *Ceteris Paribus*

When we first introduced the idea of holding other things constant, it may have appeared that these 'other things' were unimportant. The previous section, however, should have highlighted how wrong this interpretation would be. Indeed, the *ceteris paribus* assumption enables economists to emphasise the fact that price and a host of other factors determine demand. Whenever you analyse the level of demand for any property there will always be a need to consider both the price and many other related factors. To clarify this important distinction between the price determinant and the non-price determinants, economists are careful to distinguish between them when they discuss changes in demand.

Understanding Changes in Demand

We have already explained that changes of non-price determinants cause the demand schedule to shift to the right or to the left, demonstrating the fact that more or less is being demanded at each and every price. These changes are often referred to as increases or decreases of demand.

Let us consider one example in detail. How would we represent an increase in the quantity demanded of naturally ventilated commercial buildings (at all prices) due to a respected piece of research concluding that air-conditioned buildings caused **sick building syndrome**? The demand curve for naturally ventilated buildings would shift to the right, representing an increase in the demand at each and every price. This is shown in Figure 3.2.

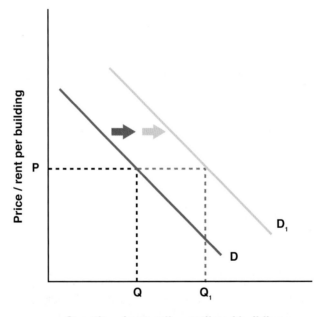

Quantity of naturally ventilated buildings demanded per year

Fig 3.2 Change in a non-price determinant

If a non-price determinant of demand changes, we can show its effect by moving the entire curve from D to D1. We assumed in our example that the move was prompted by research in favour of naturally ventilated buildings. Therefore, at each and every price, a larger quantity would be demanded than before. For example, at price P the quantity of naturally ventilated buildings demanded increases from Q to Q1.

We could use a similar analysis when discussing decreases in demand due to a change in non-price determinants. The only difference would be that the demand curve would shift to the left, demonstrating that the quantity demanded is less at each and every price.

By contrast, the price determinant causes a movement along the demand curve. This is obvious when one remembers that the demand curve represents price and quantity relationships. Changes to the quantity of demand due to price alone are often referred to as an extension or contraction of demand. This involves a move along the demand curve. When more is demanded at a lower price, this may be regarded as an extension from one coordinate on the demand curve to another. When less is demanded, due to a rise in price, demand is said to contract. Such movements along the demand curve are described further in Figure 3.3.

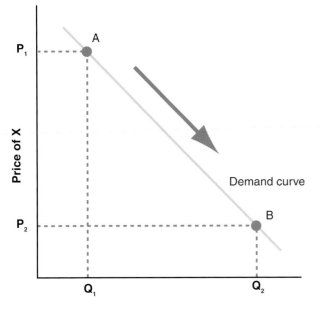

Quantity of X demanded / year

Fig 3.3 Change in price

We show the demand curve for a hypothetical good X. If the price is P1, then the quantity demanded would be Q1; we will be at coordinate A. If the price falls to P2, and all other factors in this market remain constant, then there will be an extension of demand to Q2 D from coordinate A to coordinate A.

Before we can begin to apply our theoretical knowledge of demand, it is particularly important to remember the distinction between a movement along, and a shift in, a demand curve. These rules will not only help us to understand the graphical analysis, but they will also enable us to acknowledge the numerous factors that come into play when interpreting demand.

Chapter Summary 3.2

- Four major non-price determinants are: (a) income, (b) price of other goods, (c) expectations, and (d) government policy.
- If any of the non-price determinants change, the demand schedule shifts to the right or left and we refer to an increase or decrease of demand (see Figure 3.2).
- Movements along a given demand curve are caused by price changes and these are described as contractions or extensions of demand (see Figure 3.3).

The Theory of Supply

4

Summaries to Review

Ceteris paribus (2.4)
Supply and demand graph (2.4)
Supply and demand curve (2.4)
Changing market conditions (2.5)
Equilibrium price (2.5)

Aims and Objectives

This chapter introduces the supply-side of the industry, taking a similar approach to that used for demand in Chapter 3. It completes the theoretical background to understanding markets in practice. Specifically by the end of this chapter you should understand:

- The importance of profit in making market based decisions
- The nature and determinants of supply in property markets
- Institutional frameworks that influence the property sector
- How markets work (identifying the role of expectations, elasticity, time lags, etc.)

As the chapter Summaries to Review may suggest, the theory of supply involves a similar approach to that of the previous chapter on demand and, to some extent, this gives us an intellectual start. We will not, however, fully appreciate the suppliers' side of the market until we reach the end of the text; especially as it is not until the next chapter that we explore the complex chain of events that link those involved in the development, construction, and use of property. It will quickly become apparent that the relationships between these different groups are fragmented and that each market is supplied by a distinct group of agents with their own codes of conduct.

As highlighted in Chapter 3, it is extremely difficult to envisage just one market for commercial property or housing, and it is usual to distinguish at least four sectors within each of these markets respectively. As outlined in Table 3.4, the commercial sector comprises office buildings, retail premises, industrial units and leisure outlets; some of these are owned by the occupier but most are rented. In direct contrast, the largest residential sector is made up of owner-occupied houses, with relatively fewer properties available to rent from the public and private sectors. Table 2.1 states the number of households living in each form of tenure. In every case the number of units available, for rent or purchase, depends on existing stock and newly completed stock. As a very general rule of thumb, the latter represents approximately 1% of the total stock in any one year! For example, in 2008 the total stock of commercial property increased by 0.5% and housing increased by 0.7%. Even in a boom year with relatively high completions the total rate of property growth would rarely exceed 2%. As a result, at any one particular time period the stock of property available for supply to the market is fixed.

Costs and Price

To understand the theory of supply it is useful to distinguish between cost and price. When a producer sells a good to a consumer the cost and price should not be the same. The usual assumption made by economists is that all producers (suppliers) seek to *maximise* profit! Therefore, it is most important that the cost of providing the service, or the good, is less than the selling price. To take a simple example, it is usual in construction for the cost of a project to be estimated and a mark-up for profits (risks) and overheads added before arriving at a price for the job. The contractor's mark-up is the difference between price and cost. In the present UK environment, however, many clients have become more knowledgeable and powerful; the client (or consultants acting on behalf of the client) predetermines an acceptable price and the contractor has to try to meet this figure.

The important point to reiterate is that all suppliers or businesses aim to make as much profit as possible; to the extent that, if the level of profit falls in one area of activity, entrepreneurs may move their resources to another sector where the returns are higher. To take a recent example, six new office blocks were completed in Hong Kong (during a rapid phase of change) and before they were even occupied they were replaced with luxurious apartment blocks because that way the property asset would generate far more profit. To illustrate this profit-maximising behaviour economists employ a concept of **normal profit**.

Normal profit is included in the cost of production, as it is regarded as the essential minimum reward necessary to attract the entrepreneur into economic activity. The concept of normal profit also highlights that all resources can be employed in several ways (that is, all resources have alternative uses). Consequently, what is meant by 'profit' by economists differs from its general meaning in everyday usage. To portray the general meaning of profit the following formula could be used:

$$\text{profits} = \text{total revenues} - \text{total costs}$$

For economists an alternative formula is required:

Ecomic profits = total revenues − total opportunity cost of all inputs used

The process is complicated further by the fact that, for most construction work, a price needs to be stated before the activity commences; when all the costs are not yet known. In the commercial sector rents are often fixed for five years or more before review. This property-related pricing contrasts sharply with manufacturing. Here, the producer does not have to determine the price until the activity is complete and all the costs have been revealed.

The Basic Law of Supply

The basic idea of supply has already been introduced in Chapter 2, where we explained that the **supply curve** slopes upwards from left to right, demonstrating that as the price rises, the quantity supplied rises and, conversely, as the price

Definition

Normal profit is the minimum level of reward required to ensure that existing entrepreneurs are prepared to remain in their present area of business.

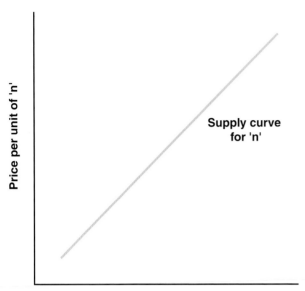

Quantity supplied of 'n'/month

Fig 4.1 The supply curve for an individual firm

The standard supply curve for most goods and services slopes upwards from left to right. The higher the price, the higher the quantity supplied (other things being equal).

falls, the quantity supplied falls. The **law of supply**, therefore, can be expressed as the opposite of the relationship stated for demand.

> **Definition**
>
> The law of supply states that the higher the price the greater the quantity offered for sale, the lower the price, the smaller the quantity offered for sale, all other things being held constant.

In other words, the law of supply tells us that the quantity supplied of a product is positively (directly) related to that product's price, other things being equal. This is displayed in Figure 4.1.

The Market Supply Schedule: in Theory

The incentives within a specific market – and the constraints faced – are roughly the same for all suppliers. Each individual firm seeks to maximise its profits, and each firm is subject to the **law of increasing costs**.

> **Definition**
>
> The law of increasing costs states that, as a firm uses more and more of its resources to produce a specific item, after a point, the cost for each additional unit produced increases disproportionately.

This law highlights that resources are scarce and generally suited to some activities better than others. It is not possible to continually increase the quantity supplied of a specific item without the cost increasing at a disproportionately high rate. In other words, when we utilise less well-suited resources to a particular production activity, more and more units of these resources have to be used to achieve an increase in output.

A firm's costs will also be affected by its fixed overheads. These vary according to the size of the firm and the nature of its activities. For example, a typical construction firm has relatively low fixed costs, as the construction contractor's output is not based in a permanent factory, with all its related fixed costs. In effect, each new construction site takes on the function of the firm's factory, and much of the fixed capital is hired as and when required. The fixed costs of a property developer would be slightly higher as they will need to maintain a permanent office, usually in a smart area, with high-tech IT equipment. By comparison, however, the firm manufacturing goods in a factory will have even higher fixed costs as the machinery will need to be paid for regardless of output.

We are now in a position to begin to appreciate the theoretical concept of a **market supply schedule**. The market supply of a product is given by the sum of the amounts that individual firms will supply at various prices. For example, at a price of £6 per unit, we might find that three firms are willing to supply 400, 300 and 200 units per day, respectively. If these three firms make up the whole industry, we could conclude that at a price of £6 the market supply in this hypothetical industry would be 900 units per day. Let us consider this example in more detail. The relevant data is presented in Table 4.1.

In Table 4.1 we see how three firms competing in the same industry perform individually at various prices. At low prices, producers B and C offer nothing at all for sale; most probably because high production costs constrain them. At higher prices, the law of increasing costs imposes constraints. By adding up each individual firm's output, at each specific price, we can discover the total supply that firms would be willing and able to bring to the market. We have highlighted the combinations at £6 per unit. As a brief educational exercise you could try to plot the market supply schedule on a graph. If you do it correctly, the supply curve for the market should be similar to that for an individual firm – a curve sloping upwards from left to right, as represented in Figure 4.1.

To take one example, in the construction market there are numerous firms that contribute to the supply of construction products, including large national contractors, material manufacturers, plant hirers and local site labourers. So, while it may be theoretically possible to estimate construction supply by summing what the firms in the market are willing to supply at various prices, the huge range of private contractors involved in construction complicates

Table 4.1 Individual and market supply schedules for a hypothetical industry

The data shows that, as price increases, supplies are willing to produce greater quantities. At the other extreme, low prices may actually discourage some firms from operating in the market. By combining the supply from each firm within the industry, the total market supply, at each price, is identified; this is shown in the final column

Price	Quantities supplied			
£/Unit	Firm A Units/day	Firm B Units/day	Firm C Units/day	Total Market supply
4	0	0	0	0
5	300	0	0	300
6	400	300	200	900
7	500	380	250	1,130
8	580	460	280	1,320
9	620	500	290	1,410
10	650	520	295	1,465

the process of simply aggregating individual supply curves. There are approximately 200,000 firms in Great Britain supplying construction-based activity and, as we have discussed in earlier chapters, the industry is clearly not one simple market. For instance, there can be little competition in the supply of products between the local builder undertaking repair and maintenance in a small town and a large national civil engineering firm. They supply separate markets. The point to note here is that we need to consider factors affecting supply in specific markets. This mirrors the approach taken in the previous chapter on demand; where we acknowledged property as comprising several different markets. As such, it is useful to envisage each market operating with distinct factors of demand and supply.

Chapter Summary **4.1**

- As a general rule of thumb, new builds represents less than 1% of the total stock in any one year. As a result, in any particular time period the stock of property available for supply to the market is fixed.
- Accounting profits differ from economic profits. Economic profits are defined as total revenues minus total costs, including the full opportunity cost of all the factors of production.
- In economics, profit maximisation is regarded as the main objective of a firm's behaviour.
- The basic law of supply is that as price rises larger quantities are supplied, and as price falls smaller quantities are supplied. There is a direct, or positive, relationship between price and the quantity supplied other things being constant (see Figure 4.1).
- Each individual firm will determine how much it can produce at various prices. Fixed overheads and the law of increasing costs affect firms differently.
- The market supply of a product is derived by the summation of the amounts that individual firms will supply at various prices. Plotting these total amounts against their related prices enables one to construct a market supply curve.
- In broad terms, the property and construction sectors comprise of many suppliers; to proceed with any analysis, therefore it is usual to consider factors affecting supply in specific markets.

Supply in the Property Industry

In the property industry, supply is not as straightforward as the elementary theory (outlined above) suggests. Property is always fixed in location, expensive to demolish and long-lasting. The institutional arrangements for funding via mortgages and loans alongside the conventions of long leases in the commercial sector create complicated time lags. As a consequence, property markets are slower to adjust than other market sectors. Indeed, as property prices, or their rents, increase the quantity supplied, in the short run, does not alter!

To put it another way, price movements in property markets tend not to affect the immediate supply available. The stock of property is fixed and supply can be described as **perfectly inelastic**.

This applies well to property markets as in the short run the same quantity of property exists regardless of the level of rent or prices achieved. This should not be interpreted to imply that property markets are not broadly competitive; it is simply stated to make a clear distinction between **short run** and **long run**

Definition

Perfectly inelastic supply describes a situation where the quantity of a good or service is fixed, regardless of its price.

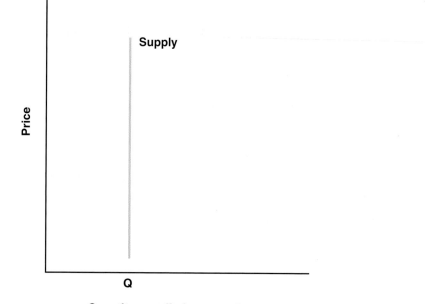

Fig 4.2 Perfectly inelastic supply

The supply curve is vertical at quantity Q, as the supply is the same no matter what the price.

time horizons in property markets. The short run is defined in economics as any period when at least one factor of production is fixed; so a change in price cannot lead to a change in supply. In the long run all factors are variable so adjustments can be made to changing market conditions.

In the short run, therefore, rental values and property prices are demand determined because adjustments cannot quickly be made to the supply of property. In fact, it is the inelastic supply relative to demand that causes property markets to be unstable and characterised by fluctuating prices. At any one specific time period, the supply of buildings is fixed and the supply curve is a vertical line. This scenario is demonstrated in Figure 4.2. It shows that the quantity supplied during a three-month period is the same regardless of price. For any percentage change in price, the quantity supplied remains constant. (Note: the same situation can be envisaged for demand; that is, a vertical demand curve represents zero elasticity at every price, too. For example, the price of electricity or gas may increase but in the short-term consumers will continue to demand the same amount of energy until they have had time to switch to more energy-efficient options.)

As introduced in Chapter 1, land is also characterised by being perfectly inelastic; that is, as property prices increase the quantity supplied does not immediately alter. Undeveloped areas can be developed and existing areas of land can change use; but both these possibilities take time.

Supply and the Price Determinant

As the law of supply states: in general terms more goods are supplied at higher prices, other things being held constant. This is because at higher prices there is greater scope for firms to earn a profit. Firms already in the market have an incentive to expand output, while higher prices may also enable those firms on the fringes of the market to enter the industry. At higher prices, therefore, the increased quantity supplied is made up by existing firms expanding output and a number of new firms entering the market. For example, in Table 4.1 we showed that in our hypothetical industry at a price of £5 per unit market supply was 300 units per day, but higher prices enticed other firms into the market and total supply increased.

In property markets, however, as house and property prices increase the quantity supplied, in the immediate time horizon, tends not to alter. The important point has already been made above; increasing the supply of property takes time. If firms have some surplus capacity, such as vacant land with planning permission already granted, they may be able to increase production fairly rapidly. But once a firm reaches full capacity supply is fixed until extra capacity can be installed. For property, therefore, this is a particular issue and we need to remember the distinction made between the short run, when adjustments to changes in market conditions have not yet taken place; and the long run when firms have had sufficient time to adjust fully to the changes in the market place. This is important because property market shocks are more likely to be seen in price movements than supply changes.

Supply and Non-Price Determinants

Until now, we have discussed supply and its related curve on the assumption that only price changes. We have not effectively considered any other determinants that influence producers' behaviour. We have constantly reiterated the *ceteris paribus* qualification, that other things are held constant. Some of these 'other things' assumed constant are the costs of production, technology, government policy, weather, the price of related goods, expectations, the goals of producers (do they wish, for example, to maximise profits or sales), and so on. Indeed, there are many non-price determinants; we shall broadly consider four.

Cost of Production

We have implied that producers are seeking to maximise their profits. Therefore, any change in production costs will, *ceteris paribus*, affect the quantity supplied. To illustrate this principle, return to Table 4.1. If unit production costs increase by £1, and this additional cost cannot be passed on by suppliers, then they will supply less to the market at each price. These changed conditions will cause the market to shrink so that, for example, only 300 units per day would be supplied at a price of £6 per unit.

In terms of economics, what is happening is that the supply curve has shifted to the left: less is now supplied at each and every price. The opposite would occur if one or more of the inputs became cheaper. This might be the case if, say, technology improves, but such opportunities seem slow to emerge in the construction and property sectors as they tend to be labour intensive and culturally inclined to invest little in research, development and training.

Government

In a similar way, taxes and subsidies also affect costs and thus supply. For instance, landfill tax increased construction costs and reduced supply at each price. A subsidy would have the opposite effect, increasing supply at each price, as every producer would be 'paid' a proportion of the cost of each unit produced by the government. For example, Real Estate Investment Trusts launched in 2007, provide tax incentives to those using their personal savings to invest into property. A more complicated issue is the impact of general taxation, as much of the demand for property is derived and depends on how others forecast their requirements. The most direct impact that the government has on markets concerned with buildings is through legislation. Obviously the industry is affected by changes in statutory regulations that apply to building, planning, energy, health and safety.

Institutional Arrangements

It would be rare for a property developer to be able to complete any project entirely alone; just consider, for example, the variety of materials and design specifications that need to be supplied and the range of financial funding that needs to be agreed for a typical project to progress. Most development involves integrating and managing a whole host of activities and processes before the final product can be delivered. A development pipeline is discussed further in Chapter 5 and the various stages are summarised in Figure 5.1. The purpose of this section, however, is to highlight the significance of institutional arrangements to the supply of property.

During the last decade the **institutional model** has captured the imagination of property economists as an explanation of the supply side of property markets.

In other words, the model recognises the importance of the legislative, financial, political and cultural norms that influence the ways in which the property sector operates. Clearly such institutional characteristics vary from one decade to the next, and can form the basis of an account for the changing nature of the supply of property.

For example, in the mid-1980s banks, building societies and insurance companies began to compete in each other's markets and the competition that ensued increased the flow of funds that were available for investment into property. Subsequently, this trend spread to the international financial network and the flow of funds supporting commercial, and residential, development acquired an increasingly international character. To a large extent, these changes to the codes of practice of financial institutions increased the rate of transactions for homes and commercial property through the nineties and into the mid-noughties, and in theoretical terms this historical period could be represented by a supply curve shifting to the right, as more was supplied at each and every price. Then the sudden financial hiatus arrived that brought about the current crisis and left markets generally struggling to find a new equilibrium.

Similarly, the period of urban regeneration that has characterised much of the property developed since the early 1990s can be attributed to institutional change. The government's Urban Task Force, which reported in July 1999, highlighted widespread decay in derelict urban districts. This led to the formation of the government-sponsored agency English Partnerships, set up to support government initiatives such as the *Sustainable Communities Plan.* The strategic role of English Partnerships involves identifying and organising land for development. Much of the land that it develops is already owned by the public sector, but from time to time private sector land needs to be acquired and infrastructure put in place. Since 2000, this work has seen the development of approximately 5,000 residential units, including housing for key workers and more than 500,000 square metres of commercial floorspace.

As a final example of changes to institutional arrangements we briefly review the standard commercial lease that is discussed more fully in Chapter 5 (under the heading Institutional Leases). For purposes of this section, we simply need to understand that until recently most commercial property

Definition
The institutional model is a new approach to understanding property markets by focusing on the rules, norms and regulations by which society functions.

Table 4.2 Property development 1985 to 2015

Time period	Institutional context	Impact on the market
1985–1995	Financial deregulation	Increased owner occupation and property investment opportunities
1995–2005	Urban regeneration	Government-led mixed mode development
2007–2010	Financial crisis	Banks become risk averse to providing loans
2005–2015	Shortening of commercial lease	Increased churn

was let for a fixed period of 25 years, with **upwards-only rent reviews** every five years. At present, however, there is a marked shortening of the lease length. As a consequence of this change, the proportion of firms with leases coming to an end will increase and the market will see more firms seeking to relocate. For example, when the typical lease was 25 years it could be assumed that every year one in twenty-five companies were seeking to review the terms of their lease and possibly relocate. The typical lease is now nearer eight years in length, so in any year we should see one in eight companies seeking to review and/or relocate. In short, there is in the region of three times more activity in the commercial property market. Table 4.2 summarises the above institutional arrangements and indicates their impact on property markets.

This discussion emphasises that, in order to understand the supply of property, we need to consider many related markets.

Expectations

A change in the expectations about future prices or prospects of the economy can also affect a producer's current willingness to supply. For example, builders may withhold from the market part of their recently built or refurbished stock if they anticipate higher prices in the future. In this case, the current quantity supplied at each and every price would decrease; the related supply curve would shift to the left.

Chapter Summary 4.2

- It is the inelastic supply of land and property that causes the related markets to be unstable and characterised by periods of escalating prices.
- Supply within the property sector is made up of several interrelated markets. Output is determined by thousands of firms that can transfer to other sectors of the industry if they think it would be worthwhile.
- The supply curve is plotted on the assumption that other things are held constant. Four important non-price determinants are: (a) costs of production (including technological changes), (b) government, (c) institutional changes, and (d) expectations.

Understanding Changes in Supply

Just as we were able to distinguish between shifts of, and movements along, the demand curve, so we can have the same discussion for the supply curve. A change in the price of a good itself will cause a movement along the supply curve, and be referred to as an extension or contraction of supply. A change in any non-price determinant, however, will shift the curve itself and be referred to as an increase or decrease in supply.

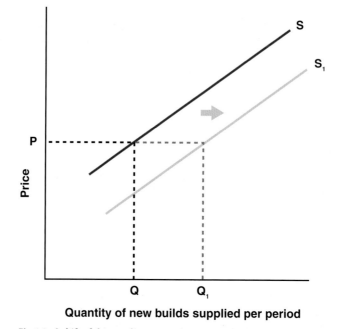

Fig 4.3 A shift of the supply curve

If prices change, we move along a given curve. However, if the costs of production fall, the supply curve shifts to the right from S to S_1, representing an increase in the quantity supplied at each and every price.

Let us consider one example in detail. If a new computer-assisted design (CAD) package that incorporates cost estimating, reduces fees relating to new builds, then design and build contractors will be able to supply more new buildings at all prices because their costs have fallen. Competition between contractors to design and build will ultimately shift the supply curve to the right, as shown in Figure 4.3. By following along the horizontal axis, we can see that this rightward movement represents an increase in the quantity supplied at each and every price. For example, at price P, the quantity supplied increases from Q to Q_1. Note that if, on the other hand, the costs of production rise, the quantity supplied would decrease at each and every price and the related supply curve would shift to the left.

For analytical purposes, it is helpful to distinguish the cause of changes in supply. In our example about CAD, it would have been wrong to conclude that price has simply fallen and quantity supplied expanded accordingly. The reason for the increase in supply, at all prices, is due to a change in technology.

Elasticity

Economists are often interested in the degree to which supply (or demand) responds to changes in price. The measurement of price responsiveness is termed price elasticity.

A numerical value for the price elasticity of supply (PES) may be calculated using the formula:

$$PES = \frac{\text{percentage change in quantity supplied}}{\text{percentage change in price}}$$

Definition

Price elasticity is a measurement of the degree of responsiveness of demand or supply to a change in price.

What the formula tells us is the relative amount by which the quantity supplied will change in relation to price changes. For example, if a 10% increase in price leads to a 1% increase in the quantity supplied the PES is 0.1.

That is a very small response. There are in effect three types of measure that economists use as a reference point to discuss price elasticity.

Price-inelastic Supply

When the numerical coefficient of the price elasticity of supply calculation is less than 1, supply is said to be 'inelastic'. This will always occur when the percentage figure for the change in supply is smaller than the percentage figure for the change in price. A PES coefficient of anything between 0 and 1 represents a situation of inelastic supply. The introductory example in which a 10% increase in price led to a very small response in supply suggests a price-inelastic response: the measured coefficient was 0.1. As explained above, in most cases where firms are supplying some form of property the price elasticity of supply, in the short term at least, will be inelastic. In fact, it has already been characterised as perfectly inelastic (see Figure 4.2).

Price-elastic Supply

When the numerical value of the price elasticity of supply calculation is greater than 1, supply is said to be 'elastic'. This will always be the case when the percentage change in supply is larger than the percentage change in price. For example, if a 5% rise in price leads to a 50% increase in quantity supplied, the PES coefficient will be 10. In other words, a small change in price elicits a large response in supply. This would be unusual occurrence in the markets for construction or property – but not impossible.

Unit-elastic Supply

This is the most hypothetical case, as it describes a situation in which a percentage change in price leads to an identical percentage change in supply. This will always produce a coefficient value of 1, since the same figure appears on both the top and bottom lines of the price elasticity of supply formula.

Chapter Summary 4.3

- If only price changes, we move along the supply curve and there is an extension or contraction of supply.
- If any of the non-price determinants changes, the entire supply curve shifts to the left or right and we refer to a decrease or increase in supply (see Figure 4.3).
- Price elasticity of supply is given by the percentage change in quantity supplied divided by the percentage change in price.
- Long-run supply curves are relatively more elastic than short-run supply curves because over a longer period of time more resources can flow into or out of an industry when price changes.

Combining Supply and Demand

So far the chapters on demand and supply have confined the discussion to isolated parts of the market relating to the consumer or producer. Obviously this separation is theoretical and only useful for educational purposes. In reality, there is a close relationship between the forces of demand and supply; and we have already explained in Chapter 2 how the interactions of supply and demand determine price. The concept of an equilibrium (or market) price at which both consumers' and producers' wishes are met was introduced in Figure 2.6. We now extend this model to consider the analysis from the supply side in any property market.

As discussed above, in both commercial and residential markets the available stock of property is fixed in the short run. New buildings may be started and completed, but this will take time to negotiate and process before they can be added to the existing stock in the market. The supply and demand analysis is presented in Figure 4.4. The solid lines show the initial equilibrium position. In the short run, the supply is perfectly inelastic; the stock of buildings is fixed regardless of the price or rent offered. In the long run, some new buildings could be added to the stock, existing buildings can be refurbished, greenfield areas can be redeveloped and brownfield sites can change use. Any of these developments would shift the vertical supply curve to the right, which is shown by the dotted line in Figure 4.4, showing an increase in quantity from Q to Q_1. Theoretically, this could lead to a fall in price from P to P_2, but assuming that property appraisals have forecasted correctly and demand has also increased at each and every price (shown by D_1) then we arrive at a new equilibrium at P_1. In short, movements in the price, or rent, assure that the quantity demanded is matched by the available supply.

Another way of expressing the nature of this lagged response in the property market is to describe it as supply-led; this characteristic is explored further in Chapter 5.

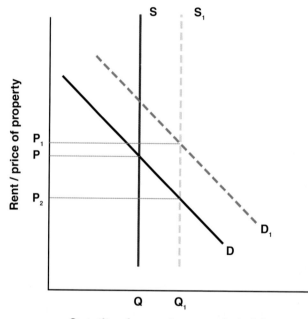

Quantity of property per period of time

Fig 4.4 Supply and demand of property

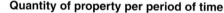

Chapter Summary 4.4

- By combining the forces of supply and demand we can begin to understand many markets.
- The concept of equilibrium demonstrates how the wishes of sellers and buyers are brought together via price.
- Price elasticity of supply is identified by the percentage change in the quantity supplied divided by the percentage change price.
- In reality, the determinants of supply and demand need to be considered simultaneously.

Tutorial **2**

✓ CHECK POINT

By this point in the text you should be able to:
- ✓ Understand the basis of theoretical analysis of property and related markets.
- ✓ Begin to understand commentary in the press and media relating to property markets.
- ✓ Recognise how commercial and residential markets can be broken down into a number of sectors.
- ✓ Recognise that the markets for property are different to the market for general goods and services.
- ✓ Begin to sense that markets and price signals can be relied upon to promote a competitive spirit that is strong enough to efficiently allocate resources.

Introduction to Tutorial 2

Chapters 3 and 4 outlined the theory of allocating resources through markets. At several points along the way, however, it has been suggested that the free interplay of supply and demand may not be completely appropriate for all property markets. Therefore, the following extract raises some specific questions about how efficiently the market mechanism allocates resources to social housing.

The principle behind these tutorial exercises is to encourage discussion and thought, and in this instance, we seek to encourage you to form an opinion about the efficiency of allowing the free market to work and to what extent government remedies should be borne in mind. Indeed the role of government forms an important theme to the remaining chapters of the textbook. So take time to carefully read and understand the extract before considering the questions at the close.

Tutorial Reading

The market for social housing

Thirty years after the Thatcher government brought in its revolutionary Right To Buy scheme, the new coalition government could be about to trigger another major overhaul of the social housing sector. The October 2010 Comprehensive Spending Review has signalled the start of a radical journey to remove the Government's deficit by the financial year 2015–2016. From the first step in the plan it appears that the Department for Communities and Local Government is expected to be one of the departments to bear the full brunt of the cuts.

Communities Secretary Eric Pickles, a politician who made his name in the late 1980s slashing spending at Bradford council, has already committed to cutting his department's revenue spending by a third, and is now considering ways of privatising social housing to unlock another £125bn.

Housing minister Grant Shapps caused controversy at the 2010 Conservative Party conference when he hinted that one of the biggest casualties of the cuts looks set to be the National Affordable Housing Programme (NAHP) – the pot of money which funds all of England's social housing and which, in 2009–2010, stood at £3.2bn.

Shapps said that the current housing funding system had failed and the government would look at new models of investment in future. 'All options are on the table [as far as the NAHP is concerned]', Shapps told delegates. 'I don't think there is anything particularly magical about funding affordable housing through capital as it hasn't been particularly successful'. He added that the £8.4bn of NAHP funding from 2008 to

Tutorial 2

2011 had not produced what he would have hoped for, and pointed out that: 'We need to be open-minded to other ways of funding people to live in affordable homes'.

Pickles and Shapps are likely to pay special attention to a recent report entitled: *Unlocking Capacity from the Affordable Housing Sector in England* published by building consultancy EC Harris. This predicts that the government could raise £80bn by spinning off housing association and local authority housing stock into a fund to sell to investors. The government, it adds, could save another £37bn at a stroke by replacing the public sector grant on the balance sheets of housing associations with private finance (see Table 4.3 for savings totalling £125bn).

At the Conservative's 2010 conference, Shapps mentioned Hyde Group's deal to raise £200m with a bond issue – the fourth issued in the social housing sector this year – which offered investors an interest rate of 5.2% secured on the 45,000 homes it owns or manages. The cash raised will be used to refinance existing debt and support the building of 1,000 homes. Shapps said: 'This successful bond issue shows just what can be done when housing associations are innovative in raising money to benefit people in social housing'.

Rebecca Bennett Casserly, group head of residential-affordable at EC Harris and author of the report, says: 'New legislation and a changing financial environment mean that new sources of funding and investment are starting to emerge. Legislation has now been enacted to allow commercial companies to be "for profit" registered [social housing] providers. Why can't existing providers reconstitute themselves to attract private equity?'

A further £6bn of additional bank borrowing could be leveraged, Bennett Casserly adds, by enabling housing associations greater flexibility to manage their housing portfolios along more commercial lines. In short, this means allowing social housing providers to cut down on the amount of loss-making social rented housing they provide and replace it with profitable 'shared ownership' schemes. These schemes – which by their nature are offered to 'key workers' rather than the unemployed – enable

Table 4.3 A radical shake-up of affordable housing could unlock £125bn for reinvestment

Challenge	Possible solutions	Potential outcomes	Potential value
A need to drive greater value for money from public funding	Unlock the latent value of existing stock to leverage additional capital	Releasing £80bn of capital appreciation from existing stock	£80 billion
		Replacing £37bn of public grant with private finance	£37 billion
Severely constrained public funding for new affordable homes	Incentivise new commercial models to attract private investment	Greater flexibility to manage housing portfolios by, for example, using half of the affordable housing stock that becomes vacant for rent	£6 billion
A need to encourage new commercial owners and operators	New providers could drive improved performance and create tougher benchmarks on efficiency	Operational efficiencies in the sector alone could save £2bn	£2 billion
			Total £125 billion

low-paid workers to buy part of their home with a small mortgage and then usually rent the other portion. The idea of increased private sector involvement in the social housing sector, while politically controversial, is finding popularity with many in the private sector.

'Housing associations and developers will look at possible partnerships as an alternative to the established patterns of providing affordable housing', says Home Builders Federation director of external affairs John Slaughter. 'The private sector will not be able to provide higher [social housing] contributions to new schemes, given that business conditions are more challenging than they were prior to the downturn'.

The prospect of a substantial cut to NAHP cash is already having a major impact on housebuilders. This is because the affordable housing units developed by house-builders under section 106 planning obligations are usually sold to housing associations, which pay for them with social housing grant. If no grant is available, developers are often forced to foot much of the bill for such housing themselves.

Here again, the government is coming under increasing pressure to persuade councils to be more flexible in their demands on property developers so that affordable housing continues to be built.

James Brown, development director at Hamptons International, says that in situations where no social housing grant is available, developers should be allowed to build profitable intermediate affordable housing through the likes of shared equity schemes rather than costly social rented housing.

'Unfortunately, many local authorities don't allow developers to do this because, within the short to medium term, they can see that this could realistically lead to very little affordable housing being delivered', says Brown.

Source: Edited from 'Homes set for a snip', *Estates Gazette*, 16 October 2010, pp 72–73.

Tutorial Questions

1. Can the free market be left to allocate housing?
2. Using supply and demand analysis explain and discuss the function of price signals in housing markets; and how this might affect the rent in the market for social housing.
3. The article suggests that social housing providers will need to adapt to changes in market conditions if they are to continue acquiring sources of funding in the future. State two examples of the changes that are envisaged in the market for social housing.
4. In what ways would the answers change if commercial property became the point of focus to questions 1 and 2?

Development, Construction and Occupation

5

Summaries to Review

Aims and Objectives

This chapter briefly overviews the main aspects of property development in which the design, construction and operation are commonly regarded as distinct stages; and this fragmentation of interests causes some tensions as we progress along the development pipeline. Specifically by the end of this chapter you should understand:

- The supply-side of the industry – the process of development

- The characteristics of the construction sector

- The demand side, by looking at occupation and buildings in use

---

The three activities represented in this chapter should form an integrated market. Unfortunately, however, the property world is diverse, disorganised and dysfunctional – in a word, 'fragmented'. As a result, this chapter examines three sets of separate relations as each sector is represented by its own culture, code of conduct and economic agents. To take one of many possible examples, a variety of professions need to liaise in the process of development and construction before occupation of a property can occur. Yet each group seem to act in isolation, as if they are in separate markets, with surprisingly few relationships between them. Table 5.1 highlights the number of disparate professional organisations and an approximate size of current membership across the activities; it only requires a little imagination to understand the conflict of interests that can emerge between those involved in the same projects.

Clearly this is a complex set of relationships. There are few shared values or systems integrating the processes and even academic research and its associated literature tend to specialise in only one sector. For example, there are several, respective, texts and academic papers on construction, development and office use; and there is active research into the economics of housing, commercial property, construction and urban issues. But it is rare for these to be considered together between the same covers. Compounding this lack of cohesive thinking, occupiers are not effectively represented as a group (either

Table 5.1 Professions associated with property development

Professional body	Approximate membership
Chartered Institute of Architectural Technologists	9,500
Chartered Institute of Building	45,000
Chartered Institute of Building Services Engineers	20,000
Institution of Civil Engineers	84,500
Institution of Structural Engineers	23,500
Royal Institute of British Architects	44,000
Royal Institution of Chartered Surveyors	110,000

Source: Relevant websites.

professionally or academically) and it is only in the last few years that they have gained sufficient respect to be referred to as 'clients' or 'customers'.

In fact, it appears that investors, contractors, building managers, architects and planners all operate in parallel but separate universes; rarely singing from the same song sheet. Consequently, there is an odd relationship between those who demand buildings for their performance attributes and those who supply them. Not surprisingly, the market for property is often regarded as supply-led and adversarial. In a similar vein, a journalist once charmingly characterised the property industry as resembling a flock of pecking chickens: fragmented, quarrelsome and, as a group, largely ineffectual.

Development

There are two types of developer, those who create built environment assets for investment clients and those who develop property for their own purposes; sometimes distinguished by the phrases **investor–developer** and **trader–developer**. In very general terms, the developer provides the entrepreneurial talent that enables property opportunities to be brought to the marketplace.

This is not as simple or as straight-forward as it sounds, and the complicated nature of development activity needs to be captured in any comprehensive definition. The following is just one of many possibilities.

Definition

Development is a complex process that involves the co-ordination of finance, materials, labour and expertise by many actors across a wide range of sectors.

In other words, a completed building represents the culmination of an intricate web of relationships and negotiations, with many of the underlying transactions completely 'invisible', and unknown, to the passer-by. Indeed, the average commercial property development will take far longer to complete from its initial conception, than the visible construction phase would suggest; something near a ratio of 10:1. In plain English, it could take in the region of 10 years to complete the various stages before construction, which would be relatively quick. Thereafter, the building has at the very least 25 years of commercial life.

Figure 5.1 illustrates some of the main events in the property development process; and it can be thought of like any other form of economic production, as it involves the integration of land, capital and labour. The time dimension is emphasised by the distance from the beginning to the end of the pipeline and managing the chain of events inevitably requires some creative vision for a successful venture.

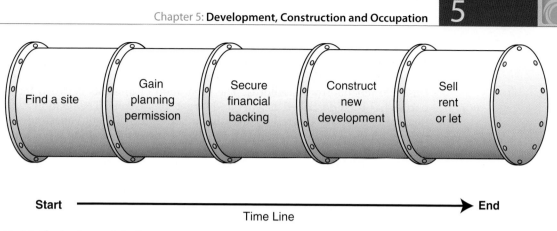

Start ——————————————————————➤ End

Time Line

Fig 5.1 The development pipeline

The pipeline analogy tends to oversimplify the process, as effective property development depends upon bringing together all the resources at the right time and place; the risks of a poorly managed project can be quite costly. In fact, it can be argued that the property development process, more than any other industry, demonstrates the importance of the entrepreneur. The essential ingredient to any successful property project is the timing of a person with vision who is prepared to take the risks necessary to bring resources together to create assets that will form a sufficient stream of future income to generate profit. Indeed, relatively few property developers own land, capital and labour in its own right; they just bring all the factors of production together. Furthermore, it is only within the past 30 years that this process has stopped being initiated by the developer relying solely on 'gut' instincts; nowadays, appraisals of property development decisions are increasingly supported by research data.

The process of development is unlike the manufacturing industry, as there is no continuous chain of events producing one building after the other, dependant on the employment of the same team of labour. Each development project, and its associated team, is different. Each unit of production needs to be negotiated, planned and designed before construction and occupation can commence. The analogy of a film set may be useful to illustrate how the various professions and trades are brought together, to do their work (complete a development) and then leave for another location to do 'similar' work for another developer.

Finally, before completing this introduction to the development process, it is worth remembering that the majority of residential property is usually speculatively developed, in the sense that it is built ('on spec') without a specific purchaser (or tenant) being identified. Commercial property is becoming increasingly developed for a named tenant; i.e. it is 'pre-let' or 'bespoke' (for sale or rent). The sharpest contrast between these two sectors, however, is in the pattern of ownership; houses are mostly owner-occupied and commercial property is usually rented by businesses on long-term contracts. The implications of this separation of interests between the ownership and use of commercial property are explored further in the next section, and again when we consider the perspective of occupation.

For Sale or Let

As Figure 5.1 indicates, at the end of the development pipeline the property is put on the market for sale, or to let. This can create an unusual conflict of interests as property primarily meets the needs of those that own them, rather than those that occupy them. This creates an interesting dilemma, as in many cases it has led to the development of mediocre buildings that pay little attention to running costs or user comfort. This is equally true of multiple-let residential or commercial properties. The crisis, however, is particularly notable in the energy-guzzling, crowded and uncomfortable office buildings that are leased to tenants from landlords. The separation of interests between these parties has been described as a 'let and forget' philosophy. The relationships that really exist are blurred by the divide between the agent collecting the rent and managing the property on behalf of a distant institution who owns the property as an investment asset! This separation between ownership and occupation is most pronounced in the terms of the standard commercial lease (also referred to as an institutional lease).

Institutional Leases

For most of the period since the Landlord and Tenant Act of 1954, the contractual agreement between the owner and the occupier of a commercial building meant that once a tenant signed a lease they remained responsible for the building and its rent throughout the subsequent 25 years. Furthermore, every five years the rent would be reviewed and could only be increased! While the legal jargon expressed it the **upward-only rent review** clause may seem anachronistic in a world of market forces, it is, nevertheless, self-explanatory and self-perpetuating; in fact, all that has happened in recent times is the introduction of 'break clauses' that allow tenants a way out of the contract.

Institutional leases give owners a surety of income and occupiers long-term commitment; but it is not market sensitive. (In the first edition of this text this lease arrangement was introduced as a classic example of market failure. The landlord has control over the freedoms to enter and exit the marketplace and at a rent that is often predetermined in their favour; such arrangements make nonsense of efficient market forces.) Up to 1990 around 90% of the commercial property owned by developers or financial institutions in the UK were rented out on this basis. Table 5.2 lists the main characteristics of the typical institutional lease.

Table 5.2 The main characteristics of a commercial lease

Traditionally run for 25 years or more
Landlord has control over any disposal of the lease by the tenant
Regular, say every 5 years, upward-only rent reviews
Tenant has full responsibility for insurance, repairs and maintenance
Tenant liability on successive assignees

To clarify what this type of lease involves consider the following analogy derived from Harris (2005). 'Just imagine that you had to rent your home and commit to a lease of 25 years, and were responsible for the cost of all repairs and insurance of the building during that time. Furthermore, should you decide to move before the 25 years are up, you must continue to pay the rent or find a replacement tenant. And that is not all, if the replacement tenant should at any time fail to pay his or her rent, the landlord could come back to you as the original signatory to the lease and demand payment. This arrangement no doubt strikes a ridiculous chord to the average occupier in the residential market, but in the commercial sector these are the type of arrangements that prevail as the norm'.

Obviously, as the pattern of shorter leases becomes more common (and it is noted that leases of five years or less are on the increase) there will be fewer rent reviews. Instead, there will simply be more firms looking to renegotiate or relocate at any point in time.

Chapter Summary 5.1

- Development is the process where land or old buildings are transformed into new uses. The process involves a number of stages identified in Figure 5.1.
- The developer as an entrepreneur can be seen in a wide variety of guises, organising different types of property for different markets.
- Generally, houses are developed for owner occupation and commercial property is usually rented by businesses on long-term contracts.
- The separation of interests between ownership and occupation is most pronounced in the terms of an institutional lease. The five typical characteristics of a standard lease are listed in Table 5.2.

Construction

One of the most striking features of the construction industry is the large number of small firms. In the UK alone, there are more than 200,000 private construction contractors and more than 90% of them employ fewer than eight people. Similarly across the other member states of the European Union, there are literally millions of contractors – employing tens of millions of people – accounting for nearly 10% of the total employment in Europe. Small firms dominate the industry for two main reasons: first, they can supply services, which do not suit the nature of large firms, such as repair and maintenance; and second they can supply labour on a subcontract basis to large firms.

Labour-only Subcontractors

It is usual in Europe for the majority of work carried out on a construction site to be done by subcontractors. To the main contractor, labour-only subcontracting offers a cheap and efficient option, as the self-employed worker is not entitled to holiday pay, redundancy money, sick leave, pension rights or any other benefits that accrue to permanent staff.

As a result of this tradition, a high level of fragmentation is associated with the European construction industry. To cite just one instance from the UK – after being in a post for six months, a construction minister remarked in an interview that, in terms of meeting all the trade associations, he was only halfway down the alphabet. The interviewer sarcastically added that: by the time he gets to Z he'll probably have moved on to his next job.

This way of working has resulted in an industry that has many interfaces which are often points of tension and conflict, which lead to increased cost and reduced efficiency. For example, some commentary of the 2010 BP oil disaster in the Gulf of Mexico claims that the problematic drilling rig would have been more efficiently managed if the services had not been subcontracted to another firm. In other words, if BP had owned and managed the platform services there would have been greater control and less chance of incidents. Figure 5.2 indicates the level of fragmentation that is typical of most construction projects; it highlights the number of negotiated contracts where tension, conflict and misunderstanding might arise and accounts for many of the industry's strengths and weaknesses.

Weaknesses

There is a recognised lack of collaboration within construction teams. For instance, a refurbishment to a Barclays Bank high street property would require up to 40 different suppliers ranging from architects to specialist contractors.

Construction

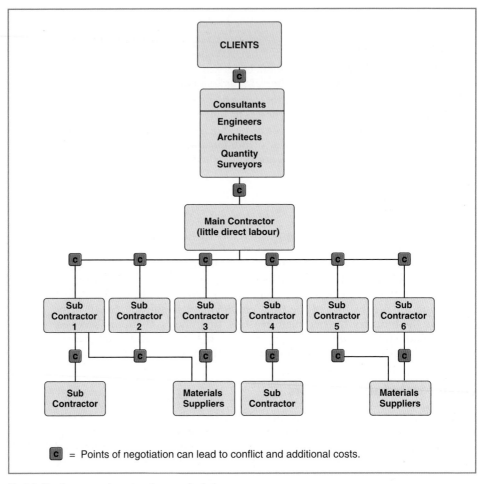

= Points of negotiation can lead to conflict and additional costs.

Fig 5.2 The fragmented construction supply chain

Similarly, Sir Robert McAlpine won the contract to construct the main stadium at the Olympics in London, but he employed more than 100 subcontractors to work on the project. Such diverse teams can lead to a lack of trust between the various subcontractors and account for the adversarial nature that often typifies relationships on site. Another weakness of fragmentation is the lack of commitment to education, training, research and safety on site. It is often suggested that contractors do not seem to learn from one project to the next – a common myth is that each building is regarded as a 'prototype'.

The generic outcome of all these shortfalls is the construction industry's seeming inability to construct on time, on budget and to the quality expected. Just studying the history of disastrous projects relating to British parliament buildings provides an extensive set of examples. The palace of Westminster (the houses of parliament) was burnt to the ground in 1834, and it took 26 years and a threefold budget increase to complete the redesign. More recently, the Westminster extension, Portcullis House, which opened in 2001, saw an increase in costs from £150 to £250 million; and a staggering 7,500 defects were recorded. Finally, the Scottish parliament went a spectacular £400 million over its initial £40 million budget and was delivered 20 months late.

Strengths

On the positive side, fragmentation enables the industry to be sufficiently flexible to deal with the highly variable workloads that accompany changing economic circumstances.

Clearly the weaknesses outweigh the strengths and this is why the various types of partnering agreements that are emerging are regarded as such promising developments. These are discussed in the next section.

Partnering

There are many definitions of **partnering** and different forms have been used in the UK, US and Japan.

The idea of partnering is only just beginning to gain momentum; and this is despite the publication of a number of government reports and academic papers written in support of its use. For example, the National Audit Office (NAO) report, published in 2001, emphasised throughout its pages that 'partnering' is the way to tackle the adversarial and inefficient working practices that characterise the construction industry. To support this development the NAO cited evidence to show how partnering could deliver cost savings ranging from as low as 2% to as much as 30% depending on the type of partnership. **Project partnering**, which is based on a client and contractor working openly on a single project, was stated to lead to cost savings of between 2 and 10%. Whereas **strategic partnering**, which involves the client and contractor working on a series of construction projects, was regarded as capable of delivering savings of up to 30%. In addition, partnering has the potential to deliver better designs, make construction safer, enable deadlines to be met with ease and provide all parties with increased profits. Examples of partnering are emerging worldwide in various forms of **public private partnerships**. One established scheme is the **Private Finance Initiative (PFI)** and this is described in the following section.

> **Definition**
>
> Partnering refers to some form of collaborative approach in which clients and contractors are increasingly open with one another in order to meet common objectives.

Private Finance Initiative

This form of partnering has a higher profile (a web search will show there has been a large number of articles in the press) and it represents some of the biggest projects presently being constructed. Projects such as: highways, hospitals, prisons, schools and government offices. Since its official launch in the UK, in November 1992, more than 650 PFI contracts have come into force, representing future commitments of around £250 billion, and similar arrangements are a growing phenomenon worldwide.

In these projects the public and private sectors collaborate. Initially, the public sector takes on the role of the developer; specifying the requirements and vetting the tenders. This public sector development role is not usually identified, as it comes very early in the chain of events, and the majority of the long-term development role is transferred to a group of private investors. The group formally awarded with the contract are referred to as a 'consortium' or 'special purpose vehicle' (SPV).

The SPV may comprise of a number of companies such as: a building or FM contractor, a bank or management company, or separate liaising companies. (Subsequently, the SPV may subcontract its responsibilities.) This complex set of relationships is shown in Figure 5.3, where the PFI relationships have been simplified into a flow diagram.

In other words, a project procured under the private finance initiative is based on a new kind of relationship between a public sector client and private sector contractors. The general procedure is as follows: private firms

> **Definition**
>
> In a PFI contract a group of private sector operators are given the contractual right to build, design, finance and manage a project for a defined period of time before it is returned to the public sector.

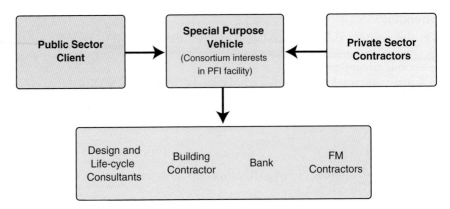

Fig. 5.3 The private finance initiative model

operating in a consortium, agree to design, build, *finance*, and *manage* a facility traditionally provided by the public sector. (Finance and manage are italicised to emphasise that a distinguishing characteristic of these schemes is that, under PFI arrangements, the private sector is expected to raise the initial finance to fund the project and thereafter to manage and/or maintain its operation.) In return, the public sector client agrees to pay annual charges and/or allows the private sector to reap any profits that can be made during the life of the contract – which may last up to 30 years or more. In this way, both sectors can be seen to be specialising in what they do best: with the public sector client setting the agenda by specifying the level of service required and the private sector contractor determining the best way to deliver that service.

These PFI arrangements have obvious advantages as the contractor no longer 'Builds And Disappears' – as in the BAD old days – because the contractor (as part of the consortium) is involved in managing the project once it has been built. When the private sector has money at risk in this way, there are far greater incentives to make sure everything is right, especially as the consortium now have to consider the running and maintenance costs.

Advantages and Disadvantages of Partnering

It is easy to see why partnering in any form is an attractive idea. In purely economic terms, it has the advantage of eliminating inefficiency insofar as costs per unit of output are reduced. Leibenstein's concept of **x-inefficiency** can be applied.

Definition

The notion of 'x-inefficiency' is used to describe a market, or firm, that is not subject to a sufficient level of competitive pressure to reduce costs.

As Leibenstein explained when a government agency or individual firm is left entirely to their own devices to choose the *activity* they carry out, its *pace*, the *quality* and *time* spent, they are unlikely to choose the activity-pace-quality-time (APQT) bundle that will maximise efficiency. In other words, if a public sector authority or individual contractor can choose what to build, how to build it, how long to spend on the project and so on, they are less likely to maximise the value of output. The resulting loss of value is what Leibenstein referred to as x-inefficiency and his solution depended on securing a more competitive market structure; to push firms beyond their usual capacity. Partnering provides such a solution as it relies on the dynamics of the market; it puts the client more firmly in the driving seat, improves the flow of information between the participants and creates the necessary incentives to complete the contract on time, to budget and to the expected quality.

A significant disadvantage is that successful partnering is far easier for big firms than small firms – and construction is still dominated by the latter. In a truly competitive perfect market all information is freely available – everybody has access to the knowledge they need for exchange to take place – and transaction costs are zero. Governments often try to ensure that these conditions prevail by standardising legal and financial procedures, in order that market participants know where they stand. However, in construction markets where partnering and, in particular, PFI is emerging these conditions do not prevail. Many firms lack the necessary resources to understand the complex legal information that is inevitably associated with these forms of procurement. Transaction costs are prohibitively high, with architects', lawyers' and accountants' fees to be met by all the participating parties. As a result, it is unusual for more than three or four consortium groups to find sufficient resources to engage in the tedious, lengthy and detailed bidding processes involved. Indeed, PFI bidding costs can commonly exceed £1 million per project. The firms that are able to take on such large-scale operations and risks are few and far between, and it is a common concern that partnering arrangements often exclude the smaller contractors.

Chapter Summary **5.2**

- The problem of fragmentation, introduced at the beginning of the chapter, is typified by the construction team. Contractors liaise with the client to supply specified products that are subsequently produced by subcontractors.
- Reports by government departments and academics have advocated various forms of partnering as a vital part of improving efficiency in the construction industry.
- Partnering has made great strides in recent years – particularly under the umbrella of the private finance initiative.
- It is easier for large firms to benefit from partnering arrangements, as small firms generally lack the resources to participate in the lengthy and protracted negotiations.

Occupation

At the heart of any development or construction process are the occupants, or users, of the building: the retailers, office tenants, manufacturers (using a warehouse or factory), restaurateurs and residents. All have different needs and requirements of the property they use. Ironically, however, relatively few of them seem to know much about the development of property, its construction or its performance. From the client or occupier's perspective, acquiring new premises can be a complex and daunting prospect. This is particularly the case with the broad band of commercial property where the client may even be portrayed as 'a nuisance' in the development and construction process.

The idea of the occupier or client being a nuisance might seem odd to economists who study the broader economy, as theoretically in competitive markets the customer is regarded as 'king', in the sense that they determine what goods and services are produced. In fact, the basis of market economics (as introduced in Chapter 2) was created on an assumption of **consumer sovereignty**. Customers in the market for cars, food and consumer durables expect value for money; products that are free from defect; goods delivered on time, with worthwhile guarantees; and reasonable running costs. In sharp contrast, however, the picture portrayed of markets in development and construction imply that suppliers take the lead as they tend not to think about the client (the occupier) but more about the next employer in the contractual chain or the next investment in the development pipeline. In short, property development is dominantly supply-led.

The occupation of property is a costly business and accommodation costs can easily exceed £7,000 per employee per year; in the West End of London, the total occupancy costs can be as much as double this figure. Aside from the rent are the associated costs of fit-out, maintenance, furniture, IT equipment, cleaning, and energy. In total these represent a significant part of business costs; yet the institutional lease described above (see Table 5.2) makes it difficult for the occupier to freely exit the market once a contract has been agreed.

Inevitably such arrangements can lead to a market sector becoming economically inefficient; and there is some debate whether property developers always act in the occupiers' best interests. This debate can be explained via the **principal–agent** concept.

Definition

The principal–agent concept focuses on the contractual relationship that emerges when one party delegates to another person the performance of a specific economic transaction.

In this instance the contractual agreement under consideration is between the client or occupier – the 'principal' – and the developer or contractor – their 'agent'. The subsequent analysis raises questions about the balance of power between the less informed occupier and the knowledgeable agent. It is possible that the hired property 'agent' may not always act in their client's best interest; especially as they might be able to get away with it because of the 'principal's' incomplete knowledge. Any situation in which one party holds most of the cards can lead to an equivalent market imperfection, and the principal agent approach is in no way unique to property markets.

A conclusion following from this type of analysis is the need for the property industry to focus on the business – 'use' – value of their buildings as opposed to its investment value; to allow the demand side into the equation and to listen to their customers. In a metaphorical sense, to see office design from the other end of the telescope; to allow occupiers to express their needs more clearly and limit the prevailing conflict of interests. These messages have often been echoed in the pages of the *Estates Gazette* and rehearsed in the academic literature since the property slump in the early 1990s and new systems such as **sale and leaseback** and **serviced offices** have emerged – both of these are outlined in the next section.

Outsourcing

Traditionally all businesses have real estate assets and it is clear that their management and maintenance form a significant part of total operating costs. **Outsourcing** aims to lower these costs. In short, occupiers have begun to regard property as a service; not as an asset!

To express it another way, commercial property is beginning to be understood as a commodity – a mere factor of production – and a new approach is beginning to emerge where property occupiers focus on their 'core' business by transferring the ownership of related processes to a separate supplier. As a consequence, companies have begun to dispose of, or separate their real estate assets from, their trading operations. In other words, the corporate sector buy in the services they need and concentrate on their day-to-day business. Initially, this process involved the provision of services such as cleaning, security, reception services, and so on. However, it soon extended to a more comprehensive package of facility management and nowadays also includes office accommodation.

> **Definition**
>
> Outsourcing is a relatively new approach to providing business services by a third party in exchange for income or rent.

The key to understanding this definition lies in the notion of transfer of control; as the client does not instruct the supplier how to perform the task but instead leaves that to them. The aim is to lower the operational costs to the lowest possible point. Outsourcing should not be confused with **offshoring**, which involves moving to a completely new location, usually overseas, to lower costs.

There are analogies with the private finance initiative approach detailed above, as in this case the occupier specifies the standards of accommodation they require and someone else provides and manages it. In this instance, however, it extends beyond the public sector and can take many forms.

Sale and Leaseback

Sale and leaseback involves a company, as owner-occupier, selling a freehold property and remaining in occupation by way of a lease. The sale releases capital for the company and reduces risks. In effect, a sale and leaseback agreement enables the property and operational aspects of the business to be split up. For example, in 1999 Shell sold the freehold of 180 of its petrol stations but continued to sell petrol by leasing back exactly the same sites. Similarly in 2005, Debenhams sold the freehold of its 23 department stores to British Land for £500 million and then leased them back to continue trading. This releases capital tied up in property assets and generates cash flow to the trading company.

> **Definition**
>
> The occupier of a property transfers the ownership and management of the accommodation to a separate company, who subsequently charges a realistic rent or occupancy cost.

In effect there are now two companies; one concentrating on operations and one on property. This helps to focus the directors' minds and they may decide that the best return for the property is to seek an alternative occupier or use. In short, the agreement ensures that the property pays its way! Moreover, this system is gaining momentum because companies want to focus on their core business.

Serviced Offices

The fully **serviced office** is a more sophisticated alternative to the straightforward sale and leaseback agreement as it entirely frees the occupier of real estate risk. The service provider looks after all of the property needs from acquisitions and disposals right down to vending and office furniture. In effect,

> **Definition**
>
> Serviced office contracts replace leases with short-term arrangements typically involving the provision of staffed facilities; shared meeting/conference space; fully equipped work environments and communications infrastructure.

this is the 'full' outsourcing scenario where the property company provides fully serviced accommodation for an agreed period and price.

The occupation charge (otherwise known as a facilities price) is based on the cost of providing the accommodation and associated facilities management services; including security, maintenance and cleaning. In return, the occupier has no responsibility for the various management issues associated with property.

Conclusion

Serviced offices and sale and leaseback arrangements are the two principle means in which occupiers can reduce their exposure to real estate and achieve some flexibility through different forms of contract. They allow a business to relieve itself of unwanted, non-core activities and introduce some certainty into their corporate planning. Hence, the highly fragmented nature of the development, construction, and occupation supply chain is slowly becoming more integrated. At the very least, the 'tenants' of the institutional lease are increasingly referred to as 'customers' in the new and diverse world of outsourcing!

Chapter Summary 5.3

- The occupiers, the users, create demand for the development and construction of property; they are, therefore, the 'real' clients that lie at the heart of the process.
- Economic inefficiency occurs whenever the forces of supply and demand are not left to freely and fairly allocate resources to a specific economic transaction. Examples seem to be abundant in the relationships set up between occupiers and developers.
- Outsourcing takes many forms, including PFI, serviced offices and sale and leaseback schemes.

Government Intervention

6

Summaries to Review

What, how, and for whom (2.1)
Productive and allocative efficiency (2.3)
Supply and demand equilibrium (2.5)
Market failure (2.5)
Shifting supply curves (4.4)
Development and the institutional lease (5.1)
Relationships between occupiers and developers (5.3)

Aims and Objectives

Chapter 6 reviews the idea that markets fail in some contexts, and that governments may be required to intervene to assure the continuance of a fair and efficient system. It raises questions relating to whether the market or government know best. Specifically by the end of this chapter you should understand:

- The causes of market failure
- A range of government options adopted to correct failing markets
- Debates about the effectiveness, and level of, government intervention
- The notion of government failure and public choice theory
- The tension between government intervention and market forces

In this text we have emphasised that most resources are allocated through relatively free markets. In Chapters 2, 3 and 4 we described how the price mechanism provides an incentive for firms to enter and exit markets in their search for profits; and how most markets tend towards equilibrium. So far, the dominant theme has been that most economic problems can be resolved by allowing the market to work freely without intervention.

The market, however, does not always work. That is to say, there are problems in the way some markets operate that prevent the price system from attaining productive and allocative efficiency. This seems to be the case particularly when markets involve, or impact on, the environment; when goods are not privately managed but commonly owned; when the product has a 'lumpiness' in terms of its location, longevity and expense; and when ownership of resources or information give one of the parties in the transaction an unfavourable advantage. In such cases, non-market alternatives need to be considered. One of the most important non-market forces is government, and this chapter reviews the role of government intervention within failing markets. We shall also look at the problems that governments can face in seeking to achieve efficient outcomes, and this is discussed at the end of the chapter.

There are, therefore, two central concepts to expand on, namely the idea of **market failure** and its antidote **government intervention**. Historically, there has been some tension in determining the balance between the two, but most economists recognise a need for at least some minimal level of government intervention. As Milton Friedman, one of the most influential champions of the free market forces has stated: 'The existence of a free market does not of course eliminate the need for government. On the contrary, government [intervention] is essential both as a forum for determining the rules of the game and as an umpire to interpret and enforce the rules decided on'.

Definition
Market failure may be defined as any situation where the unrestricted price system causes too few or too many resources to be allocated to a specific economic activity.

Market Failure

Whenever the forces of supply and demand do not allocate resources efficiently there is said to be some form of market failure, and interventionists use these instances to justify a government role.

To take just one of the examples suggested above it is clear that the majority of environmental problems, such as polluted seas, devastated forests, extinct species, acid rain and the vaporising ozone layer are associated with market failure. To some extent this is shown by the amount of current government policy that is aimed at reducing environmental impacts emerging from Westminster and Brussels.

Economists have identified many causes of market failure and in this chapter we shall examine six, which are listed in Table 6.1.

Table 6.1 Causes of market failure

Time-lag
Unequal distribution of income
Producer power
Asymmetric information
Externalities
Free-rider problems

Time-lag

Due to the inflexible nature of certain markets, the forces of supply and demand are not always sensitive to price changes. Property markets are a case in point, as they are often structured in such a way that aspects such as information flows, financial arrangements, government legislation, and professional requirements restrict the dynamics of the market. As discussed in Chapter 5, economists focus on these factors in the institutional model to account for the inflexible and sluggish nature of property markets.

Consequently, property markets are characterised by a pattern of cyclical booms and slumps as they struggle to arrive at a stable market price. As described in Chapter 5, property development can be a lengthy and fragmented process. For example, it takes approximately 18 months to two years to complete a house from the planning approval stage and up to 10 years to deliver a modern office block. As a result, price instability within property and associated markets is quite common; and in Figure 6.1, we present the annual percentage change for house prices and the total return on commercial property over a 30-year period. (The total return combines the capital growth and the rental income.) Both sets of indices portray the unstable cycle that has been experienced.

The Cobweb Theorem

To account for these successive cycles, property economists sometimes use the **cobweb theorem**, which is based on two distinguishing features of the construction industry.

1. The decision of builders to change their output is heavily influenced by current market prices. For example, house supplies in two years' time are dependent on today's prices.

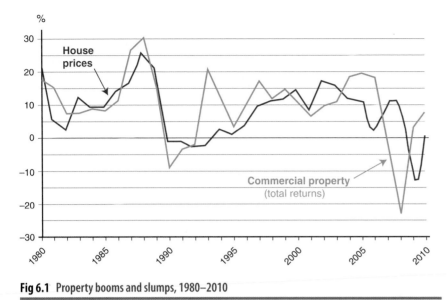

Fig 6.1 **Property booms and slumps, 1980–2010**

The graph shows the unstable, cyclical, nature of property values between 1980 and 2010. The data plotted refers to the UK.
Source: IPD and CLG

2. There are numerous property developers and they all make decisions to adjust their scale of production in isolation from one another.

The result of these distinguishing features is that, if buildings are scarce in one time period, then high market-clearing prices will prompt construction firms to begin new projects. This rise in production will in due course depress market prices, which sets off a major contraction in the scale of production. We show this process in Figure 6.2. Let's assume that the fixed amount of property available in the short run causes the market-clearing price to rise to P_1. The supply curve indicates that, at price P_1, construction firms would like to produce Q_2, although they cannot do so immediately. Building contractors begin to make plans to adjust output based on the current market price and try to produce Q_2. After a time-lag, a potentially unstable situation is likely. Indeed, assuming the pattern of demand remains unchanged, and output Q_2 is achieved, prices will be forced to drop to absorb the excess supply. This will ultimately result in a contraction of production, leading once more to higher prices. Note that, in this example, market prices move above and below the equilibrium level and are not stable. This price instability could be greater or less depending on the elasticity of the supply and demand curves.

The pattern of oscillation around the equilibrium point is accounted for by the inherent time-lag in the development cycle, by imperfect information, and by the inflexible nature of the development and construction phases. The oscillating pattern also provides an explanation for the name of this model – the cobweb theorem. (It is also referred to as the hog cycle, as it was first used to explain the time-lags needed to breed and fatten pigs before they could be taken to market.)

Obviously, there are limitations to this generalised theoretical model. First, builders are aware of the cyclical nature of their industry and therefore attempt to make adjustments to relate starts to expected prices rather than current prices. Second, they can choose to manipulate their stocks by holding property, and/or land, off the market during the low price part of the cycle.

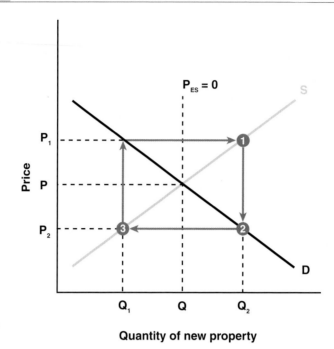

Fig 6.2 Cobweb theory of property market adjustments

In the short run, the market is faced with a perfectly inelastic supply curve, as shown by the dashed line (PES). The longer-run supply curve S indicates that at price P1, construction firms would like to build Q2. However, when Q2 is eventually completed, the price will need to fall to P2 to absorb the excess supply. This will result in a subsequent contraction of supply as shown by position 3. The shortage of supply will cause prices to be bid up and the process continues.

Nonetheless, the economic analysis is still useful since it highlights the root of a problem.

Unequal Distribution of Income

According to economists, who gets what, when, and how is resolved by the market system. (This approach has already been explained in Chapter 2.) Clearly, for the price (or market) mechanism to operate fairly we all need to be able to 'cast our votes' with purchasing power. Left to its own devices the free market will allocate nothing to those who cannot pay. That is, those who can sell their labour, or other factors of production, will have significantly better life chances than their retired, unemployed, disabled or underprivileged counterparts. Consequently, all post-war governments have used policies, with differing levels of intervention, to redistribute income from the rich to the poor. These policies, and others, designed to resolve failings of the market, will be reviewed in the middle section of this chapter. For now, it is sufficient to say that those who have no money are unable to function in the market.

In contrast, if producers dominate a specific sector, or work in close collusion with their competitors, unfettered markets can prove to be very rewarding.

Producer Power

Firms in dominant market positions do not have to 'price-take'; they can 'price-make', or become involved, through **collusion**, in price-fixing. Several of the known instances of illegal practice and other unfair competition arrangements have involved firms in construction and development. For example, in 1990 the lease arrangement between breweries and pubs led to the six largest brewers controlling 75% of the pub outlets and this was deemed to give these producers an unfair advantage. The competition commission subsequently instructed them to sell a significant share of the property. Similarly, the cement and plasterboard manufacturers have been investigated for using their dominant producer position to control price and quality in their market sectors.

These problems of unfair trading are not just a contemporary phenomenon; indeed as long ago as 1776, Adam Smith, the founder of modern economics, expressed suspicion of contracts between rival firms. He observed that 'people of the same trade seldom meet together for fun and merriment, but the conversation ends in a conspiracy against the public or in some contrivance to raise prices'. Consequently, it is recognised that as competition declines, the price (or market) system often becomes less efficient in allocating resources. A good example is the way that firms who tender in competition for similar jobs on a regular basis may form a type of informal agreement where they provide **cover prices** to share the available work around on a regular basis; inevitably this leads to higher prices than those determined by a competitive market.

Asymmetric Information

Whenever there is a problem of one-sided information there is a strong possibility that the market will not reach a fair outcome; it will fail. As pointed out in the previous section, problems created by a dominant firm, or group of colluding firms, typically favour the producer. In fact, any contractual agreement that is loaded in favour of one party contributes towards market failure.

The problem of an imbalance of information between the occupier of property and its supplier is neatly summarised by the **principal–agent** concept, which was introduced and defined in Chapter 5. In most cases, this idea boils down to the supplier (the *agent* – as the concept describes them) having an unfair market advantage. The *principal*, buying the product or service; the owner or tenant in the case of property, has less access to information. As a consequence, most property transactions are determined solely on price. For example, a volume house-builder could choose to incorporate more insulation or add a grey water system to run alongside the conventional set up, but these upgrades would increase the relative price of their product. On the other side of the transaction, conventional buyers tend not to understand or trust such upgrades. It could be argued, therefore, that information asymmetry generally tends to lead to a decline in quality, as markets tend to favour cheaper products. In the end a vicious circle accrues where 'bad' products tend to drive comparatively 'good' products out of the market. This is particularly apparent in those markets where suppliers are not rewarded for delivering quality information or cannot find ways to disclose it sufficiently; and where buyers (such as tenants and occupiers) cannot discriminate between the qualities of different products. In short, **asymmetric information** can lead to adverse selection.

Externalities

These are **third-party** effects that occur as spillovers from market activity. In the traditional market agreement, there is a deal struck between a buyer and seller: a good or service is exchanged for money. Alongside this two-party activity various spillovers spread to third parties. That is, people external to the market activity are affected hence **externalities**. These externalities may be classified as positive or negative: as benefit or cost.

For example, consider a hypothetical world where there are no government planning departments. A property developer moves into a street and converts two large Victorian houses into eight flats. The price (rent) eventually charged will reflect only the costs incurred by the developer during the refurbishment. On completion of the development, however, neighbourhood costs are created. There are now parking constraints, traffic congestion and related road problems as eight homeowners try to negotiate the two generous spaces initially allocated to the two houses. The indirect costs that the neighbours inevitably experience are referred to as a negative externality or external cost.

Not all externalities are negative. Some property developments may improve the value of nearby residencies. That is, some of the benefits associated with the development may spill over to third parties. These positive externalities may be termed external benefits.

One way of taking into account the positive and negative externalities is via **cost benefit analysis**, but first of all some related terms need clarifying.

Private Costs and Benefits

Until now, we have been dealing with situations where the costs and benefits of any market activity have been accounted for directly by individuals. The prices paid were assumed to cover all the costs and justify all the benefits that occur.

Social Costs and Benefits

In this chapter, however, we have raised the possibility that, in some instances, third-party costs and benefits are experienced. Hence, not all of the costs and benefits remain private (i.e., internal to the two parties involved). External costs and benefits also exist. When we add these external costs and benefits to the private (internal) costs and benefits we can identify a total picture: a (net) **social price**.

A fuller analysis of costs and benefits is presented in the next section, which deals with ways to correct market failure.

Definition

A social price involves considering the private costs and benefits alongside the external cost and benefits.

Free-rider Problems

The last piece of analysis leads us to the **free-rider** problem. Whenever external benefits greatly exceed private benefits, the good or service concerned becomes unprofitable. For example, if you pay for several lampposts to light the pathway and pavement outside your house, the private benefit would be too small relative to the cost. Yet the external benefit to your neighbours from the street lighting would be significant, as they would have a brighter pathway for free. The problem is that the market system cannot easily supply goods or services that are jointly consumed. For a market to work efficiently a two-party agreement is preferable. If non-paying parties cannot easily be excluded from the benefits of a good or service, we have the problem of the free rider. Good examples of this situation are the markets for sewerage services, paving, street lighting, flood control, drainage, fire-protection services, law enforcement, roads, tunnels and bridges. In short, goods and services supplied to collective markets are typically managed and paid for by the government.

Correcting Market Failure

Governments intervene in various ways to correct market failings. Historically, the preference had been for correction via legislation, but increasingly correction is sought via market instruments. Some of the options, used and proposed, during the last decade are outlined in Table 6.2. This indicates, in a general way, the broad range of approaches to tackling the different types of market failure; as the press would describe it: stick, carrot and tambourine approaches play a part. To clarify what this means, in the next sections we discuss some of the relevant policies designed to resolve the six causes of market failure.

The final section examines the effectiveness of these measures. To preview the approach, Table 6.5 (on page 92) provides a general summary.

Government Taxation

Taxation in various forms has been used to control the economy for hundreds of years. Traditionally, it was used to simply raise funds to provide essential public goods and services. Nowadays, it is increasingly used to alter the pattern of private expenditure. The tax burden is shifting away from 'goods' such as employment, and towards 'bads' such as pollution and environmental damage. This complex balance is reviewed and developed each year in the Chancellor's Budget.

Table 6.2 Government policies to address market failures

Market failure	Government taxation	Regulations	Information and Publicity	Government spending
Time-lag	Community infra-structure levy		Energy performance certificate	
Unequal distribution of income	Progressive income tax	National minimum wage		Provision of merit goods
Producer power		Competition policy	Code of practice	
Asymmetric information	Differential rates of fuel duty	Building and planning regulations	EU directive on energy performance; EU eco-label scheme	
Negative externalities	Land tax; Climate change levy; Aggregates levy	Water quality legislation	Cost-benefit analysis	
Free-rider problems	Tax relief for cleaning up contaminated land	EU landfill directive		Provision of public goods

The Chancellor of the Exchequer usually makes his annual budget statement in March. He takes the opportunity to announce new legislation and report on forecasts of the economy. The prime purpose of the Budget, however, is to review changes to taxation and government expenditure. Underlying these changes is the policy of the government of the day, which determines the nature of the changes made. The March and April issues of the *Estate Gazette* will always report and debate Budget changes relevant to property. In the next section, we concentrate on the taxation policies of the last decade that have been specifically introduced to improve the dynamics of the property market and the distribution of income.

Land Tax

The idea of some form of land tax was first proposed more than a century ago by Henry George, an American economist. His radical idea was that a single land tax could raise sufficient funds to pay for all public goods and services. This premise is sometimes referred to as the **Henry George theorem**.

> **Definition**
>
> The Henry George theorem has come to play an important part in property economics as it suggests that, under certain circumstances, there is a relationship between the value of taxable land in an urban community and the amount of funds needed for public services in the same area.

In short, Henry George advocated that all public expenditure should be raised from a tax on land. The justification of this proposition was his belief that increases in land value are a major cause of inequality and injustice and the government should, therefore, tax ownership of land and natural resources in preference to taxing effort and enterprise.

It was not until 1909, however, that such a levy was first imposed; and it only survived 11 years before it was abandoned. A further five attempts to tax the increase in land value resulting from property development subsequently failed during the last century. For a brief outline of this complex history see Table 6.3.

A new form of betterment levy, or land tax, was brought into force by the government in April 2010, namely the **community infrastructure levy**.

Table 6.3 Brief history of land tax

1879	Henry George publishes his ideas on progress and poverty, suggesting that all taxation should be raised from a single land tax
1909	The first attempt by government to introduce a land tax; a 20% duty chargeable on the increased value of land when sold
1920	Caused uproar and was abandoned
1932	Town and Country Planning Act gave local authorities the power to collect up to 75% of the increase in land values brought about by re-zoning land for building
1940	Planners concluded that the betterment levy was not effective
1947	Labour introduces the development charge in the 1947 Town and Country Planning Act
1952	Abandoned by the Conservatives
1967	Harold Wilson introduces a betterment levy set at 40% of profit
1970	Edward Heath kills it off
1978	Development land tax (DLT) reintroduced, set at 80% of the increase in land value. Subsequently reduced to a rate of 60% by the new Thatcher government
1985	DLT abandoned, as it costs more to administer than it collects
2010	Community infrastructure levy introduced

This is a tariff which local authorities in England and Wales can impose on new developments in their area in order to secure funding for roads, public transport, schools, health centres or sports facilities, etc.

The actual rate of levy will be assessed locally and applied equally to all developments. One way of determining the amount is to review the difference in land value before and after permission is granted. For example, when land designated for agricultural use in the South East is reclassified to residential use it increases its value more than 200 times; from £13,400 per hectare to £2.7 million per hectare, respectively. In the North East the respective residential land is 100 times the value of agricultural land. The new community infrastructure levy, therefore, could be based on a charge of a small percentage of the uplift in the value of land resulting from the granting of planning permission. It has been estimated that the levy could bring in a total of £700 million per annum.

Income Tax

All post-war governments have supported systems that redistribute income through different taxes. In very general terms, the amount paid depends on a tax allowance and a tax rate. An allowance is a sum of money that a person is allowed to earn, or keep, free of tax; and the tax rate determines the percentage that is deducted by the government. **Inheritance tax** and **capital gains tax** are obviously a greater burden to the rich than the poor. In the following section, we simply focus the explanation on the general taxation of annual income as a means of redistribution.

The main principle of income taxation involves taxing high-income earners more than the lower paid; so as a person's income increases, the percentage of income paid in tax increases. To express it more formally, the marginal tax rate is greater than the average tax rate, which means that as income increases the tax bracket changes (this happens at specified intervals and a higher specific rate is applied). For example, before 1988 a broad range of rates applied and they increased in steps of 5% from 40 to 60% (40, 45, 50, 55, 60), as income increased. The current tax regime is, however, far simpler. Table 6.4 shows the tax rates announced in the 2010 Budget. A similar system is employed throughout Europe and is referred to as **progressive income tax**.

Another form of taxation that enables the government to redistribute income in favour of those in need is **National Insurance Contributions (NICs)**. These contributions are deducted from those in employment and, in effect, they are another form of income tax; although they are paid by employers and employees and the self-employed. The employer's contributions can be regarded as a kind of payroll tax and for employees it is another deduction from gross income; although NICs are less progressive than income tax. Subsequently, the payments create a fund that entitles people in less fortunate times to claim housing benefit, job seekers' allowance and state pensions.

Finally, it is important to note that it is not necessary for an actual cash payment, or tax allowance, to be paid to the poor in order to redistribute

Table 6.4 Taxable income

Each tax band includes a personal allowance: £6,475 for financial years 2009–2011. From 2010–2011 an extra tax band is added for incomes above £150,000

£ per year	2009–2010	2010–2011
Basic rate: 20%	£6475–£37,400	£6,475–£37,400
Higher rate: 40%	over £37,400	£37,401–£150,000
Additional rate: 50%	NA Over	£150,000

Source: Adapted from HM Revenue and Customs.

income, as the government also provides **benefits in kind** and various essential goods and services. Some of these are discussed below, under the heading of government spending.

Market-based Instruments

As stated at the beginning of this text, modern governments believe that free markets, in general, provide the best means of allocating resources; as unless you express a price for outputs they tend to be taken for granted. Hence, you can see from Table 6.2 that the government has begun to use taxes to put a price to environmental issues such as climate change and waste. These green taxes may be discussed under the heading of **market-based instruments**.

> **Definition**
>
> A market-based instrument is a levy or tax that operates through the price mechanism to create an incentive for change.

In other words, taxes are regarded as one possible way to internalise external costs into the price of a product or activity. Interestingly, the most recent examples of taxes introduced to reduce negative externalities all relate to property and its construction.

Landfill Tax

The landfill tax was introduced in October 1996. It was imposed to provide an incentive to minimise waste and promote recycling – to internalise the costs to the community of waste going to landfill. Depending on the nature of the waste, the tax can be as much as £48 per tonne. This is potentially a significant penalty: in a typical year as much as 70 million tonnes of construction and demolition waste ends up as landfill waste – of which, rather surprisingly, 13 million tonnes (nearly 20%) is reported in government documents to comprise materials delivered and thrown away unused. The government has indicated that it expects to make annual increases in the standard rate of landfill tax, and by 2013 it is projected to be £72 per tonne. These rates send a signal about the need to reduce the external costs associated with the large volume of waste sent to landfill, and should provide economic incentives to develop alternative forms of waste disposal, such as reuse or recycling.

Climate Change Levy

The climate change levy commenced in April 2001. It is a tax on the business use of energy, and it covers the use of electricity, gas, coal and liquefied petroleum gas (LPG) used by the non-domestic sector. The levy is imposed on each business energy bill according to the amount of kilowatts used. There are differential rates for different energy sources. The levy is nearly three times higher for electricity (0.0043p/kW) than gas or coal (0.0015p/kW). This differential has been introduced because the use of each type of fuel creates different levels of greenhouse gas emissions – which cause climate change. The levy has caused energy costs in the commercial sector to increase by 10–15%.

The purpose of the climate change levy is to encourage businesses to internalise – that is, pay for – the negative externalities associated with the greenhouse gas emissions that they are responsible for generating. Firms using environmentally friendly energy technologies, such as photovoltaic systems, energy crops and wind energy, or combined heat and power systems, are exempt from the levy.

Aggregates Levy

The aggregates levy came into effect in April 2002. It is a tax applied to the commercial exploitation of rock, sand and gravel. It applies to imports of aggregate as well as to aggregate extracted in the UK. Exports of aggregate are not subject to the levy. The purpose of the levy is to give businesses operating in the UK an incentive to compare the full costs – including all negative externalities – of using alternatives or recycled materials with virgin equivalents.

To explain it another way, the levy has been established to reduce the noise and scarring of the landscape associated with quarrying. These environmental costs could not continue to be ignored, and the levy is meant to encourage the polluter to pay. The intention is that the construction industry should reduce its demand for primary materials, recycle as much as possible and reduce waste on site. The immediate benefactors from the removal of these negative externalities would be those communities living close to the quarries. It is interesting to note that their opinions were sought in the preparatory research that established the aggregate levy at a rate of £1.60 per tonne.

Regulations

In the history of government intervention there are more examples of regulation than anything else. This generalisation does not only apply to regulations designed to improve markets in the built environment, but also to the economy as a whole. In this section, therefore, we could address all types of market failure; we shall, however, concentrate on those relating to problems of externalities, producer power, asymmetric information and income distribution.

To begin with, an example that has many implications across the property and construction sectors is the government's responsibility to prevent businesses denying accountability for the environmental impact of their products and services. This seems to be particularly important where habitat needs to be conserved, water quality needs to be maintained, carbon emissions need to be reduced, sites of scientific interest need to be protected, or building standards need to be observed. Legislation of this type is well-established – for instance, the present system of **planning regulations** has a history of more than 50 years and the equivalent set of **building regulations** is more than 25 years old.

It has been argued that, broadly interpreted, the property and constructions sectors have become one of the most highly regulated areas of business. First, property developers need to obtain planning permission from the local authority and second, building standards must reach certain minimum requirements before the property can be sold or let. Planning and building regulations are examined next.

Planning Regulations

The government sets national planning policy and this is interpreted and enforced by local authorities. In effect, local authorities decide what can be built and where. These regulations form a major constraint to the way resources are used, as the planning system determines the supply of land available for particular uses taking into account various externalities. In economic terms, interventions at the macro level affect the market mechanism and the way resources are allocated in local property markets.

In setting the national planning policy the government needs to recognise that the UK is one of the most crowded countries in the world. For example,

England accommodates a population of more than 51 million in only 4% of the EU land area; and this alone makes decisions about the future too risky to leave to the free market. Areas such as national parks, green belts and sites of scientific interest need to be protected, and in England around half the land is effectively precluded from development. People need to be assured of decent homes, offices and shops in accessible environments. Clearly, this affects productivity, innovation, investment and enterprise and there are concerns over the speed, flexibility and transparency of the present planning system. More than 150,000 planning applications are processed each year, but only half of these are decided in the target time frame of 13 weeks.

Planning regulations affect market failures in many ways, most obviously in the avoidance of externalities such as incompatible land use: to take a classic example, an investor in a new hotel can be reasonably confident that a concrete plant will not be given permission to locate next door. Planners call this the benefit of certainty. Other important benefits of planning that avoid shortcomings in the market system include the provision of infrastructure such as pipelines, parks, roads, sewerage and highways.

Building Regulations

According to the Building Act of 1984, building regulations can be made in England and Wales for the purposes of securing the health, safety, welfare and convenience of people in and around buildings, to further the conservation of fuel and power, and to prevent waste, etc. Responsibility for complying with the regulations rests with builders and developers. The aim is to assure the public that a certain level of technical accuracy has been achieved and environmental impacts reduced.

Building regulations set a baseline of minimum standards to be expected from the industry; as such they lag behind the standards imposed by the equivalent sets of regulations in North European countries. This is particularly the case in terms of energy efficiency, and even though building regulations have been rapidly updated and revised a staggering amount of energy could be saved by going beyond the expectations of the building regulations.

Minimum Wage Legislation

A regulation that affects the economy more broadly is the legal right to a National Minimum Wage. With a few exceptions, this entitles all workers in the UK aged 16 and over to be paid a minimum amount per hour. This is regardless of the kind of work they do, or the size and type of company they work for. The rate has been reviewed every year since it commenced in 1999, with increases taking place in October. The rates from October 2010 range from £3.64 an hour for workers aged 16 and 17 to £5.93 an hour for those people over 21 (with a mid-rate of £4.92 for workers aged 18 to 20). The aim of this legislation is to prevent the market exploiting those that sell their labour to employers. It particularly protects the young and those who are unable to negotiate a fair wage. Obviously it does not apply to the self-employed.

Competition Policy

It is widely recognised that businesses that are open (in the sense that there are no barriers to entry), transparent and fair form the basis of a strong economy. Consequently, levels of competition are monitored by governments across all sectors of the economy and various bits of legislation have been put in place, over the past 50 years, to prevent monopolies, and other unfair practices developing between firms. The **Office of Fair Trading (OFT)** and the related **Competition Commission** currently employ over 200 staff to investigate markets that appear uncompetitive, and during the last 10 years there have been investigations into allegations of unfair competition in industries as diverse as insurance, crematoria, horse racing, construction, mobile phones and airports. Two relevant examples to follow up are the competition commission report on supermarkets and the Office of Fair Trading (OFT) enquiry into the nature of bid rigging across construction contracts.

The competition commission report into supermarkets was conducted between 2006 and 2008 and was primarily prompted by concerns over the increasing dominance of Tesco in the grocery market. The root of the problem lay in the fact that Tesco, Asda, Sainsbury's and Morrisons had built up empires that together accounted for 75% of the grocery market, and there were growing concerns over their pricing tactics in relation to small independents and the way they used their holdings of development sites to block the expansion of rivals. The enquiry focused on Tesco, as it was the biggest in the grocery group, twice the size of its nearest competitor. It had a land bank of 185 development sites, and had made rapid inroads into the convenience store sector. In 2006, it was reported that £1 in every £7 spent in retail was spent in a Tesco store; the proportion would have been higher if the ratio was expressed for grocery only. Some argued that Tesco had such a dominant hold on the grocery sales that the market had become inefficient. The final report concluded that there were potential losses to consumers and the possibility in *some* areas of limited competition. But, providing planning limits were followed on new stores, and plots in certain regions designated as lacking competition were sold, the market would continue with a reasonable level of efficiency.

The OFT enquiry into bid rigging in the construction industry in England was carried out during 2008 to 2009. This enquiry looked into the allegation that collusive behaviour by contractors bidding for construction work in England was damaging transparency and fairness in the market. The investigation uncovered 240 infringements across 112 construction companies. These companies were fined millions of pounds for engaging in bid rigging activities as the government tried to emphasise that this is not an efficient, fair or ethical way to conduct business.

Alongside the two general regulatory agencies (Office of Fair Trading and the Competition Commission) are the specialist regulatory offices overseeing the communication industries (**OFCOM**), water services (**OFWAT**), gas and electricity industries (**OFGEM**). These utilities are historically structured in such a way that one company often has substantial control over the market, and that is why their development in the private sector has always required a nominated ombudsman or regulator. Once you have fully grasped this idea you will appreciate that a significant amount of economic activity in the private sector is 'regulated'. Indeed, those industries that are explicitly regulated include telecommunications, water and sewerage, electricity networks, gas and oil distribution, nuclear power, roads, rail and airports. The implications of a regulated and unregulated private sector are explored further in the reading on page 187.

Publicity and Information

Now we come to a more *laissez-faire* approach where information is gathered by the government in an attempt to support and influence market decisions. This is particularly important when markets lack transparency due to asymmetric information and externalities need to be measured and publicised. Examples take many forms: from the simple government campaign to raise awareness or publicise findings, through to legislative requirements to formally gather information to support a market transaction. This approach is sometimes referred to as the tambourine effect, as it is often aimed at capturing people's imagination and getting them all to dance to the same tune. Some examples follow.

Government Agendas

The energy-efficiency campaigns aimed at householders and businesses to raise understanding of what to expect in terms of standards and payback periods, and the more recent EU energy-labelling scheme that was designed to encourage environmentally friendly purchasing represent good examples of Government trying to help society avoid inertia and ignorance. Both schemes were set up to form a greater symmetry between consumers and suppliers in an effort to create more transparent markets and increase efficiency.

These campaigns contrast with a newer approach that falls in this category where codes of conduct are made explicit by the government. Examples include *The Code of Practice for Commercial Leases in England and Wales*, which was introduced in 2002 and *The Agenda for Sustainable Construction*, which was first introduced in 2000 and revised in 2008. Both of these publications were considered preferable to government legislation. In the first case, the government wanted to encourage greater flexibility in the commercial property market; reducing lease periods and the need for upward-only rent reviews. With the sustainable construction agenda the government wanted the sector to change its traditional ways of working; on the basis that it made business sense. The latter agenda is discussed at some length in Chapter 9.

The common thread between *The Code of Practice for Commercial Leases* and *The Agenda for Sustainable Construction* is the government's use of the publications to gently nudge sectors of society to do things that are in the market's best interests.

EU Directives and Legislation

At the other extreme governments can choose to legislate about the level and quality of information required to support market efficiency. The **energy performance certificate** that is required by law to support property transactions is an excellent example. Following the EU directive on the Energy Performance of Buildings, all residential and commercial property now needs to be supported by an energy performance certificate indicating its current level of performance and suggesting ways that the energy rating could be improved. This is important to governments because across Europe nearly 50% of energy consumption and carbon emissions typically arise from the way our buildings are lit, heated and used; so even a comparatively minor change in the way we use energy has a significant effect in reducing overall energy consumption. The certificates are designed to raise awareness about user costs and how energy could be saved. The document needs to be made available whenever a property changes hands; that is, whenever there is a new tenant, lease or owner. In short, energy performance certificates are a type of benchmark, enabling buildings to be compared with one another whenever they change hands or ownership.

Cost–Benefit Analysis

Another option for governments seeking to raise awareness and spread information is to use an investment appraisal technique known as cost–benefit analysis. This method of resource allocation includes externalities as part of its process; in other words it manages to include aspects that most methods of resource allocation omit. In these analyses, the external costs and benefits are considered alongside the internal (private) costs and benefits to provide a complete picture. For this technique to work, all issues need to be expressed in a common denominator for a 'total price' to be calculated. As a result, what may not be viable in conventional financial accounting terms may appear viable in a broader cost–benefit appraisal.

Cost–benefit analysis helps to clarify the significance of externalities but it is easier in theory than practice; two common problems are acknowledged. Firstly, the externalities that are identified rely upon value judgments. For example, following the Deepwater Horizon oil spill disaster, 40 miles off the coast of Louisiana, which ran from April to July 2010, there were several protracted debates between the American government and BP determining areas of responsibility. Clearly the firm responsible for the oil rig (BP) should pay compensation for the loss of 11 human lives following the initial explosion on the rig, but would they be held as equally responsible for the loss of marine life in 2020 and beyond? This brings us to the second problem associated with externalities, namely that all the issues need to be expressed in monetary terms for a 'total price' to be arrived at. This problem is resolved, where possible, by employing the concept of opportunity cost. For example, when completing the cost–benefit analysis of London's third airport, noise pollution was quantified on the principle of how much it would cost in treble-glazing to restore the houses to their foregone quiet existence. But one would need to be more creative in the use of the concept to put a value to loss of marine life in the Gulf of Mexico, or the visual damage caused to the sea, or the long-term climate change costs caused by spraying chemical dispersants into oily waters.

Despite the difficulties, many cost–benefit analysis studies have been completed by the public sector in their efforts to publicise the community-based nature of some investments. High-profile examples include the building of motorways, the construction of the Channel Tunnel, the relocation of Covent Garden Market, and the proposal to build a third runway at London Heathrow airport. But on a local scale it is precisely this type of appraisal that is used to justify 106 agreements, or **planning gains**, where the developer, in return for planning permission, has to enter into an agreement to compensate the local community for the social losses that their scheme imposes by providing community facilities such as a library, town hall, playing field or park.

> **Definition**
>
> Cost–benefit analysis involves identifying monetary values for *all* the internal and external costs and benefits of a project to enable a total (social) price to be stated.

Government Spending

The final area that we identified as a cause of market failure related to the free-rider problem. The problem here is **excludability.** The benefits of some goods or services – due to their very nature – cannot be excluded from non-payers. Even supporters of the free market, from Adam Smith to Milton Friedman, have recognised that there are a few goods and services that the market mechanism does not supply effectively. These are called **public goods**.

In order to explain the precise nature of public goods, it is helpful to begin at the other end of the spectrum and clarify the definition of private goods. Indeed, so far in this text, private goods have been at the heart of the analysis. We have mainly discussed the activity of those involved with private property. Any private good (or service) is distinguished by two basic principles. One can be termed the **principle of rivalry** and the other the **principle of exclusion**. This means that if you use a private good, I cannot use it; and, conversely, if I use a private good, you cannot use it. For example, when I use the services of an architect, he or she cannot be working at the same time on the design of your building. We compete for the architect's services; we are rivals for this resource. The services of architects are therefore priced according to levels of demand and the available supply of their time; the price system enables them to divide their attention between customers.

A feature of public goods, however, is that they can be used several times. In other words, they can be jointly consumed by many people simultaneously without any discriminatory price system being applied to exclude. National defence, street lighting and overseas representation are standard textbook examples of pure public goods.

A distinction is sometimes made between *pure* public goods, which are defined as being both non-excludable and non-rivalrous, and *quasi* (near or impure) public goods, which do not have both of these characteristics. The major feature of **quasi-public goods** is that they are jointly consumed. This means that when one person consumes a good, it does not reduce the amount available for others. A server providing a wireless connection for those subscribing to a network is an example of a quasi-public good.

Finally, there is one last group of goods that is provided by government because of the external benefits that they bring to society. These are referred to as **merit goods**. Merit good provision differs from country to country since it depends upon what the government of the day regards as socially desirable. The decision involves selecting certain goods or services and providing them free, or below cost, to all citizens either through subsidy or government production. Examples of merit goods in the UK are museums, ballet, health, education and local authority housing. The important feature is that there is nothing inherent in any of these particular goods that makes them different from private goods; they can be supplied through the market (and in some countries they are) but because they are deemed important, due to their related positive externalities, the government becomes involved.

Chapter Summary **6.2**

- Governments can use several instruments to correct market failure. For example, there are: various tax regimes, legislative and regulatory frameworks; systems for gathering and distributing information; and the provision of public and merit goods.
- Externalities can be internalised by taxation and/or legislation.

Is Government Correction Effective?

There is an acknowledged gap between the design of policy and its effective implementation. In short, the intention of government intervention is not always achieved. The assumption that the alternative to a failing market is a brilliant government is misleading. Governments can fail too. As evidence, several of the corrective measures discussed above have limitations. These are briefly summarised in Table 6.5 and examined further in this section.

Table 6.5 Market failure and government interventions

Causes of market failure	Example of intervention	Nature of problem
Time-lag	Community infrastructure levy	Measurement
Unequal distribution of income	National minimum wage	Who benefits
Producer power	Competition policy	Enforcement and assessment
Asymmetric information	Building and planning regulations	Enforcement and assessment
Externalities	Taxes and levies	Measurement
Free-rider	Provision of public goods	Tax burden

Distribution Problems

An obvious problem is assuring the delivery of government policy to those it was designed to benefit. In other words, if the government intervenes to protect the poorer classes of society, is it the poor who actually reap the rewards?

There are two possible routes to follow. The universal route involves benefits being made available to *everyone* regardless of need. For example, the national health trust provides a state-subsidised service that is available to everyone. The other route involves selective payments that are paid according to need and often involve a form of means testing. For example, housing benefit is only available to those on incomes below a certain level.

The irony is that government intervention initiated to redistribute income often does no more than maintain the existing differentials. A classic example of a system that was set up to promote welfare, but which distorted the market even further, is **rent control**. These controls were first introduced in 1915, when 90% of UK families resided in homes rented from private landlords. Ninety years later this figure had fallen to around 10%. This rapid decline was caused, in part, by the constant renewal of legislation relating to rent in various attempts to keep the cost of housing as low as possible.

Rent control, as with any maximum price legislation, causes a disincentive to the supplier because the control enforces a 'price ceiling'. Consequently, private landlords respond by reducing the number of dwellings available for rent. They either sell their property on the open market for higher-priced uses, such as owner occupation, or put fewer funds into maintaining them. The result is that the supply of rented accommodation decreases and quality deteriorates.

The reality of this unfortunate scenario, initiated to help the poorer tenant, can be clarified using a supply and demand diagram (see Figure 6.3).

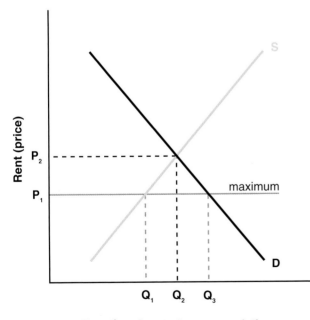

Quantity of rented accommodation

Fig 6.3 Rent control: maximum price legislation

The free market equilibrium price is P2. The government imposes a maximum price for rental accommodation of P1. Consequently demand increases to Q3, but supply is reduced to Q1. The final outcome is an excess demand of Q1, Q3.

The diagram in Figure 6.3 shows the demand for rented accommodation at the controlled maximum price of P_1 is Q_3. At this controlled price, however, landlords are only willing to supply Q_1. The distance Q_1Q_3 represents the excess demand that remains unsatisfied due to the imposition of rent control. The final result is that the rent control only benefits the relative few who are fortunate enough to find and live in rented accommodation. It is also evident that the effect of applying such a control distorts the free-market solution. This is not what the present government supports. Consequently, the private rented sector has been deregulated since 1988, and provided with tax incentives in an attempt to revive it.

Measurement and Assessment Problems

Government attempts to reduce time delays, to minimise unfair competition, and prevent negative externalities require careful assessment and measurement. For example, the **polluter pays principle** is all well and good providing that the guilty party is easy to identify and that it is possible to determine a fair price for them to pay. Given that many externalities manifest themselves in global or national environmental issues and involve free goods, such as air, the ozone layer, habitat, flora, waterways, peace and quiet, their measurement and assessment causes endless problems.

To analyse these problems further, it may help to consider Figure 6.4. Here we have the demand curve D and the supply curve S for product X. The supply curve includes only the private costs (internal to the firm). Left to its own devices, the free market will find its own equilibrium at price P and quantity Q. We shall assume, however, that the production of good X involves externalities that are not accounted for by the private business. These externalities could be air pollution, destruction of a green belt, noise pollution or

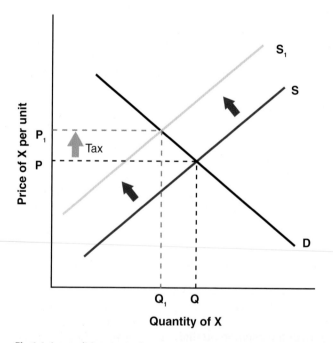

Fig 6.4 Internalising external costs

The supply curve S represents the summation of the private costs, internal to the firm. The curve to the left, S1, represents the total (social) costs of production. In the uncorrected situation, the equilibrium is Q, P. After a tax, (P1 – P) the corrected equilibrium would be Q1, P1.

any neighbourhood cost. We know, therefore, that the social costs of producing X exceed the private cost. This can be illustrated by shifting the supply curve to the left, since it indicates that theoretically the costs of producing each unit are higher. (You may remember from Chapters 3 and 4 that changes in price and non-price determinants – such as a tax – are represented in different ways in graphical analysis.)

The diagram highlights the fact that the costs of production are being paid by two groups. At the lower price P, the firm is only paying for the necessary private inputs. The difference between the lower price P and the higher price P_1 is the amount paid by the community – the external costs. For these external costs to be internalised, the government would need to introduce a tax equal to P_1–P. This should result in fewer resources being allocated to this activity – with less demand and supply Q_1 – as the tax would lead to higher prices and force potential purchasers to take into consideration the costs imposed on others.

It is easy to see, therefore, that in an unfettered market, external costs are not paid for and resources are over-allocated to environmentally damaging production. A tax should help to alleviate the problem, but the practical issues of precisely how much tax and who will be burdened with the expense are difficult questions to resolve.

Enforcement Problems

The success of any policy cannot rely solely on a strong theoretical argument. Political support, voter appeal and luck are equally important. In other words, just because a government has carefully debated and passed through parliament a new policy, launched a publicity campaign, or initiated another set of regulations does not automatically guarantee its success.

Rule-based measures, such as regulations, create a whole range of associated costs. There are the compliance costs of implementing, enforcing and administering the legislation. For example, the building regulations are devised to set minimum standards; such as how much insulation should be used, what kind of windows should be fitted and how efficient the heating boiler should be. Yet in recent history no builder has been prosecuted for non-compliance! This rather startling fact was highlighted in October 2004 when the Building Research Establishment conducted a study to examine the rumour that building controls officers were not vigilant in making sure that building regulations had been complied with. The study investigated 99 new dwellings, spread across 12 geographical areas in England, and found that in 43% of the new houses the regulations had not been enforced. Part of this enforcement problem may be explained by the fact that building controls officers are no longer solely employed by the local council. Nowadays, builders may hire 'approved inspectors' to certify their houses. In these cases if the inspectors are too tough, they won't be hired again; so they face a conflict of interests.

The Environment agency has presented a similar scenario on the basis that it has insufficient funds to carry out the number of inspections that the directives emanating from Westminster and Brussels require.

Even when regulations are enforced, there is little incentive for property developers, or builders, to be innovative. In fact, some analysts argue that it's precisely the heavily regulated nature of the property sector that creates the conservative attitudes that typify the industry. As there is usually no incentive to improve on the regulatory standard that has been set, often firms will do only the minimum that is required. As a consequence, the property industry suffers from inertia, which is not particularly sustainable in the long term.

Tax Burden

In the UK, the government collects almost £550 billion in various taxes each year. Spending on law and order, defence, the environment, international co-operation and transport alone accounts for approximately 25% of this expenditure. In effect, the average citizen in the UK must work from 1 January to March or April just to pay all their taxes.

This **tax burden** is clearly a significant proportion of any citizen's income, and it raises some of the thorniest questions that any government has to face. In the UK, and much of the developed world, public spending grew relatively unchecked until the early 1970s, but now many governments choose to exercise some restraint by following the **golden rule** – which, in simple terms, means that governments should not allow current spending to exceed current receipts. The golden rule forms a central plank of modern government and it is discussed further in Chapter 7.

Finally, it is worth noting that income taxes can be a major disincentive to work effort, as once tax has reached a certain level further tax increases will lead to tax avoidance and possibly even illegal evasion. This problem is acknowledged by the flat tax movement that advocates a single low tax rate as the ideal system. This idea has gained some support in Hong Kong and Singapore, and several former communist countries such as Estonia, Russia, Ukraine, Slovakia, Romania and Albania. Most of them have adopted income tax rates of less than 20%; while other countries influenced by the flat tax argument have simply reduced the number of tax brackets that are used.

> ### Chapter Summary 6.3
> - Neither universal nor selective benefits necessarily reach the target group.
> - A method for internalising external costs is to impose a tax. But it is difficult to set tax rates so that the polluter pays the correct amount.
> - Just because a government has rubber stamped some regulatory procedures or launched publicity campaigns, does not automatically mean that better practices will be effectively enforced.
> - Governments provide a range of public goods and services. Inevitably, these entail associated costs that need to be financed by tax revenue.
> - Notionally it is possible to perceive that there is a limit to how much taxation a nation will tolerate.

Government Failure

To conclude this chapter we recognise that market failure cannot simply be remedied by government action; that is, perfect governments do not resolve imperfect markets. As a result, modern economic texts tend to acknowledge the occurrence of **government failure**.

> ### Definition
> Government failure is said to occur when government intervention makes a situation worse rather than better. Ironically, it often occurs as a result of interventions introduced to deal with market failure.

Government failure is understandable since the political process, by its very nature, is likely to be inefficient in allocating resources. When choices are expressed through the market mechanism, the price forces individuals to absorb most of the costs and benefits. Politicians, however, allocate resources more on the basis of judgment. Government judgments are often skewed by lack of financial incentives, gaps in information and pressures applied by different stakeholders.

The basis of this idea is derived from a branch of economics and political science known as **public-choice theory**. This studies the ways that government decisions are made, working from the premise that politicians are basically driven by a desire to please their supporters and be re-elected; in short, they are motivated by self-interest.

Furthermore, the sheer scale of managing a nation from the centre is problematic. As we have discussed above, there are problems of distribution, measurement, enforcement, and funding. These problems lead to inefficiency and a wasteful use of resources. Indeed, the more wide reaching and detailed an intervention becomes, the less likely it is that the benefits will justify the costs.

In recent years, therefore, there has been a tendency to believe that, in general, markets provide the best means of allocating resources. Indeed, the idea of justifying less and less intervention by government is becoming increasingly popular. Even in the difficult times following the financial crisis of 2007 to 2010 it was argued that the problem could be left to the virtues of the market; to adjust, absorb and emerge stronger than before. In 2010, Anatole Kaletsky developed this argument in a clear historical review of financial crashes and made the case that market capitalism *always* survives and flourishes. (For the student who wants more of the Kaletsky thesis they should see the details in further reading.)

Government systems, by comparison, tend to become bureaucratic, inflexible and excessively expensive to run. As government intervention increases, individual liberty is reduced and the competitive spirit declines. The present trend, therefore, is to provide incentives through the market system wherever possible; to reduce the scale of state intervention. How far government intervention can be reduced is debatable. It is not, however, solely a question of economic efficiency but one of politics too.

Chapter Summary 6.4

- Government failure is a recently acknowledged phenomenon; it highlights that intervention through policy initiatives do not necessarily improve economic efficiency.
- Government failure is caused by a number of factors, such as poor judgment, lack of information, inadequate incentives and the scale of the problem.
- The notion of government failure is currently being used to justify a reduction in the scale of state intervention in the UK.

Tutorial **3**

✓ CHECK POINT

By this point in the text you should be able to:
- ✓ Understand commentary in the press and media relating to government policy.
- ✓ Understand the nature of the fragmented property development process and appreciate the complexity of the government sector trying to manage it.
- ✓ Recognise that both the free market system and the government have limitations in allocating resources efficiently.
- ✓ Begin to sense that historically there was a sentiment that the state was somehow wise and paternal; whereas today it appears that society prefer to celebrate the idea of the market and free enterprise.
- ✓ Understand that economy, and related property markets, are difficult beasts to tame or manage.

Introduction to Tutorial 3

The following reading is based on an extract from a report on the current state of the construction (and property) industry and its future direction. *Never Waste a Good Crisis: a review of progress since Rethinking Construction and thoughts for our future* was authored by Andrew Wolstenholme, the Managing Director of Balfour Beatty, on behalf of Constructing Excellence in October 2009. This is one of many high powered reports that have looked at construction and property firms during the last 50 years, urging them to become modern, integrated, sustainable, reliable, safe and efficient organisations, etc. There is further coverage of industry specific government reports in Chapter 9. The aim here, however, is to offer the opportunity to examine some of the results that follow from intervention. An extract from the Wolstenholme report is, therefore, highly appropriate as it reviews progress from 1998 when the Egan report – *Rethinking Construction* – highlighted problems with the traditional supply-side of the industry, to 2009 when recession took hold and demand collapsed. In Wolstenholme's words, 'the economic crisis offers a perfect opportunity to think again. We cannot afford to waste it...'

Tutorial Reading

How do we progress from here...

[Egan's] *Rethinking Construction* [1998] was published when the economy was growing and therefore provided a favourable commercial environment for initial acceptance of its recommendations. The decade that followed was arguably a golden age for the UK economy and for construction. The effect of this, whilst clearly beneficial in many respects, was that there has been no major commercial imperative to seek radical transformation, such as occurred in the offshore oil or automotive industries in the 1980s. In the absence of any industry wide impetus for change, different sectors of the industry have progressed at varying rates.

The chart below shows a breakdown of the £125bn built environment industry between the private and public sectors and the financial basis for each sector. In some sectors, to draw on the title of the 2008 BERR Select Committee report, it can be said that 'construction matters' – in other words that the cost, programme and quality of the delivery all support the business case. In other instances, sadly, 'construction does not matter' and has minimal impact on the business case – the private housing market seems to fit into this category, for example, where land prices and location have been the dominant factors.

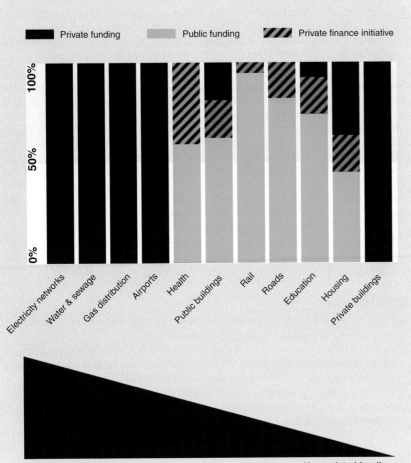

Tutorial 3

Built environment expenditure by sector
Source: Wolstenholme, 2009:13.

So which sectors have shown improvement and how have they achieved it? Inevitably, it has tended to be the major clients with repeat construction business who have developed in-house 'intelligent client' teams. Successful teams have consistently integrated their processes and achieved results through a sustained programme of change – many adopting the Egan principles and adapting their business model to incentivise and promote best practice.

In the water and airport sectors, the regulator provides an added impetus to achieve better value capital investment. As a result, the supply chain has to demonstrate increased value over time to survive in post. Some of the larger retailers have also demonstrated partnering arrangements, no doubt in response to the intense competition from within the sector.

Tutorial 3

The public sector has made some significant moves in the right direction. NHS Estates' Procure21, Defence Estates' Prime Contracting, Birmingham City Council, Manchester City Council and Hampshire County Council are all examples of best practice for collaborative working in integrated teams…

Looking to the future, there is no doubt that the recession has undermined confidence in Egan's idea of client-driven change. Egan did not envisage that good clients would not always have new work, nor that client framework agreements may not provide the expected long-term stability for contractors. The era of client stability and leadership may be over, as the credit crunch seems likely to limit funding for some years to come. Instead, we now need the supply side to take on the leadership role and embrace the challenge of delivering more value for less budget. The current economic downturn should focus suppliers' minds on the need for more radical change if they are to survive, let alone thrive, in the upturn when it comes. 'Never let a good crisis go to waste', as President Obama's Chief of Staff commented in early 2009…

Source: adapted from, Wolstenholme (2009): *Never Waste a Good Crisis: a review of progress since Rethinking Construction and thoughts for our future.* Constructing Excellence: London.

Tutorial Questions

1. Comparisons are often drawn between the automotive and offshore oil industries. Identify at least two reasons for the comparison.
2. Various forms of government intervention mean that much of the demand for construction output is derived from the public sector: (a) Identify the two most obvious examples, and (b) broadly interpreted what percentage of total construction demand is currently derived from the public sector.
3. What would you recommend to the government to increase the pace of change in the construction industry?

Managing the Macroeconomy

7

Summaries to Review

Macroeconomics (1.2)
The mixed economy (2.2)
Interventions to correct market failure (6.2)

Aims and Objectives

This Chapter builds on Chapter 6 as it looks at Government intervention from a macroeconomic perspective. It introduces the broad objectives and policy framework that Governments manage. Specifically by the end of this chapter you should understand:

- The nature of business fluctuations overtime
- The concepts of economic growth, price stability, full employment, balance of payments, and environmental responsibility
- Fiscal and monetary policy instruments used to control an economy
- The impacts that the macroeconomy make on the property sector
- Problems of managing the property sector; such as the circle of blame
- The basis of the financial crisis 2007 to 2010

As many famous economists have emphasised, there is widespread agreement about the major economic goals of economic policy; but there is less agreement about the role that policy instruments can and should play in achieving these goals. In this chapter, we review the goals and policies that are common to all governments and consider the role of economic management. The goals and policy of government have direct importance for anyone who needs to understand and manage property, as the demand for buildings is always derived from activity in other sectors.

Property economists and planners also need the ability and confidence to interpret economic statistics relating to the wider economy and this is the subject of Chapter 8; so Chapters 7 and 8 should be read as a related pair.

Business Fluctuations

In most years, economic output, income and employment increase; and as a consequence, a steady upward trend is experienced in property markets. In fact, over the last 100 years the UK economy has averaged approximately a 1.5% annual increase in economic activity. There are, however, periodic fluctuations that detract from this steady trend; and we identified a similar cyclical pattern in property markets in Chapter 6 (see Figure 6.1, on page

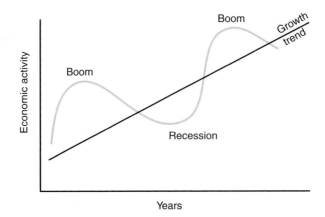

Fig 7.1 Business fluctuations

79). At times business activity slows right down and even becomes negative; while at other times it accelerates rapidly and may even double in pace. The former is a **recession** and the latter a **boom**. The concept is portrayed in Figure 7.1.

One way of defining the fluctuations portrayed in Figure 7.1, is to focus on the changes in output that occur around the general line of growth.

These cycles are experienced in each industrial sector, at different rates and during different time periods, and their combined effect inevitably relate to activity in the broader economy. At times, the overall business climate is buoyant: few workers are unemployed, productivity is increasing and not many firms are going bust. At other times, however, business is not so strong: there are many unemployed workers, cutbacks in production are occurring and a significant number of firms are in receivership. These recurrent ups and downs in economy-wide activity used to be called **business cycles**. But the term no longer seems appropriate because '*cycles*' implies predetermined or automatic and, nowadays, we do not experience automatic recurrent cycles. The general nature of economic activity in the 21st century tends to be characterised by subtle changes of pace, and are more accurately referred to as **business fluctuations**.

The nature of business fluctuations, portrayed in Figure 7.1, was first identified in 1860 by Juglar, when it was referred to as a trade cycle, and he suggested that it took eight to 11 years to progress through a complete cycle from one boom to another. Since then, other economists have challenged this time measurement with various cycles being identified ranging from three to 50 years. More importantly, over time the nature of the cycle has changed; periods of expansion have increased, while contractions have become shorter. This change in nature is partly due to the intervention of governments who, since the 1940s, have begun to accept a responsibility to prevent the economy getting caught in periods of low output and high unemployment. As explained above, nowadays these periods are increasingly referred to by the more neutral term of business fluctuations.

The overall growth trend rate is of increasing importance. For example, it took Britain 100 years, following the industrial revolution in the 19th century, to transform into a modern industrial economy. America and Japan progressed through similar journeys in 60 and 30 years, respectively. At present, it seems quite probable that China will make the same transformation in just a 20-year time period. In short, the steeper the incline of the overall growth line the faster the scale of change.

Definition

Business fluctuations are characteristic of the aggregate economic activity of a nation; typified by a period of expansion, which is subsequently followed by a recession that leads back to another boom period.

In fact, of all economic goals a sustained increase in economic growth is arguably the most important to governments worldwide. It does not matter which political party is in office, or which nation is under consideration, all governments seek certain broad economic goals. These can technically be referred to as **macroeconomic objectives**. It is generally agreed that five main ones dominate; and economic growth is the top priority.

> **Chapter Summary 7.1**
> - One characteristic common to all economies are business fluctuations above and below the general upward trend.
> - Modern economies seek to achieve five macroeconomic objectives and long-term growth is the number one goal.

Five Macroeconomic Objectives

In general terms there is a universal political consensus about the five dominant macroeconomics objectives that need to be achieved. These are: a sustained rate of economic growth, price stability, full employment, a positive trade balance with overseas partners, and effective protection of the environment. Each of these objectives is considered in turn below; and related macroeconomic statistics for the UK economy are presented in Table 7.1.

Sustained Economic Growth

The long-term objective of all governments is to achieve steady increases in productive capacity. Governments measure **economic growth** by the annual change in the rate of output, and the commonly used measure of economic output is **gross domestic product (GDP)** – the *gross* (total) *domestic* (home) *product* (output). To express it more formally: GDP represents the total money value of all the production that has taken place inside a specific territory during one year.

GDP figures are used worldwide as a proxy for a country's progress towards prosperity: since the more money a country makes, the higher its GDP growth, the assumption is that increases in GDP mean that the citizens of that country are enjoying a higher standard of living. In simple terms, the GDP can be regarded as the annual domestic turnover; or to extend the analogy, a giant till ringing up all the transactions taking place inside a country. To accurately portray the rate of change of actual output, GDP must be corrected for price changes from one time period to another. When this is done, we get what is called 'real' GDP. As

Table 7.1 UK macroeconomic statistics

The data is taken from various government sources. Three points need to be emphasised, economic data is subject to revision, it is calculated in different ways by individual nations, and proper comprehension relies on footnotes.

	1995	2000	2005	2009
Inflation[1]	2.6	0.8	2.0	2.2
Unemployment[2]	2.3	1.6	1.5	2.4
Economic growth[3]	2.8	3.1	2.2	−5.0
Balance of payments[4]	−9.0	−19.2	−33.0	−18.0

[1] Consumer price index (percentage increase in previous year).
[2] ILO unemployment (annual average, in millions).
[3] Annual percentage increase in 'real' GDP.
[4] Current account (total for whole year, £ billions).

such, a more formal measure of economic growth can be defined as the rate of change in real GDP over time (usually one year). As the footnotes indicate, the growth data in Table 7.1 has been corrected accordingly and it shows that the growth rate of the real GDP was on a steady upward path in the decade to 2005; in fact, apart from the exceptionally severe recession experienced during 2009, the period from 1995 to 2008 were years of positive growth in the UK – and this upward trend was the norm in most Western economies.

The performance of several countries and an outline of how GDP data is calculated are reviewed in Chapter 8.

Stable Prices

Stable prices are crucial for business confidence as it is much easier to work within a consistent economic environment; as persistently rising prices cause problems for most sectors of an economy. If prices continually change, entrepreneurs are hesitant to enter into contracts as they cannot work out the long-run results of their investments. This is compounded by the problems caused by the changing interest rates and fluctuating foreign exchange rates that often accompany inflation. Stability means that the costs and prices of any project or investment can be estimated with greater certainty and transparency, allowing businesses to plan with confidence. Indeed, economists define the associated effects of inflation on business as **menu costs**. These costs arise due to the need to revise existing contracts, new tenders and bids for work as inflation sets in. Obviously, as inflation rates become higher and more volatile, menu costs become more demanding and, in extreme circumstances, they might include costs associated with alterations to vending machines, the costs of printing revised price lists, the time spent renegotiating, and so on.

Consequently, price stability has become the primary objective of most governments that wish to secure long-term growth and full employment. It is no longer believed that tolerating higher rates of inflation can lead to higher employment or output over the long-term. Today's target is to keep inflation within 1–3% and retail prices are monitored on a monthly basis by the **consumer price index (CPI)**. A sample of annual CPI statistics for the UK economy covering the period 1995–2009 is presented in Table 7.1. As the table shows, the general trend for inflation has been to stabilise around 2%, and this is regarded as encouraging, not as an end in itself, but due to its economic significance in meeting all other government objectives.

Price stability is so central to understanding modern macroeconomic management that this text would be incomplete without some explanation of its measurement and this is dealt with in the next chapter.

Full Employment

Full employment does not mean that everybody is employed and in any dynamic economy some unemployment is unavoidable. For example, there will always be individuals moving in and out of employment, as they change from one job to another; and there will always be seasonal, technological and overseas factors that cause fluctuations in the number of jobs available in the different sectors. Therefore, full employment represents, say, 95% employment at any one point in time. The problems arise when there are large numbers of unemployed for long periods of time; as a large pool of unemployed labour represents wasted resources.

Unemployment has many costs, not only in terms of loss of output but also in terms of human suffering and loss of dignity. As a result, all governments record the number of workers without a job, although the precise way unemployment is measured changes from time to time. At present, unemployment in the UK is estimated in two ways: by the number of people registering for unemployment benefit and through a labour force survey. The former is known as **claimant unemployment** and the latter is referred to as the **ILO measure** as it is produced according to a standardised system that is used across Europe, by the International Labour Organisation. (As a general rule the ILO count is greater than the claimant count by approximately 0.7 million; the distinction between the two is discussed further in Chapter 8.) Unemployment is either expressed as a percentage rate of the total workforce of 28.8 million; or as an absolute number. As Table 7.1 implies, the unemployment rate has been below 10% for over a decade, with unemployment reaching a high of approximately 2.4 million during the recession in 2009. The figures in Table 7.1 also suggest that lower levels of unemployment are associated with declining rates of inflation.

Understanding unemployment statistics can form an important part of the feasibility study for many types of property development as it varies according to occupation, regional location, social class and even marital status! Chapter 8 therefore will complement your understanding of interpreting and measuring unemployment.

External Balance

All international economic transactions are recorded in a country's **balance of payments** statistics. The ideal situation represents a position in which, over a number of years, a nation spends and invests abroad no more than other nations spend or invest in it. Economic transactions with other nations can occur on many levels and, for accounting purposes, these transactions are often grouped into three categories: current account, capital account and financial account. Of these three, the most widely quoted is the current account. This involves all transactions relating to the exchange of visible goods (such as manufactured items, which would include building materials), the exchange of invisible services (such as overseas work undertaken by consultants) and investment earnings (such as profits from abroad). In any one year, one nation's balance of payments deficit is another nation's balance of payments surplus – ultimately, however, this is not sustainable and, in the long run, debts must be paid.

The data in Table 7.1, which is described more fully in the next chapter, show a worrying trend, insofar as the UK current account figures are all negative amounts, and this has been the typical portrait for the past 20 years. However, in addition to buying and selling goods and services in the world market, it is also possible to buy and sell financial assets and these are recorded separately in the financial account. The UK's annual position on the financial account is usually in balance. A final qualifying remark regarding foreign trade is to recognise that balances of payment figures are notoriously difficult to record accurately. (In fact, of all the statistics shown in Table 7.1, the balance of payments estimates are subject to the biggest amendments.) In practice, therefore, statistics relating to the external balance need to be considered in a broader historical context.

Environmental Protection

As discussed in Chapter 6, free markets do not deal effectively with the spillover (third-party) effects of many economic activities. As a consequence the environment has gained a high political profile in recent years. There is an increasing recognition that a healthy economy depends upon an infinite resource base, and protection of the environment forms an important strand of the sustainable development agenda adopted by most governments across the world. The UK agenda is outlined more fully in the final chapter.

Governments increasingly have to intervene to influence resource allocation, preserve biodiversity and reduce pollution. At present, there is a broad-ranging debate arising from concerns that some economic activity damages the environment, and politicians are beginning to consider environmental protection together with other macroeconomic goals. An interesting current example lies in the sharp increase in the price of crude oil; the barrel price has more than doubled in the last three years. This reflects a combination of factors, including supply constraints, an increase in demand and speculation concerning possible interruptions to supply because of the conflict in Iraq. Environmental economists, however, are keen to dispute the importance of this development on the basis that markets need an incentive to become less dependent on oil.

The objective of protecting the environment, therefore, covers a broad range of concerns, from global warming, fossil fuel depletion, harnessing renewable energy through to maintaining biodiversity and changing cultural attitudes to waste and recycling. At present, however, there is no agreed way of monitoring the performance of environmental protection and there is no indicator for this objective in Table 7.1. We will briefly consider the implications of this omission when considering the measurement of national output in Chapter 8, as one development is the monitoring of various toxic emissions as a ratio of GDP. We will also consider the measurement of the ecological footprint that is gaining status in international circles, as this may eventually become the indicator used to monitor environmental progress.

Priorities: An Historical Perspective

During the 20th century, governments have gained enormous influence over the performance of the economy. All governments, in all nations, now seek the same objectives in their quest for economic stability. It is only the order of priority of the five macroeconomic objectives that depends on the government in office. The notion that the government should undertake actions to stabilise economic activity is, in historical terms, a post-war phenomenon. For example, the White Paper on Employment published in May 1944 stated that the government accepts responsibility for the maintenance of high and stable levels of growth and employment, and these themes dominated government macroeconomic agenda for the next 30 years.

Since the 1980s, however, the order of priority changed and governments made the control of inflation their number one objective. For example, a budget statement made in the late-1990s emphasised that: 'Price stability is a precondition for high and stable levels of growth and employment.' As the political and economic scene evolves, it is quite possible that during the 21st century, the objective of protecting the environment will sufficiently raise its profile to demote inflation, employment and growth from their current positions as high-profile government objectives. In other words, while there may be some doubt at present about the priority attached to environmental issues, internationally the interest in climate change, renewable energy sources, reduction of waste and other issues of sustainability is gathering momentum. (More on this new emerging agenda is reviewed in Chapter 9.)

Chapter Summary 7.2

- To achieve economic stability, five main macroeconomic objectives are pursued: (1) steady growth, (2) stable prices, (3) full employment, (4) external balance, and (5) environmental protection.
- The order of importance attributed to macroeconomic objectives depends on the government in office.

Government Policy Instruments

All governments, regardless of political persuasion, employ the same types of policy instrument to achieve their macroeconomic objectives; again, it is only the emphasis that seems to change. The instruments can be grouped into three broad policy categories, namely: fiscal, monetary and direct.

Fiscal Policy

In the UK, fiscal policy emanates, on the government's behalf, from HM Treasury. **Fiscal policy** consists largely of taxation (of all forms) and government spending (of all forms). The word fiscal is derived from the Latin for 'state purse' – and this is most appropriate as taxation is the main source of income from which governments finance public spending. In other words, fiscal policy is concerned with the flow of government money in and out of the Treasury; and an indication of the scale of the various receipts and expenditure are shown in Figure 7.2.

An important element of the current fiscal framework is to make sure that both sides of the government balance sheet are managed efficiently, and the scale of borrowing is reduced. In theory, any public sector debt must be held at a prudent and stable level in relation to GDP, and borrowing is only acceptable to cover capital expenditure. In technical terms, these two Treasury rules are:

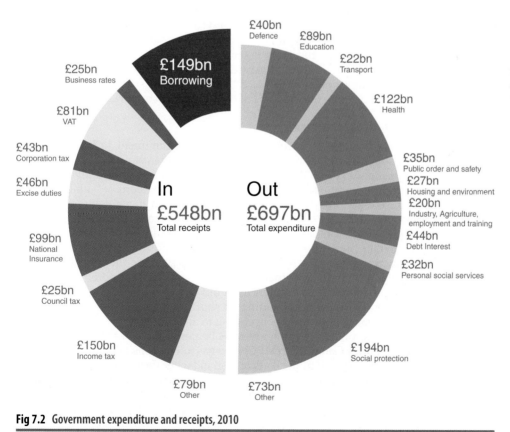

Fig 7.2 Government expenditure and receipts, 2010

Source: Adapted from Budget data June 2010

1. The **golden rule**, which states that over the economic cycle the government can only borrow to finance capital investment and not to fund current day-to-day spending.
2. The **sustainable investment rule**, which states that over the economic cycle public sector debt expressed as a proportion of GDP must be held at a stable and prudent level.

These two rules provide a benchmark against which the government can judge its fiscal performance, as the basic principles appear relatively straightforward: spending that produces benefits that are consumed in the same year as the spending occurs is classed as current spending and should not be funded by borrowing. Whereas spending that produces a stream of services over several years is classed as 'capital spending' and can be funded within reasonable parameters by public sector borrowing. The problem that remains is that much of the current spending is demand determined and society has become used to a certain level of state provision and support, particularly during recessionary phases; and the level of public sector debt has, over time, reached an unstable level. Consequently, the current UK's fiscal framework is being slimmed back, via large public sector cuts, to bring the share of GDP devoted to public expenditure below 40%; and to reduce the level of interest payments associated with budget deficits. In short, at the current time there is considerable pressure to improve the fiscal position and cut government debt.

Monetary Policy

Monetary policy is implemented by the Bank of England (UK's central bank) on behalf of the government. In other words the **central bank** has responsibility for monetary stability and financial regulation, and it has a certain level of independence to use the tools it feels are necessary to manage the macro objectives. The tools in current use are: the monitoring of interest rates and the quantity of money circulating the economy; and the supervision of financial sector to regulate the overall level of debt that they support.

Interest Rate Manoeuvres

Since the 1990s, governments have made a commitment to bring inflation under control by monitoring and manipulating interest rates. This is done on the understanding that the prevailing rate of interest significantly influences spending decisions, and, in particular, affects the decisions of both businesses and households on whether to borrow (that is, to incur debts) to pay for consumption and investment goods. As interest rates become higher, and more volatile, businesses and consumers generally become less confident about making new investment and negotiating future contracts. To follow one sequence, higher interest rates will tend to increase the cost of financing house purchase, reduce demand and lower prices. Therefore, other things being equal, higher rates of interest should encourage saving and discourage investment and consumer spending. In short, changes to interest rates have a strong influence on the level of spending in an economy.

The process of changing interest rates begins at the monthly meeting of the **Monetary Policy Committee (MPC)** who has full responsibility for determining the rate of interest used by the Bank of England when dealing with other financial institutions trying to raise funds in the money market. The official **base rate** is sometimes referred to in monetary circles as the **repo rate** (the rate that a central bank is willing to lend funds to other banks). Subsequently this determines the rate of interest that top quality banks charge each other for loans (this rate is sometimes called LIBOR which is short for the London inter-bank offer rate).

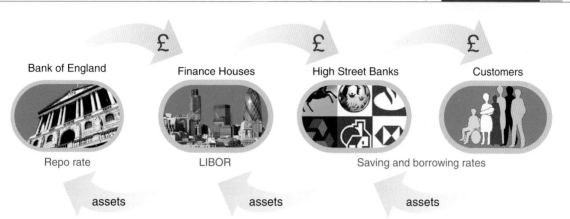

Fig 7.3 The money market

In turn, dealings in the inter-bank market affect the interest rates adopted in the wider economy by all other credit agencies such as the high street banks when trading with their customers. Obviously, no bank would lend to customers at a lower rate than the one at which it borrows as they are in businesses to make a profit not a loss! Hence, when banks find themselves facing higher funding costs, and more difficult times, they tend to increase the rates charged on their loans; and they might even decide to ration the quantity of credit they are willing to extend – in effect both of these actions were captured in the phrase **credit crunch** that dominated the headlines throughout the period 2007 to 2010.

The important point here is that the official rate (known as the base rate or repo rate) is the reference point that ultimately affects the whole spectrum of interest rates used across the economy. The sequence of events is neatly captured in Figure 7.3 where it would help to assume that the rate of interest always changes in marginal increments as we progress from the Bank of England to the ordinary customers of commercial banks. The credit crunch dimension simply means that the gap between the official repo rate, and all other rates significantly widened; highlighting that, in relative terms, borrowing costs had increased and savings rates had decreased.

Quantitative Easing

A related impact of the repo market is that it enables the Bank of England to manage the quantity of money circulating in the economy. For example, if the Bank wishes to inject money into the economy it can purchase assets (UK government bonds or similar high-quality debt issued by private companies) from insurance companies, pension funds, banks or non-financial firms. Whichever avenue is used the outcome is that the seller's bank account is credited. This process is sometimes known as **quantitative easing**, and is portrayed in Figure 7.3 by the related flows that swop money for assets between institutions.

This approach means that spending may be boosted in a variety of ways. As suggested above, the sellers of the assets have more money so they may go out and spend it, thus helping to boost growth. Or they may buy other assets instead, such as shares or company bonds, and this will push up the prices of those assets, making the people or institutions who own them, better off; so they may go out and spend more. Furthermore, banks will find themselves holding more reserves and this could lead them to boost their lending to consumers and businesses; so, once again, borrowing increases and so does spending. That said, if banks are concerned about their financial health, they may prefer to hold the extra reserves without expanding lending.

Financial Regulation

The financial crisis that emerged from instability in the American markets during 2007, and subsequently spread across global financial markets from 2008 onwards, was largely due to a lack of supervision that resulted in the combination of asset losses and a collapse in funding liquidity that seriously shocked economies worldwide. In response, the authorities took measures to recapitalise the banking sector, partly through quantitative easing, and put in place new levels of supervision to assure that it would not be repeated. In the Bank of England's case it was given a stronger remit to monitor the balance sheets of the financial system as a whole. In other words, the Bank accepts full responsibility for the work of colleagues at the **Financial Services Authority**, who supervise and regulate commercial banks and other financial intermediaries operating in Britain. As the Governor of the Bank of England remarked at the time: 'the Bank cannot effectively perform its role as lender of last resort without first-hand knowledge of the health of the banks to which it might provide support'.

Co-ordination of Fiscal and Monetary Policy

An important point to stress at this juncture is that fiscal and monetary policies are equally important in the government's attempts to manage the macroeconomy. A change to either policy has broad effects on many of the core macroeconomic objectives. Consequently, all governments employ both fiscal and monetary instruments; although the emphasis alters from government to government.

Until the mid-1990s, the Chancellor of the Exchequer directed the operation of both UK fiscal and monetary policy. Although this theoretically meant that there could be a high degree of co-ordination between both arms of macro policy, in practice this was often not the case. On coming to office in 1997 the Labour government introduced a new monetary regime, which gave a greater clarity of roles and responsibilities between the Bank of England and the Treasury. Fiscal policy, however, continues to be more complicated as there are various instruments that are only effectively reviewed annually in the Budget. Monetary policy, by contrast, is relatively straight-forward as it is primarily focused on inflation and related policy decisions are reviewed monthly.

Direct Policy

Many other government economic policies tend to be more 'objective specific' compared with the broad macro fiscal and monetary policy options we have considered so far. We refer to these instruments as **direct policy**, but it is also known as direct control or direct intervention. A feature of this type of policy is that it tends to have less impact on overall market prices than the broad macro changes to tax or interest rates.

Direct policy tends to be of a legislative nature. Conventional economic textbook examples include legislation designed to control prices, wages or imports to assist with the stabilisation of prices and trade; legislation to support research and development, education and training to influence long-term growth; and general support to encourage small businesses. Good examples of direct policy within the area of property economics include building and planning regulations to protect the environment, and specific initiatives such as the Rethinking Construction movement (the Egan Report) and the sustainable construction agenda introduced to change cultural attitudes towards productivity, safety and the environment. These initiatives are aimed at stimulating growth, stability and environmental performance within the sector; they form the focus of Chapter 9.

Macroeconomic Objectives and Policy

The basic macro objectives and policies discussed above are summarised in Figure 7.4; a see-saw is used to illustrate the trade-offs that exist between the two sides. Trade-offs, however, also occur between one objective and another, and one policy and another. In other words, effective macroeconomic management is not an easy task; as economic growth, price stability, employment, the current account balance, fiscal deficits and interest rates are all interlinked.

Let us briefly consider the current financial crisis (the credit crunch), as an example requiring macroeconomic management. Although the initial problem was triggered by instability in the US financial markets in mid 2007, it soon spread across the world's banking counters, with serious implications for the UK during 2008 to 2010. To be precise, the international financial system had come close to collapse in the autumn of 2008, following the failure of Lehman Brothers, and the subsequent panic across global markets prompted unprecedented action by central banks. For example, the Bank of England cut the official rates of interest several times and supplied billions of extra funds as they tried to stabilise the financial system.

Regardless of the monetary policy, banks and building societies (the lenders) raised the cost of borrowing and restricted the supply of loans in

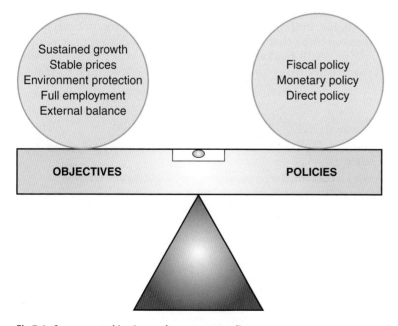

Fig 7.4 Government objectives and government policy

The see-saw in this figure portrays how macroeconomic objectives are balanced by various government policies in an attempt to create a stable economy.

their efforts to remain solvent. In other words, interest rates in the high streets increased across the financial sector (despite all efforts by the central banks to lower them). This action was unprecedented as the usual practice (outlined above) was for interest rate manoeuvres to mirror adjustments in exactly the same direction as changes made to the official (repo) rate – and usually on the same day. Institutions in the financial market post 2008, however, were less quick or symmetric in their rate changes as they began to revise the margins and increase the costs of borrowing; to move to a new equilibrium.

As a result, consumer and investment spending was cut back – and this action in turn reduced employment opportunities. Increases in unemployment typically put a strain on the fiscal stance as the unemployed no longer pay income tax (reducing government revenues) but they receive benefits from the state (increasing government spending). Similarly, bankrupt businesses no longer pay corporation tax on their profits but they too receive benefits from the Treasury. The **public sector net cash requirement (PSNCR)** – the government's annual deficit – consequently increased. In turn, this provoked a debate about the need to cut back government spending in other areas, leading to further unemployment. As output falls, then obviously economic growth slows down. Yet, as economic growth declines, there is the possibility of relatively less environmental damage. To sum up, despite government policy, the recessionary impacts of the credit crunch led to a severe contraction of output, a sharp rise in unemployment, an explosion of government borrowing and a possible halt on the pace of environmental damage.

This period of macroeconomic instability highlights the complex nature of macroeconomic management. It also emphasises the global nature of macroeconomic activity, the potential incompatibility of some macroeconomic objectives and instruments, and highlights the uncertainty that surrounds the impact of one macroeconomic instrument. A further point of complication is the fact that few policies have an immediate effect – a time-lag is inevitable. Indeed, the Bank of England's macroeconomic model works on the assumption that interest rate changes, and asset purchases to ease conditions on credit markets, can take up to one year to effect demand and output, and nearly two years to play out all the effects on the inflation rate.

Chapter Summary 7.3

- All governments use a combination of fiscal policy, monetary policy and direct policy.
- Fiscal policy is concerned with government expenditure and taxation.
- Monetary policy is concerned with achieving price stability and regulating the overall level of debt by manipulating interest rates and the quantity of money circulating the economy.
- Effective management of the macroeconomy is complex due to the linked nature of the objectives and policies.

Managing the Property Sector

As you might expect, fluctuations in the property sector share a similar pattern to the broader economy and in this instance they are referred to as property cycles.

Economists have a long history of studying such cycles, and a search on EGi will bring up literally hundreds of related articles from the stored archive dating back to January 1986; a more advanced search will throw up more than 30 in-depth items written in the last decade. The articles contain many explanations for property cycles of which the following is just one scenario. An increase in economic activity leads to 'overheating'; this is characterised by shortages of labour and stock and a consequent rising of prices. In turn, this leads into a downturn, characterised by falling output, rising unemployment and increasing stock levels. Some businesses collapse and properties become vacant and cheaper to rent or buy. Eventually, this generates opportunities for a new upswing, which takes advantage of the various cheap unemployed resources.

Another way of explaining this would be that property markets respond to macroeconomic factors: employment, levels of output, income, levels of inflation availability of debt finance and shifts in societal preferences etc. Finally, we need to recognise that property investment is managed across several classifications and locations for several different purposes.

Figure 7.5 shows the actual business fluctuations experienced by three sectors of the UK economy: manufacturing, services and construction. The figures demonstrate that, over a 25 year period, there is a general pattern between sectors. The important point, however, is that although output generally moves in a similar direction across industries, the magnitude of fluctuations differs greatly.

The sector most commonly exposed to changes in the rate of business activity is construction (and property). Figure 7.5 shows output growth in construction has hit highs of 17% and lows of –9%. The manufacturing sector is also volatile, but to a lesser degree – and over the same period, the peaks and troughs have varied by 7% in both directions. By contrast, the service sector has experienced relatively moderate peaks and troughs in business fluctuations.

What is notable, particularly in the comparison between the construction and service sectors, is the fact that construction cycles show far greater amplitude than the equivalent cycles in general business activity and precisely the same can be said of property. In other words, periods of decline and expansion are

Definition

The property cycle is the compounded result of business fluctuations from the wider economy, which are coupled with cyclical tendencies inherent in property markets.

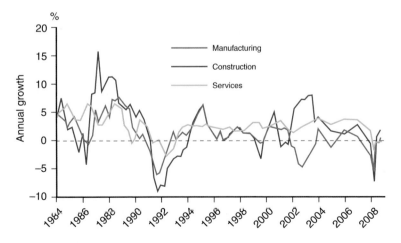

Fig 7.5 UK output growth by industrial sector

All sectors rise and fall together over the business cycle but volatility is most pronounced in construction.

Source: Economic & Labour Market Review (January, 2010)

far more volatile in the construction and property sectors than in the general economy. This type of analysis forms an important basis of forecasting economic behaviour and it will be explored further in the next chapter. Finally, it should be noted that there is a tendency for investment in new construction to shift to spending on repair and maintenance as economies develop. In short, as GDP increases the proportion of new construction work decreases.

This line of analysis is not meant to portray an unmanageable or depressed industry, as property is, without doubt, a permanent and important sector of any economy. Indeed, it is arguably the most important sector of any economy. It is certainly not like other sectors that may expand and contract and then disappear. Property and construction sectors are here to stay and they will always have work – to maintain and lease existing stock, to replace demolished stock and to sell or let new stock. The management of these activities are mostly left to market forces.

From the government perspective of managing the economy, the construction and property sectors clearly have important roles to play. Employment in construction on public works such as building hospitals, schools, roads and other infrastructure can be used to prompt further employment elsewhere in the economy, and the quality of the houses and offices procured by the government can be used to lead by example. So the departments concerned with roads, housing, health, education, energy, defence and the environment represent major clients of the construction industry and it is an oft-quoted statistic that around 40% of construction activity is derived from the public sector. It might not seem so surprising therefore to find that the UK explicitly target policy towards the construction end of the property market.

In the UK, the Department for Business Innovation and Skills (BIS) has various business sector units that maintain one-to-one relationships with the leading firms in each industry to represent the interests of their respective sectors in the development of government policy. For instance, there is an established Construction Sector Unit based in BIS, which aims to: increase the productivity and competitiveness of the industry; provide effective links between the industry and government; and encourage the industry to contribute to sustainable development. However, up until 2010 there was no specific mention of the broad property sector, which no doubt accounts for the distinct lack of cohesive thinking about its overall role and how it could best serve the economy. Yet during the fierce debates leading up to the comprehensive spending review in October 2010, a newly formed Government Property Unit emerged to encourage savings across government departments. A first stab estimate suggested that around 480 leases were due to expire, or break, in the following six months, with a rent roll of £47 million per annum, and many of these represented buildings that were not being fully utilised. There were also concerns about the wasteful use of energy in many of the buildings, rented and owned by the government that needed to be addressed in a co-ordinated and strategic manner.

In effect, this means that the construction industry has had representatives at government level to speak on its behalf for more than a decade and the government is developing a mechanism to deliver its messages from the top down. The broad commercial property sector, on the other hand, relies largely on the Royal Institute of Chartered Surveyors for general representation at government level. The problems that the government subsequently face in encouraging sustainable development are the subject of Chapter 9, but part of the problem is unfolding here. Clearly links need to be forged between property developers, architects, contractors and occupiers! And the argument we began in Chapter 5 and shall pursue in the final chapter rotates around more joined up thinking.

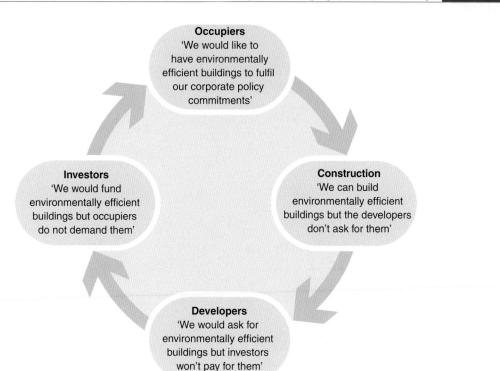

Fig 7.6 The circle of blame

In the UK, and elsewhere, there is a mindset that tends to fragment the responsibility for change. Construction firms argue that they can only adopt holistic approaches if clients ask for them. Developers imply that there is no demand for sustainability, and investors are hesitant to fund risky new ventures. There is a so-called 'circle of blame' that perpetuates the existing traditional approach to construction. This idea is captured in Figure 7.6, which characterises four typical views from the industry.

Since this idea first appeared in the *Estates Gazette* in August 2001, the 'circle of blame', or 'cycle of blame', as some prefer to call it, has become a standard part of the academic literature dealing with sustainability. It effectively emphasises the conservative nature of the property and construction sectors, and serves as a good way to highlight the fragmented interests that exist and the need to transform the vicious circle of blame into one that is a virtuous circle for the good of society.

Chapter Summary **7.4**

- The symmetry between business fluctuations and property cycles is complicated. Construction output declines as a percentage of GDP as economies mature, yet the variation from one year to the next can be quite volatile.
- The Department for Business Innovation and Skills has an established unit to co-ordinate activities across the construction sector and a new unit to oversee Government property.
- In the UK, and elsewhere, there tends to be a fragmented approach to sustainable development; and this is a particular problem with sustainable property.

Measuring the Macroeconomy

8

Summaries to Review

Macroeconomics (1.2)
Official and specialised data (1.2)
Business fluctuations (7.1)
Macroeconomic objectives (7.2)
Managing the property cycle (7.4)

Aims and Objectives

This chapter builds on the macro objectives introduced in Chapter 7 and provides some insight into the nature of official statistics. Specifically by the end of this chapter you should understand:

- Economic growth and how it is officially measured
- Inflation and how it is officially measured
- Unemployment and how it is officially measured
- International trade and how it is officially measured
- The ecological footprint and how it can be measured
- The contribution that economic data makes to interpreting business fluctuations and economic forecasts

---

Every month a new economic statistic is announced and the aim of this chapter is to understand how these statistics are produced. It is not sufficient to simply collect a press release from the website of the appropriate government department or to look at an official government publication; it is important to understand what lies behind the numbers. Sources of data were generally introduced in Chapter 1 (see pages 13 and 14) but the purpose here is to grasp a broad understanding of how official statistics are collated and what they mean. We concentrate on the main macroeconomic objectives, which were introduced in Chapter 7. The key sources of this data are identified and briefly described in Table 8.1 (overleaf).

The main aim of any statistical series is to reliably reflect an accurate portrayal of the phenomenon being measured; simply changing its format, or the way it is collated, does not alter the *actual* level of unemployment, inflation, economic activity, trade or whatever. For example, during 1979 to 1994, the UK government made more than 30 changes to the ways that official unemployment figures were recorded. These changes had the cosmetic effect of reducing the unemployment figure, but all that had changed was the way unemployment was estimated; the same numbers of people were still unemployed!

To manage and forecast the economy, or make a property related decision, on the basis of official data, therefore requires confidence and insight into the complexity of the data measurement. This is particularly important in an age

Table 8.1 A guide to official sources of statistics

UK National Accounts
This is published annually in the autumn by the ONS, and is considered to be an important source of data for the UK macroeconomy, since it provides a comprehensive breakdown of GDP. As with other ONS publications, recent editions have become more user-friendly. For example, it contains notes explaining how to interpret the accounts, a subject index and a glossary of terms. In economic circles, the accounts are often referred to as the *Blue Book*; the colour of its cover.
Monthly Digest of Statistics
As the name implies, this is a collection of statistics published monthly, by various government departments and other organisations. It covers a wide range of topics, including economic, social and demographic. In relation to this chapter, it is a source of data on national accounts (including balance of payments), prices, production and government finance.
Economic and Labour Market Review
A monthly publication covering issues broadly relating to the economy, including commentary on how the statistics are produced and interpreted. In terms of data each issue regularly includes a couple of pages detailing the latest macroeconomic indicators, an update on the latest releases and a directory of online tables. It is the best publication to use to access the latest data relating to this chapter.
Bank of England Inflation Report
This is produced quarterly alongside the Bank's Quarterly Bulletin. The inflation report serves a dual purpose. First, it provides a comprehensive review of various specialised indices and commentary on their forecasts. Second, it is the official publication responsible for making the minutes of the monetary policy committee available to the public.
UK Balance of Payments
This is published annually in the autumn by the ONS. It is the main source of data for economic transactions between UK residents and the rest of the world. It presents accounts of inward and outward transactions and shows how they are made to balance. It includes notes on how to interpret the accounts, a subject index and a glossary of terms. The accounts are often referred to as the *Pink Book*; the colour of its cover.

when statistical information is subject to increasing levels of scrutiny. Frequent use of the term *estimate* acknowledges that, although macroeconomic statistics are rarely 100% accurate, they provide a good indication towards the right ballpark. Indeed, effective statistical analysis can confirm where we are, where we have been and, hopefully, where we are going.

Measuring Economic Growth

As explained in Chapter 7, measurement of economic growth relies on the monitoring of changes in real Gross Domestic Product (GDP) from one year to the next.

A detailed breakdown of GDP is given in the *United Kingdom National Accounts: the Blue Book*, which is published annually and held for reference at most libraries. The national accounts provide a systematic and detailed description of the UK economy and, by following agreed international accounting conventions, comparisons can be made with other countries. Indeed, the national accounts are far more important than for just indicating changes in GDP; they form a central reference for those who wish to broaden their understanding of the relationship of the industrial sectors of the economy and its measurement. It is not our intention, however, to delve into the minutiae of this system, but just to establish a number of reference points and the general measurement concepts necessary to allow sufficient confidence to discuss the role of property and construction within the broader economy.

To begin the analysis, we consider a simple economy without a government sector, a financial sector or an overseas sector – that is, our starting point is a simple two-sector model economy and we analyse only the relationship

Definition

Real GDP represents the total money value of all the production that has taken place inside a specific territory during one year; adjusted to allow for inflation.

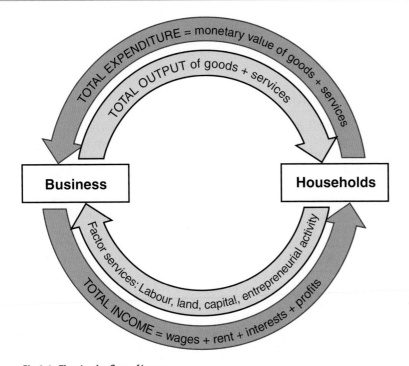

Fig 8.1 The circular flow of income

between households and businesses. The complications of the real world will be considered later. The model is presented in Figure 8.1.

To make the model effective, the following assumptions are made:

- Households receive income by selling whatever factors of production they own.
- Businesses sell their entire output immediately to households, without building up any stocks.
- Households spend their entire income on the output of the businesses.

These three assumptions seem realistic. Businesses will only make what they can sell. Production does involve paying for land, labour, capital and enterprise, and these services generate income payments – rent, wages, interest and profit – which, in turn, are spent. The model of the circular flow outlined in this way suggests that there is a close relationship between income, output and expenditure. These relationships are presented in a traditional format in Figure 8.1.

From Figure 8.1, it is clear that businesses reward the owners of factors of production (land, labour, capital and enterprise) by paying them rent, wages, interest and profit. In turn, these factor rewards (incomes) form the basis of consumer expenditure. Therefore, as the model suggests, it is possible to measure the amount of economic activity during a specified period by adding up the value of:

total output or total income or total expenditure

In effect, it is only necessary to adopt one of these three approaches since conceptually they are identical – and even in the national accounts they rarely differ by more than 0.5%. The small discrepancy is due to each of the totals being calculated using different statistical methods.

During the past 20 years, the totals have significantly increased in size, progressing from GDP figures expressed in billions to the recent totals that exceed a trillion. To appreciate better the magnitude of the numbers involved, readers are advised to look at a copy of the *UK National Accounts*. The first set of tables summarise all three methods of measurement – namely, the **output approach**, the **expenditure approach** and the **income approach**.

GDP: Economic Growth

Before considering any figures, we must fully understand what they convey and the significance of any changes in their size. In simple terms, **gross domestic product (GDP)** can be regarded as the annual domestic turnover or, to employ the analogy used in Chapter 7, the result of a giant till ringing up all the transactions that occur within a specific territory.

An alternative measure is **gross national income (GNI)**. This is similar to GDP, but includes a net figure for employment, property and entrepreneurial income flowing in and out of a nation's economy from overseas.

In other words, GNI aggregates all the activity that generates income to a specific nationality. In practice, GDP and GNI represent similar amounts; for example, in 2008 GDP in the UK totalled £1,446 billion (i.e., approximately £1.4 trillion) and GNI was £25 billion more at £1,471 billion. In European states, GDP and GNI rarely differ by more than 1 or 2%, but the difference may be substantially larger in less developed economies.

When GDP figures are adjusted from current prices to constant prices, to allow for inflation, it is possible to calculate the **real value** of any change in economic activity between one year and the next. Effectively, economic growth can only be declared if 'real' GDP has increased. If real GDP has declined, this is described as a **recession**. In the majority of years following the Second World War the recorded figures have been positive.

The UK shares a common set of accounting conventions with other countries, and this allows international comparisons of GDP and GNI to be made quite easily. Figures for five selected countries are shown in Table 8.2. The final column, which shows GDP growth, is obviously expressed relative to economic activity in the previous year. The term 'real' confirms that inflation has been removed from the calculation, with each year's GDP values being expressed at an agreed base year (to convert current prices to constant prices).

Worldwide economic activity tends to be on an upward path and, as Table 8.2 shows, all of the selected economies grew strongly during 2000–2008. In particular, there were large increases in China and India, although both countries were growing from a relatively low economic base. Furthermore, these two countries have populations in excess of 1 billion each! To facilitate international comparison, therefore, it is necessary to take into account the

Table 8.2 GNI for selected economies

| Country | Gross National Income (GNI) | | Gross Domestic Product (GDP) |
	($ billions) 2008	(£ per capita) 2008	(% real growth) 2000–2008
China	3,899	2,940	10.4
India	1,216	1,070	7.9
Japan	4,879	38,210	1.6
UK	2,787	45,390	2.5
US	14,466	47,580	2.5

Source: *World Development Indicators.*

population size of the country. This is achieved by expressing GNI on a **per capita** basis; by dividing total GNI by the total population to arrive at an amount per head (see the dollars per capita column in Table 8.2).

The statistics in Table 8.2 are taken from *World Development Indicators*, a comprehensive annual set of data produced by the World Bank. The current publication lists data for 206 national economies in alphabetical order. In previous years, however, this data was presented in rank order according to GNI per capita. The concept of 'rank order' demonstrates the importance of these figures as they are used to create a type of league table, in which (in 2008) the United States (US) comes ahead of the United Kingdom (UK), since the gross national income (GNI) divided by the population is higher. On a per capita basis, the US and UK are among the top ten richest countries in the world; with the Scandinavian, Dutch, Irish and Swiss leading the pack. Indeed, in Norway a population of 5 million share a $415 billion economy making it the richest country in the world with $87,000 per capita. At the other extreme, India and China, with their large populations, are relatively poor. Following conventions defined by the World Bank, India is a lower middle income country as its annual per capita GNI is between $975 and $3,855; some of the very poorest people of the world have an annual income of less than $500 per capita (which is possibly less than some students in the Western world earn each month – even while they are studying).

GDP: Construction and Property

Construction is a significant part of the total economy. In 2008, construction in the narrowest sense of the definition produced slightly less than 10% of UK GDP. In comparison, manufacturing produced about 17% of GDP, and agriculture accounted for just 1%. The lion's share of economic activity fell into the service category, which broadly accounted for around 75% of GDP.

In terms of property much of the current activity that GDP measures are accounted for by repairs (maintenance and improvements) and new builds. These are included in the construction industry activities (a breakdown of the figures were presented and discussed in Chapter 1, on page 11). Monies related to the services associated with the transfer of land and existing buildings is more difficult to allocate to one specific industry, but it accounts for about £45 billion per year.

Part 4 of the *Blue Book* presents a collection of data that can be derived from the accounts. For example, Table 8.3 is based on details showing the market value of assets in the UK; some figures for the years 2000 and 2009 are shown. The details can be used as an estimated measure of the wealth of the UK, as they represent the stock of existing assets, such as the ownership of property, plant and machinery, agricultural land, farming stock, vehicles and certain types of military equipment. Intangible assets, such as patents, the rights to mineral exploration, and artistic works, have been placed under the heading of miscellaneous.

According to the figures in Table 8.3, at the end of 2009 the total value of commercial and industrial property was £559 billion. At the same date the residential property was worth £4,048 billion (i.e., £4 trillion, which is approximately three times the value of the annual GDP). Finally, it is worth emphasising that these figures are always based on current market prices, and this explains the decline in value of commercial and industrial property as the contrast that is being drawn is between two stark comparisons: namely, the buoyant market of 2000 and a market in recession during 2009.

Table 8.3 Balance sheet of national wealth (£ billions)

Assets	2008	2009
Residential buildings	2,107	4,048
Agricultural assets	54	53
Commercial and industrial property	574	559
Civil engineering works	523	725
Plant and machinery	366	506
Vehicles including ships, aircraft, etc.	114	172
Miscellaneous	510	880
Total Wealth	**4,248**	**6,944**

Source: Adapted from *UK National Accounts*, 2010 (Table 10.2).

GDP and Environmental Accounts

The final part of the *Blue Book* focuses on environmental accounts, the so-called **satellite accounts**, which detail oil and gas reserves, atmospheric emissions, and energy use, etc.

Satellite accounts enable an assessment of the environmental impact that has taken place alongside the economic activity. Much of the data in the section is detailed in units of physical measurement or volume; in short, not monetary units, and this allows the calculation of environmental features to be analysed in relation to economic change. For example, by expressing changes in real GDP in relation to energy used (measured in millions of tons of oil equivalent), it is possible to calculate the amount of energy required to support a certain level of GDP; or more simply the energy consumed per unit of output. With efficiency gains it is possible for energy, and emissions, per unit of output, to decline. The official word used to refer to this is to 'decouple' one from the other, or in plain English to accept that it is not inevitable for economic growth to always produce an equivalent deterioration in environmental quality.

Academic work has been progressing along these lines since the 1960s and the satellite accounts are now being developed to inform sustainable development policy and evaluate the environmental performance of different industrial sectors. More of this will be taken up in the next chapter.

Conclusion

To end this section we need to add one, or two, small caveats about national accounting data. First, the figures recorded in national accounts are official activities 'put through the books'. Alongside these formal, legal activities, there are informal, illegal, activities, such as unofficial work carried out for cash-in-hand, which is difficult to include. In the widest sense, however, national accounts should include all productive output. So, although some economic activities are hidden and difficult to measure, estimates are made. For example, estimates relating to the smuggling of alcoholic drink and tobacco products, and the output, expenditure and income directly generated by that activity, have been included since the 2001 edition of the *Blue Book*. A small percentage is also added to construction data to allow for informal output.

Second, it should be mentioned that economists are beginning to question whether national accounts are a perfect measure of welfare, since they clearly glorify the materialistic society in which we live. GDP numbers cannot capture our true overall well-being as a nation. As the satellite accounts remind us, economic activity also produces external costs, such as pollution, noise and accidents. Similarly, leisure, happiness and health cannot be measured simply

Definition

Satellite accounts describe areas or activities not dealt with by the core economic accounts, as they often use a different metric to money.

in terms of income, output or expenditure. Monetary values do not encompass everything that we care about; some things will always remain beyond price.

> ### Chapter Summary **8.1**
>
> - National accounts measure the annual level of economic activity, and economic growth is identified by changes in 'real' GDP.
> - The simple circular flow model highlights (a) that households sell factors of production in return for incomes, (b) that businesses sell goods and services to households, and (c) that there is a close relationship between income, expenditure and output.
> - GDP represents the total money value of all production created within a country during a year. GNI includes the income generated for the nationals of that country by overseas activities.
> - The narrow definition of construction suggests that activity in the sector accounts for approximately 10% of GDP; whereas property is better assessed in terms of its contribution to wealth (see Table 8.3).
> - In most countries, informal output means that economic activity is under-reported in national accounts.
> - There is some debate regarding the validity of GDP figures as an accurate measure of a nations well-being.

Measuring Inflation

As introduced in Chapter 7, an important objective of a stable and competitive economy is a low inflation rate, and the explicit aim of monetary policy since 1997 has been the control of **inflation**.

> ### Definition
> Inflation is a *persistent* increase in the general price level.

The italicised word in the definition is important, as any increase in the price level must be sustained to be categorised as an inflationary situation. The continuous annual price rises, such as those experienced in the UK and across Europe, are definite examples of inflation.

Table 8.4 shows the annual average change to the *retail price index* for the period 1970–2009; this is the broadest of the UK official measures and is sometimes referred to as the headline rate of inflation. In the 1970s, the inflation rate was high and very volatile – for example, it changed from 7.1% in 1972 to an all-time high of 24.2% in 1975. The 1980s, relative to the 1970s, could be classed as a decade of **disinflation**; that is, prices continued to rise each year but the overall rate began to slow down. The period 1990–2009 can generally be characterised as one of **low inflation**, with annual inflation rates running below 4%. In the not too distant future, the UK may even experience **deflation**, which is defined as a sustained fall in the general price level. Deflation is, in effect, the complete reverse of inflation even to the extent that it typically results from a fall in aggregate demand, in response to which firms reduce prices in order to sell their products.

Inevitably, as a form of price instability, deflation also has adverse economic consequences and it poses particular difficulties for economic management – one being that if inflation rates fall below zero (become negative), the Bank of England monetary policy committee would not be able to reduce interest rates

Table 8.4 Annual average UK inflation rate (%)

1970–1979	12.5
1980–1989	7.5
1990–1999	3.2
2000–2009	2.6

to stimulate demand. The macroeconomic aim, therefore, is to achieve price stability; to steer a course between inflation and deflation.

Measures of inflation involve representing changes in price over a period of time. The statistical device best suited for this purpose is **index numbers**. Index numbers are a means of expressing data relative to a given **base year**. They enable the cost of a particular range of products to be expressed as a percentage of the cost of the same group of products in the specified base year. The basic principle is shown in Figure 8.2. What is put into the basket for the base year and comparative year must be the same. That is, the system is dependent on comparing the price of a good or service that is identical or as near as possible, from one time period to the next.

Cost of Living Indices

The most commonly used price indices in the UK are the **retail price index (RPI)** and the **Consumer Price Index (CPI)**. The two indices are very similar and for our purposes can be dealt with under the same heading. In each case, they provide an assessment of the prices of goods and services purchased by the typical household. In fact, a good way to think about the RPI and the CPI is to imagine a 'supermarket shopping basket' full of goods and services on which people typically spend their money; but in this case it includes everything from food and housing to entertainment. Movements in the RPI or the CPI, therefore, reflect changes in the cost of living.

To be completely accurate, the cost of the basket should be calculated with reference to all consumer goods and services purchased by all households, and the prices measured in every shop or outlet that supplies them. In practice, however, this is impossible, and both the CPI and RPI are calculated by collecting a sample of prices from various outlets in various locations. The sample currently represents a selection of 650 goods and services, typically purchased by households. The prices of these indices are collected across

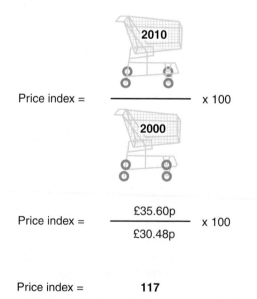

$$\text{Price index} = \frac{\boxed{2010}}{\boxed{2000}} \times 100$$

$$\text{Price index} = \frac{£35.60\text{p}}{£30.48\text{p}} \times 100$$

$$\text{Price index} = \mathbf{117}$$

Fig 8.2 Calculating a price index

In the example, two baskets of goods are compared and a base year of 2000 is selected. 2010 expressed in relation to 2000 gives a price index of 117; in short, an increase in price of 17%.

different types of retail outlets in 150 geographical areas in the UK. Currently, the cost of living indices are compiled on the basis of approximately 120,000 separate price quotations that are recorded every month.

An important objective is to make sure that the basket is representative of the current consumer goods and services typically purchased by households. Hence, the basket is reviewed each year to keep it as up-to-date as possible, and to reflect changes in buying patterns. Items are dropped from the basket when they become more difficult to find in the shops or no longer typical of what most people spend their money on. For example, purchases of vinyl records were common during the 1960s and 1970s. However, with the advent of compact discs and the download of music, records now form a niche market and have not been included as a representative item since the early 1990s. Similarly, spending on conventional CRT (cathode ray tube) televisions has decreased and no longer warrants inclusion, and spending on flat panel televisions has taken their place. It is equally important that new items are added to represent emerging markets, consequently rose wine, hardwood flooring, satellite navigation systems, and DAB radios, have all been added as new items in the last few years. In other cases, new items are selected as direct replacements for similar products that leave the basket, as they currently represent a greater proportion of the market. For example, in 2010, garlic bread replaced pitta bread; a bottled fruit drink replaced a carton of fruit drink; liquid soap replaced a bar of soap; and electrical hair straighteners and tongs replaced hairdryers.

Finally, the annual review of the basket needs to consider not just the list of items to be priced, but also where the prices are collected, and hence purchases and hire over the internet has been added in recent years. The level of detail that informs these annual reviews should be noted as it underlines the level of importance attached to the official measurement of economic variables.

The various items in the RPI and CPI basket are given a statistical weighting to take account of their importance to the typical household. The items that take more of people's incomes are given a higher weighting. For example, the statistical weight for food is higher than that for tobacco and alcohol, as changes in food prices affect everybody, whereas tobacco and alcohol prices only affect smokers and drinkers. The statistical weights attached to the broad commodity groupings for the CPI are shown in Table 8.5. The percentage distribution of the goods and services of the 650 items in the basket is also indicated.

Table 8.5 Statistical weights given to the CPI in 2010

Item	Percentage of weights	Percentage of basket
Food and non-alcoholic beverages	10.8	22
Alcohol and tobacco	4.0	4
Clothing and footwear	5.6	11
Housing and household services	12.9	5
Furniture and household goods	6.4	11
Health	2.2	3
Transport	16.4	6
Communications	2.5	1
Recreation and culture	15.0	17
Education	1.9	1
Restaurants and hotels	12.6	8
Miscellaneous goods and services	9.7	11

Source: ONS Guide, *The CPI & RPI Shopping Basket*, 2010.

The contents of the baskets used for the RPI and CPI are very similar but not identical. The RPI basket includes several items chosen to represent housing costs, including mortgage interest payments, council tax and rent, all of which are excluded from the CPI. In contrast, the CPI basket includes the fees paid by people living in communal accommodation such as nursing homes, retirement homes and university halls of residence. These so-called institutional households are excluded from the RPI, as its focus is exclusively on private UK households. In addition, the CPI also includes some items to represent costs faced by foreign visitors to the UK. These subtleties form the main technical differences between the two cost of living indices.

The more distinct difference is in their use and origin. The RPI has been established as a means of measuring price inflation in the UK, since 1947. The CPI has its origin in a system that is common to the European Union (EU). It was previously called the **harmonised index of consumer prices**, and it provides a direct contrast with other members of the EU. It became the official index used by the UK government to target inflation in January 2004. The CPI tends to produce a rate of inflation that is lower than the RPI equivalent, and on average the difference is roughly 1%.

In order to distinguish between the two, it might be useful to think of a headline rate and an official rate. The **headline inflation rate** is the one that appears in the press and usually refers to the RPI. The **official rate of inflation** forms the target for government purposes and, at present, is the CPI. The current target is to keep inflation rate around 2%; subject to a margin of 1% on either side. Finally, a passing reference should be made to the retail price index excluding mortgage interest payments (RPIX) as this had been the official government cost of living index from January 1998 to December 2003 and it is still published on a monthly basis. The three measures are compared in Table 8.6.

Specialised Indices

The same approach is used to produce various specialised indices. For example, the Investment Property Databank (IPD) compiles a property price index by comparing specific capital and rental values for 11,000 commercial properties on a regular basis. Its data goes back to a base year in 1981.

Similarly, there are a number of house price indices. The largest two mortgage lenders – Nationwide and Halifax – publish a house price index each month, based on comparisons of the prices of four different house types across 13 regions of the UK. These two financial institutions base their indices on the mortgage offers they have made in the previous month. Houses costing over £1 million are excluded, as it is assumed that this may distort the average picture.

A more comprehensive but less up-to-date measure comes from the Land Registry. This index is based on stamp duty land tax (SDLT) transactions and, therefore, covers every property deal in England and Wales. However, it is slow to reveal what is happening in the market since SDLT is paid at the end of the property transaction and that can be four or five months after the sale price has been agreed; and house prices can rise by as much as 20% within

Table 8.6 Abbreviations used that refer to UK inflation indices

CPI	Inflation measured by the Consumer Price Index (this has been the official UK government measure since January 2004).
RPI	Inflation measured by Retail Price Index, in use since 1947 (it commenced with 200 representative items in the basket, today there are 650).
RPIX	RPI *excluding* mortgage interest payments. Removes heavily weighted items from the basket. RPIX was the UK official government measure from 1998 to 2003.

three months. Recently, the websites *Hometrack* and *Rightmove* have added two further indices to the set. They collect information at the local level from estate agents on asking prices and agreed prices; they also cover far more properties than Nationwide and Halifax. All these indices are monitored and revised by the Department of Communities and Local Government to form a further measure of house prices; the CLG house price index.

Each house price index produces a marginally different estimate of house price inflation. This is because the indices are dependent both on the sample data that has been used to make up each specific basket and the way that each index is subsequently calculated. For interest, we contrast three measures of house price inflation in Figure 8.3.

House price indices are important because they are used by the government and the monetary policy committee as an indicator to assess the economy.

Many other institutions and professional bodies also produce specialised indices that are relevant to the property sector. For example, the Royal Institution of Chartered Surveyors produces the **Building Cost and Information Service (BCIS)**. This comprises of a building cost index and a tender price index.

The building cost index measures changes in costs of labour, materials and plant – that is, it covers the basic costs faced by contractors. The basket is compiled from nationally agreed labour rates and material prices. The index also includes forecasts to help predict any changes in prices that may occur in the period between submitting a tender and project completion. This is useful because the long time duration of large contracts means that work is often let at fixed prices before work commences.

The tender price index involves an analysis of successful tenders for contracts worth more than £250,000. It includes movements in wage rates, discounts, plant costs, overheads and profit – that is, it indicates the basic cost of construction work to the client. In effect, the tender price index is a measure of the confidence in the industry about its current and future workload. When demand for the industry's services is high, not only do contractors' margins increase but so do the margins of their suppliers and wage rates, and you would expect to see rises in the tender price index. Conversely, when demand for the industry's services decline, all these factors decrease and thereby exert downward pressure on the price index.

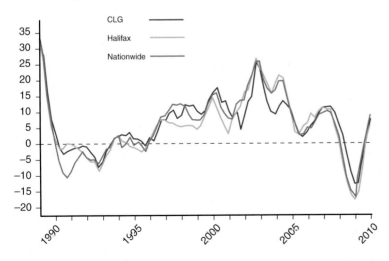

Fig 8.3 UK house price inflation

There are methodological differences in the way indices are calculated; these are highlighted when inflation is at extremes.

Source: ONS live tables, 2010.

The gap between these two indices suggests something about market conditions. During a recession you would expect to see the indices converge, with tenders certainly at a lower level than during a boom. The explanation is simple: when there is less work available, contractors will be satisfied just to get a contract and cover their costs; when the market is buoyant, tender prices will increase as contractors take advantage of the opportunity to more than cover their costs.

The important aspect in the compilation of any price index is to assure that the prices being recorded are for comparable items. For example, apples must be compared with apples, not with oranges; the baskets that are used for comparisons must be consistent! As indicated at the start of this section, a change in the measure of inflation does not alter the *actual* inflationary pressure in the economy; it remains the same regardless of the index used to measure it.

Chapter Summary 8.2

- Controlling inflation (a persistent increase in prices) has been a main economic priority for UK governments since 1997.
- Price indices compare the current cost (the cost today) with the cost of the same item(s) in a base year.
- The RPI and CPI are both used as measures of the cost of living (general inflation) in the UK.
- There are several specialised price indices, such as the Nationwide and Halifax house price indices, the BCIS price and cost indices, and the IPD index, which is designed to specifically measure changes in commercial property markets.

Measuring Unemployment

Of all the factors of production, unemployed labour is the most worrying. As acknowledged in Chapter 7, unemployed labour has many costs – in human suffering, in loss of dignity, and loss of output. This is why a common objective of government is to achieve full employment, and policy-makers monitor the official unemployment figures that are published each month.

In historical terms, the problem of unemployment has declined. A portrait of unemployment for the 60 year period from 1930–1990 was presented in the first edition of this text (published in 1994). It began with a very high rate of unemployment of over 20% in the depression of the 1930s and showed that after the war, and the government's acceptance of responsibility to try and secure full employment, the rate of unemployment tended to be exceptionally low. In fact, for much of the 30 year period from 1945–1975 unemployment was 3% or less. Thereafter, unemployment levels above 3% began to appear and rates of 4 and 5% are now quite common. In Figure 8.4 the average unemployment rate, over the period 1995–2010 is shown to be around 6.3%, but the *general trend* since the recession at the beginning of the 1990s has been downward.

Unemployment data that records previous occupations is more difficult to find. However, the occasional surveys that have been published, strongly suggest that the rate of unemployment in the construction sector is more volatile as it tends to exaggerate what is happening in the broader economy. Estimated data is presented in Figure 8.4; all the rates in this figure have been **seasonally adjusted**. This means that the figures have been statistically smoothed to allow for changes in employment opportunities that occur from month to month. For example, the construction sector typically experiences

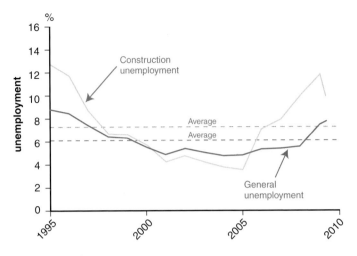

Fig 8.4 Unemployment 1995–2010

higher rates of unemployment during the winter months than during the rest of the year; so to seasonally adjust the calculation, this specific period is excluded from the annual average in the data presented in Figure 8.4.

How Official Terms are Defined

In conceptual terms the numbers of unemployed are expressed relative to the total number employed. To make sense of this we need to look at the official definition.

> **Definition**
>
> The unemployment rate is measured as a percentage of economically active people who are able and willing to work, but cannot find a job.

The way the statistics are calculated, the unemployment rate can be stated for a region, age group, industrial sector, or any other chosen group of the population. It can also be expressed as an absolute number. The percentage rate is preferable, because it measures the proportion of the economically active population who are unemployed and so takes account of changes in the size of the population over time, as well as changes in the level of unemployment.

The Economically Active and Inactive

The economically active consists of people who are employed, as well as those who are unemployed. To reiterate, in other words, the labour supply should be recognised to consist of people who are employed, as well as those people defined as unemployed.

In less formal terms, the economically active includes the following four main groups:

1. Those in employment such as employees.
2. The self-employed.
3. Those on government training schemes.
4. Those registered as unemployed and probably claiming benefit.

The **economically active** should not be confused with all those of working age, such as those involved in full-time education, those in early retirement, housewives and those who are not at present seeking work; the

> **Definition**
>
> The economically active are persons over 16 who work for pay or gain or consider themselves as 'available' for such work.

Table 8.7 The labour market in 2010

Total population aged 16 and over	49,711,000
Minus those classed as economically inactive	18,372,000
Equals total economically active	31,339,000
Minus unemployed (ILO definition)	2,510,000
Equals total in employment	28,829,000

Source: *Economic and Labour Market Review,* June 2010.

so-called **economically inactive**. Or to put the emphasis the other way, the economically inactive should not be confused with those who are registered as unemployed!

The statistics in Table 8.7 should help to clarify the distinction between the different classifications that divide the labour market; in particular those classified as economically active and those who are inactive.

Claimant and ILO Unemployment

There are two official measures of unemployment regularly published in the UK. The most frequently referred to in the press is **claimant unemployment**, which is based on a monthly total of those claiming benefit. This is very easy to collect since it is based on a computer count of all those officially registered as willing and able to work but presently claiming jobseekers' allowance. This official measure is recognisably suspect: it excludes all those who are not eligible for benefits: it *officially excludes* all men aged over 60 who, since April 1983, no longer have to sign on to claim benefit; and it also excludes those who register as desiring work at commercial agencies but not with the job centres because, owing to marriage or similar circumstances, they are not eligible for benefit. It includes some fraudulent claimers of benefit, such as those who work as well as 'sign on'.

The alternative is the **ILO unemployment rate**. This is a standardised unemployment measure, which is based on a quarterly survey of around 60,000 households (i.e., approximately 120,000 people aged 16 or over). The survey defines unemployment as: those without jobs who say that they have actively sought work in the last four weeks or are waiting to take up appointments within the next fortnight. This so-called labour force survey follows an internationally agreed definition recommended by the International Labour Organisation (ILO), an agency of the United Nations. Although the ILO measure is not so easy to calculate, and is subject to some sampling error, it has the advantage of being used internationally. In short, most countries back-up their count with a survey-based measure of unemployment. This enables international comparisons since they all use the same definition and similar sample size. It usually indicates a larger number of unemployed; and it is slowly becoming adopted as the official measure of unemployment in the UK.

Summing Up

The monthly review of labour market statistics discussed above distinguishes between those who are unemployed and those who are economically active or inactive. In other words, the data is designed in such a way that it shows the proportion who are engaged in paid work and indicates the extent to which people would be engaged in such work if their personal circumstances were different, or if jobs that attracted them were available. Figure 8.5 summarises the structure that we have discussed.

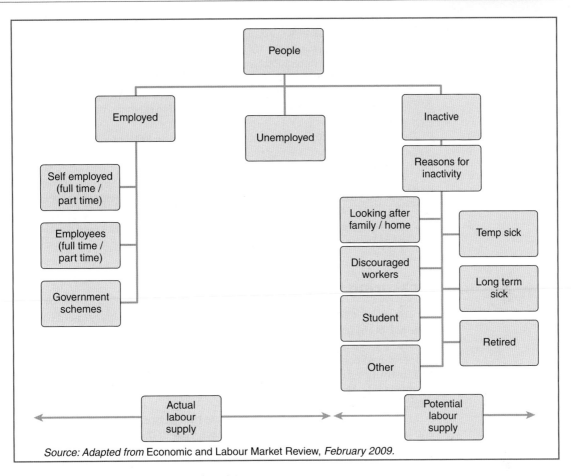

Source: Adapted from Economic and Labour Market Review, February 2009.

Fig 8.5 The structure of actual and potential employment

Obviously the actual labour market is far from static, with people moving between different categories as their personal, and overall, economic conditions change. The data merely provides a snapshot of those who are unemployed and those who are economically active, on a particular day of each month. Obviously, the members of each group will not be static, as there are constantly large numbers of people joining and leaving the pool of unemployed labour. Those joining the pool are referred to as the *inflow* and those leaving it are referred to as the *outflow*. If the inflow and outflow are equal, the unemployment rate remains the same. If the number leaving jobs and flowing into the reservoir of the unemployed exceeds new appointments, the unemployment rate rises.

To judge the severity of unemployment problems, therefore, we need to be able to examine more details relating to the duration, region, gender, age, and qualifications of the unemployed and economically inactive – and estimates of such data are published each month. This is important as property developers, for example, need to assimilate as much insight as possible into an area to understand its viability for development.

> ### Chapter Summary **8.3**
>
> - Unemployment rates in the UK during the post-war period have risen from a low of 3%, and since 2000 have settled at around 5%; at the current time they are closer to 8%.
> - The economically active includes: (i) employees in employment, (ii) the self-employed, (iii) those on government training schemes, and (iv) the unemployed.
> - The economically inactive includes: (i) students in full time education, (ii) those who are long-term or temporarily sick, (iii) those looking after family/home, and (iv) those who have retired early.
> - There are two official measures of unemployment: claimant unemployment and ILO unemployment. The former relates to those in receipt of benefits, the latter is based on a survey.
> - Unemployment statistics can be analysed in detail, and this could support decisions in the property sector.

Measuring International Trade

As stated in Chapter 7, figures relating to trade and investments across national boundaries are notoriously difficult to record accurately, and there are also many cultural barriers to developing successful strategies to invest in property and construction abroad. As a consequence, it is only the larger firms and institutions that get involved at the international level. However, in order to appreciate the international implications, an open economy perspective must be introduced.

In terms of measurement the economic transactions between UK residents and the rest of the world are presented each year in the *United Kingdom Balance of Payments: the Pink Book*. At the simplest level, these international accounts provide a measure of all the *money* coming into the country from abroad less all of the money going out of the country during the same period.

Examples of the relevant economic transactions include: the export and import of goods such as oil, food, raw materials, machinery, equipment, computers, white goods and clothing; the export and import of services such as international transport, travel, finance, tourism, insurance, computer software, accountancy and legal activities; and income flows relating to investments and the ownership of financial assets such as dividends and interest earned by non-residents on investments in the UK and by UK residents investing abroad.

> **Definition**
>
> The balance of payments is a record of one country's trade dealings with the rest of the world.

In short, the accounts record the international trading position, plus its lending and its borrowing. Dealings that result in money entering the country are credit (plus) items while transactions that lead to money leaving the country are debit (minus) items.

Of all the measurements discussed in this chapter these are the least reliable. For example, the difficulties of obtaining data on the investment in foreign property, such as second homes abroad that generate rental incomes to their owners and add capital value to their wealth, are notoriously difficult to produce reliable estimates. In 2003/2004, the value of foreign property ownership was estimated to be £23 billion – this was more than double the equivalent estimate made four years earlier. Exchange rate variations, price changes and methods of valuation all complicate the picture.

Fortunately, at the introductory level, much of the relevant analysis of property economics resides within the boundaries of one nation, so it could be argued that this set of macroeconomics statistics is at present less important than others. For instance, construction represents less than 1% of the activities recorded on the credit or debit side. But international transactions have considerable implications on an economy's performance and should not be entirely ignored at any level of study. So it will be dealt with, albeit relatively quickly.

The balance of payments details three sets of accounts:

1. The most basic flow is the balance of payments on *Current Account*. This provides a record of transactions arising from trade in goods and services, certain investment incomes and some transfer payments. Strictly speaking it should not, therefore, be confused with a simple **trade balance**, since the current account balance also includes some international investment income flows and current transfers; and together these two items alone represent around 40% of the current account credits and debits. The UK has consistently run a current account deficit every year since 1983, and it is this set of data that is commonly referred to in the newspaper headlines and media. To sum up, therefore, the current account basically measures flows. If a country records a current account deficit it means the residents are consuming more than they are producing. To pay for the difference they need to run down their assets or increase their liabilities, and this is where the other two accounts come in.

2. The balance of payments on *Capital Account* is relatively small in comparison and the amounts involved constitute less than 1% of the whole balance. It itemises transactions related to international movements of non-produced, non-financial assets (such as copyrights). This includes land purchases and sales associated with embassies and other extraterritorial bodies. Capital transfers entries are required where there is no quid pro quo to offset the transfer of ownership of fixed assets, or the transfer of funds linked to fixed assets (for example, aid to finance capital works), or the forgiveness of debt. The capital account has remained in surplus for the past 25 years; and, to a limited extent, it counterbalances the current account deficit. However, it is most unlikely that the current account and capital account would ever fully balance and this brings us to the third, and important, set of accounts detailed in the *Pink Book*.

3. The balance of payments *financial account* provides a record of the transactions associated with changes of ownership of the UK's foreign financial assets and liabilities. In other words, transactions relating to portfolio investments, derivatives and other financial assets are traded to balance the books. For example, in the event of a balance of payments deficit on the current account outflows will be greater than inflows and the supply of pounds onto the international exchange market will be greater than the demand for the same pounds. In short there will be an excess supply of pounds on the foreign exchange markets. The central bank, the Bank of England, will need to offset this excess supply by buying them with foreign currency. As such, it will need to run down its reserves of foreign exchange. In recent years, the UK has had to borrow from abroad to finance a continuing current account deficit, which has resulted in inward investment (UK liabilities) exceeding outward investment (UK assets).

In very general terms, therefore, the current account can be regarded as a measure of the flow of assets and liabilities across international boundaries, whilst the financial account records the total value of the stock of assets and liabilities at a specific point in time; and together one total counterbalances the other.

Problems occur, however, if the public sector has few financial reserves, or faces limits on how much it can effectively borrow or raise in tax income.

For instance, when the Greek government's finances collapsed in April 2010, it had already borrowed to the hilt in the international financial markets. Furthermore, evasion and corruption were endemic in Greek society and this made it difficult to generate significant funds in taxes from the collapsing economy or to find anybody within Greece willing to lend it money. As a result, Greece experienced a genuine balance of payments crisis.

The final caveat to note is the balance of payments must always balance since the accounts are constructed such that this must be true by definition. But there can be measurement error and unreported borrowing from abroad and other illegal activities. As a consequence, balance of payment figures are always being revised in retrospect and the initial estimates are provisional in the most generous of senses.

> ### Chapter Summary 8.4
>
> - The balance of payments reflects the value of all transactions in international trade, such as the trade in goods, services, financial assets and transfers.
> - In relative terms the accounts are the most difficult set of data to interpret and/or trust for reliability. This is due in part to complications caused by exchange rate variations, price changes, methods of valuation, illegal transactions, etc.
> - Much of the relevant introductory analysis of property economics resides within the boundaries of one nation, but the significant implications of international transactions demands that it is opened up as a subject warranting more advanced study.

Measuring Environmental Impacts

A current government issue gaining in importance is the question of environmental sustainability; and how the drive for worldwide economic growth is forcing governments to acknowledge the planet's limits. For the past 50 years, or more, academics have debated the need to establish a standard international measure that effectively monitors the broad usage of environmental resources; and this is now becoming increasingly urgent. Various *ad hoc* measures have been trialled, and many of these defer to GDP as a reference point, but now some consensus is emerging that governments need a specific yardstick to monitor and measure the total global environmental impacts placed by humanity on the ecosystem. In other words, an authorised metric designed to capture environmental activity in a similar way to GDP capturing economic activity.

The metric most likely to meet this role is the **ecological footprint**. This system provides a way of measuring how far the economic demands we place upon the planet – as individuals, nations and regions – are in line with the resources it can provide. Measurements currently exist for 150 countries for each year from 1961 to 2006. They are produced by an organisation called the Global Footprint Network, which uses data provided by the United Nations. A major source of interest and funds for its work comes from the EU. The Global Footprint Network's vision is to make the *ecological footprint* as prominent a metric as GDP by 2015.

Measuring the Ecological Footprint

The basis of the measurement focuses on the environmental resources needed to sustain life in terms of producing food, energy, water and timber and carrying away the associated wastes. The significance of the environment for businesses and households of all types is succinctly represented by Figure 8.6.

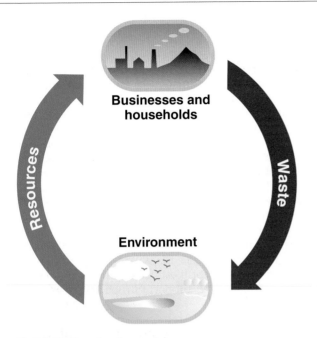

Fig 8.6 The flow of environmental resources

The environment is the resource base that provides renewable and non-renewable resources that enable production and consumption to be achieved. At the other end of a product's life, the environment is also expected to provide a sink facility to assimilate the waste matter, such as the emissions from fossil fuels. (In this analysis we should not forget that the environment also provides opportunities, as an amenity, for various leisure pursuits.)

Measurements can be expressed in many ways. For example, the world's ecological footprint in 2006 was 17.1 billion global hectares or 2.6 global hectares per person. Such data means very little unless it is expressed in relation to what is actually available. In other words, the basis of the measurement for a country's footprint requires an assessment of the total area required to produce the food and fibre that it consumes, absorb the waste from its energy use, and provide space for its infrastructure. This is done by taking each country's resource use and comparing it to what is actually available. The convention is to state the data with reference to the global hectares available per person. This is explained next.

> **Definition**
>
> The ecological footprint is an accounting tool used to measure how much productive land and water an individual, city or country requires to produce all the resources it consumes and to absorb all the waste it generates.

Global Hectares Per Person

The calculation begins with the assumption that the productive and assimilative land upon which life depends could be anywhere in the world. This seems reasonable as people of one nation usually consume resources and ecological services from all over the world. The ecological footprint calculations are, therefore, stated in *global hectares*. A **global hectare** (gha) is 1 hectare of biologically productive space. In 2006 (the most recent year for which data are available), the biosphere had 11.9 billion global hectares of biologically productive area corresponding to roughly one-quarter of the planet's surface. The 11.9 billion global hectares is approximately composed of 3.7 billion (gha) of cropland, 1.7 billion (gha) of grazing land, 4.9 billion (gha) of forest land, 1.2 billion (gha) of fishing ground, and 0.4 billion (gha) of built-up land. Non-productive, marginal areas, with comparatively low levels of **bioproductivity**, such as deserts, barren land, ice caps, and deep oceans, are not included in the

11.9 billion global hectares of biologically productive land and sea area on the planet.

To express the capacity available to each person, the 11.9 billion global hectares of productive area (the earth's surface, land and sea) are divided by the number of people on the planet – approximately 6.6 billion (2006 figures). The result is 1.8 global hectares per capita. This means that, in principle, the average amount of ecological productive capacity (the biocapacity) that exists on the planet per person is 1.8 global hectares.

If each person could survive on 1.8 hectares, or less, the world would be sustainable. However, the latest ecological footprint accounts put together by the European Environment Agency and the Global Footprint Network indicate that we are far away from achieving sustainable development. The figures show that, on average, every person on earth is taking 40% more from the planet than it can naturally regenerate. In the language of sustainable development, to meet today's needs we are raiding our children's inheritance, leaving them with less for the future. This is particularly evident in the high-income countries of Western Europe and the US where people are living beyond their means: to sustain their present lifestyles requires a productive area equivalent to two-and-a-half planets to support Europe and five for the United States of America!

The most extreme example is the United Arab Emirates as they have the highest per capita ecological footprint in the world at 10.3 global hectares, meaning that if the rest of the world consumed natural resources at the same rate, 5.5 planet earths would be required to sustain that level of lifestyle. This high per capita ecological footprint highlights how residents of the UAE use more than their 'share' of the world's natural resources and that this present lifestyle level is not sustainable!

A brief summary of the latest available data is presented in Table 8.8; for comparative purposes the same countries as those selected in Table 8.2 (on page 120) have been stated. Analysing the two tables, therefore, indicates the consumption of resources required to maintain the present levels of economic activity (GNI). It is evident that the low and middle-income countries represented by India and China, respectively, have smaller ecological footprints than their equivalents in high-income countries. But all the countries shown exceed their own ecological capacity, which is shown by the negative figures in the final column. The **ecological deficit** measures the amount by which a country's footprint exceeds the global space available to that specific nation. Interestingly, relatively few countries (approximately one-third) portrayed the opposite position; where national (biological) capacity is *not* used for consumption, or absorption of waste, by the population of that specific nation.

Table 8.8 The ecological footprint of selected economies

2006 data	Population (millions)	Total ecological footprint (global ha/person)	Biocapacity (global ha/person)	Ecological deficit (global ha/person)
China	1,328.5	1.8	0.9	−1.0
India	1,151.8	0.8	0.4	−0.4
Japan	128.0	4.1	0.6	−3.5
UK	60.7	6.1	1.6	−4.5
US	302.8	9.0	4.4	−4.6
World	6,592.9	2.6	1.8	−0.8

Source: *National Footprint Accounts*, 2009.

The so-called **ecological reserve**, however, does not necessarily remain unused, as it may be occupied by the footprints of other countries through production for export. This is obvious as the **biocapacity** column shows the productive space available in a given year to a specific territory. In all of the countries shown, the biocapacity (determined by the resources available within their borders) is smaller than their ecological footprint, which is based on the resources they actually consume!

This paints rather a daunting picture, as the only way to reduce a nation's ecological footprint, or more importantly the global ecological footprint, is by populations becoming smaller, or making reductions in the average consumption per person or increasing resource efficiency through changes in technology. The latter includes the reduction of carbon emissions by transferring from fossil fuels to renewable energy sources.

The Ecological Footprint and Buildings

The ecological footprint process is easy to exemplify within the property and construction sectors. Together these two sectors consume resources and generate waste on a scale that completely dwarfs other sectors of the economy. In the first place, it is the environment that provides the land on which buildings and infrastructure are located. In addition, it is the environment that provides many of the resources that are used to make building material products. Construction and buildings in use account for 40% of the total flow of raw materials into the global economy every year, 25% of virgin wood used and 50% of total energy use. It is also the environment that is ultimately responsible for assimilating and processing the waste that arises from the various phases of a property's life, from construction through to demolition. In other words, without the environment there would be no resources for construction and no way of managing some of the waste and outputs arising from the processes involved in maintaining the building stock and associated infrastructure.

As a consequence, changes in the ways that property is designed and used could have significant impacts on the scale of the ecological footprint. At present, a significant part of the ecological footprint is the energy footprint, as carbon emissions make up approximately half of the total footprint. These could be reduced to zero by adopting buildings designed to harness renewable sources, so-called carbon neutral solutions based on wind, sun or geothermal sources. Similarly, the **embodied energy** that accounts for a significant amount of the energy used at the construction phase could be reduced by recycling materials and/or conserving buildings, and sourcing materials locally to avoid unnecessary transportation.

The energy usage of a building over its average life, which could extend to 60 years or more, could make significant contributions to a nation's use of global sources by being more carefully designed, specified, used, and managed. This theme is developed further in the next chapter, where we will explore the barriers and opportunities offered by the built environment to contribute to sustainable development.

Conclusion

Following the above explanation, you can begin to understand the controversial nature of adopting the ecological footprint measure as it forces us to compare the current ecological demands with the capacity of the earth's life-supporting ecosystems, and it suggests that we are not living within the sustainable limits of the planet. Ecosystems are suffering, the global climate is changing, and the further we continue down this path of unsustainable consumption and exploitation, the more difficult it will become to protect and restore the biodiversity that remains. Governments will be unable to address this question properly until it has an agreed way to monitor and measure the problem; the need for this agreement is becoming increasingly urgent.

Chapter Summary **8.5**

- The ecological footprint measures the natural resource consumption required to support the existing standard of living. Calculations have been carried out for 150 nations.
- The Global Footprint Network's vision is to make the *ecological footprint* as prominent a metric as the Gross Domestic Product (GDP) by 2015.
- The global ecological footprint changes with population size, average consumption per person, resource efficiency, changes to technology, recycling, and attitudes to conservation.

Measuring Business Fluctuations

In Chapter 1 we defined macroeconomics as focusing mainly on aggregate behaviour: that is, events that many firms tend to experience. We pointed out how in a recession, although many firms and industries will be performing poorly, this doesn't mean that all firms are doing badly. During a recession some firms will get lucky by introducing a new product consumers really want. In short, some sectors will feel the recession bite more than others.

The measurement data used to investigate the nature of business fluctuations centres on identifying the turning points. For this to make sense it might be helpful to review the economic cycles introduced in Chapter 7. In Figure 8.7, we revisit in more detail the various phases that characterise business fluctuations, using recent economic activity as a reference point.

Beginning on the left-hand side of the graph in Figure 8.7, a **depression** is characterised by heavy unemployment, low consumer demand and surplus productive capacity plus low business confidence – such a situation has not been recorded since the 1930s; and prior to the current crisis the UK economy had not experienced a period of prolonged negative growth since the early 1990s. The **recovery**, or expansion phase, is easy to identify as employment, income and consumer spending all begin to increase; investment also increases and business expectation becomes more favourable. In a very general sense the economy of the UK had been on one long upward path since the mid-1990s. At

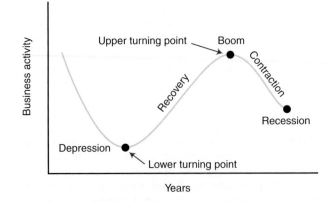

Fig 8.7 Phases of economic activity

the peak of the **boom** industries are working at full capacity and bottlenecks begin to appear in the supply chain, which leads to price increases. After an indefinite time period the economy begins to slow down, or contract, as it moves towards the final phase shown in Figure 8.7, the **recession**; at this point consumption, employment and investment all begin to fall and business expectations become negative. Recession was a common phenomenon across many economies following the financial crisis of 2007/2009.

It is important to remember that no two cycles are the same; that is why the preferred term nowadays is fluctuations. This was explained in Chapter 7, where it was stated that the extent and depth of each fluctuation varies considerably. For example, the recession phase over the years has tended to shorten in duration, to the extent that a distinction is now made between a long-lasting downturn in which output declines and a shorter less severe downward trend. The former is denoted by the term a depression and the latter a recession. The key difference between a recession and a depression is that the former tends to be short-lived and output soon returns to its trend value.

In contrast, during a depression the economy loses momentum and the downturn lasts so long that it seems unable to recover; arguably such a full-blown depression has not been experienced since the 1930s. Table 8.9 shows the average length of the economic cycle and the related periods of contraction and expansion experienced in the United States since 1854 (the figures are derived from data recorded by the National Bureau of Economic Research – NBER – which is an American research agency that is officially responsible for determining the beginning and end of economic cycles in the United States). Table 8.9 highlights that periods of expansion seem to last longer and longer as time progresses, and contractions are getting shorter in time duration. In other words, the average length of one cycle measured from peak-to-peak, or trough-to-trough, has extended in time from 48 months to 73 months (i.e. from four years to approx six years). In historical terms, therefore the period of contraction has become less and less problematic since the last great depression in the 1930s. However, according to the business cycle dating committee, the recent downturn in economic activity began in December 2007, and officially reached its lowest point in June 2009. Equivalent UK data shows a peak to trough decline of 6.4% in economic activity between Mar 2008 and Sept 2009. In other words, the financial crisis that began in 2007 led to an 18-month recession that was experienced earlier in America than the UK.

One way to measure business fluctuations, therefore, is to assess the trends in the economy by calculating changes to GDP over a period of time. Nowadays, real declines in GDP are not common; but it is possible to identify that the growth has slowed to be less than the long-run trend. Another possibility is to measure the time duration from one boom and the next.

There is a more specialised collection of economic statistics that enables us to go slightly further and predict where an economy might be heading. Their origin dates back to the 1960s and they are still referred to as **cyclical indicators**. They enable governments and business organisations to forecast what is

Definition

The official definition of a recession is when an economy has experienced at least two successive quarters of negative growth.

Table 8.9 Recessions and expansions, 1854–2009

Historical cycles	Contractions*	Expansions*	Length of cycle*
1854–1919 (16 cycles)	22	21	48
1919–1945 (6 cycles)	18	35	53
1945–2009 (11 cycles)	11	59	73

*Average duration measured in months
Source: *NBER*, August 2010.

happening in an economy. The predictions are based on a composite set of statistics that are regarded as running ahead of the general economic trend. They are based on the understanding that things do not happen simultaneously – some indicators may point in an upward direction while others portray a downward trend, especially at the 'peaks' and 'troughs' (the turning point) of a cycle. For example, when GDP growth is strong, unemployment falls and, as an economy moves into recession, unemployment starts to rise. The labour market can, therefore, be seen as a lagging indicator of the general business trends. By contrast, changes in residential property values have proved to be good lead indicators of inflation; as prices in residential markets tend to correlate with the headline rate of inflation in the UK.

Statistics that are assumed to precede the general trend of the economy by changing six to twelve months ahead of the main trend are referred to as **leading indicators**. This group is broken down into two subgroups: a longer leading index (which looks for turning points about one year ahead) and a shorter leading index (which indicates turning points approximately six months ahead). Examples of leading indicators are housing starts, new car sales, business optimism and the amount of consumer credit. **Lagging indicators**, by contrast, alter in retrospect, usually about one year after a change in the economic cycle – they confirm what we already know and, in forecasting terms, are not so important. Examples of lagging indicators include unemployment, investment in building, plant and machinery, levels of stock, and orders for engineering output. Economic statistics that are thought to trace the actual cycle are called **coincident indicators** and the obvious example is GDP figures.

Construction and Property Cycles

As you might expect, fluctuations in construction output and property markets share a similar pattern to the broader economy and they are referred to as building cycles and property cycles, respectively. Economists have a long history of studying these specialised cycles in order to gain a better understanding of business fluctuations. The symmetry between business fluctuations and building and property cycles is, however, complicated by the fact that economic development is usually associated with a shift from investment in new construction to spending on repair and maintenance. In other words, as GDP increases the proportion of new construction work decreases. There is an inevitable decline in the share of construction in GDP as economies mature. In fact, it has been observed that newly developing countries experience as much as double the rate of expenditure on construction than their more developed counterparts.

Another notable comparison between the construction and property sectors and the rest of the economy is that building and property cycles have shown far greater amplitude than the equivalent cycles in general business activity. In other words, periods of decline and expansion are far more rapid in these markets than in the general economy. This can be seen in Figure 8.8, where the annual percentage change in construction is plotted against the annual percentage change in the whole economy. The comparison clarifies two points: firstly, both construction and the economy as a whole experienced positive rates of growth from 2000–2007; and secondly, the rate of change is far more volatile in the construction sector, highlighted by the negative figure in 2008 for construction, whereas the general economy did not arrive at a negative position until the following year. The relevance of these observations will become apparent as we consider one of the main purposes of measuring macroeconomic variables: namely, economic forecasting.

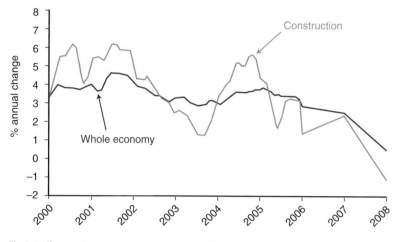

Fig 8.8 Changes in economic activity 2000–2008

Forecasting the Economy

Economic statistics provide a key resource for the government, academia and the wider business community, such as those working in the property sector, to interpret economic events. To take a simple example, some forecasters suggest that the sight of an increasing number of cranes on the skyline means that we are about to witness the start of the next recession. But this could be regarded as a dangerous presumption as there are many other variables that need to be used as a basis for forecasting. The art of forecasting involves completing a picture using as much existing data as possible and combining this analysis with anecdotal evidence to arrive at an overall view.

To avoid too many subjective judgments, models tend to be computer-based, using mathematical equations to link a number of economic variables; these variables can be categorised into two main types exogenous and endogenous. **Exogenous variables** are external to the economy insofar as they are determined by world events and policy (examples include oil prices and exchange rates). **Endogenous variables** are dependent on what goes on within an economy (examples include employment and inflation). There are more than 120 exogenous variables, and hundreds of endogenous ones – and the larger, traditional models of the macroeconomy contained upwards of a thousand relationships. The present trend, however, is for models to be smaller and rarely exceed 20 core equations.

Treasury forecasts are informed by more than 20 models managed by institutions in the city and beyond. In Table 8.10, we present the May 2010 forecast for the UK economy up until 2014. This table summarises the Treasury interpretation of the averages of the 20 independent forecasts; it does not show the range of comparisons making up the forecast. For example, the highest and lowest forecast for a percentage change of GDP in 2011 was 3.4 and 0.9%; in 2012, the respective figures were 4.0 and 1.3%.

Problems of Forecasting

Understandably, it is difficult to accurately predict the behaviour of millions of consumers and businesses to the last detail; and economic forecasts often have a margin of error. In fact, the Bank of England recently coined the term 'data uncertainty' to describe the difficulty of making policy judgments when the

Table 8.10 Economy forecasts, 2010–2014

The table summarises the independent average forecasts. Inflation is projected in percentage terms across on two measures (CPI and RPI), and unemployment is based on the claimant count.

Average projections	2010	2011	2012	2013	2014
GDP growth (%)	1.1	2.1	2.4	2.7	2.5
CPI	2.5	1.7	1.9	2.2	2.2
RPI	3.6	2.9	3.0	3.3	3.4
Claimant unemployment (mn)	1.67	1.67	1.62	1.48	1.37
Current account (£bn)	−21.4	−19.3	−12.5	−10.0	−11.7

Source: *Treasury*, May 2010.

statistical indicators they use are subject to change. To paraphrase an analogy used by Norman Lamont, during his time as the Chancellor of the Exchequer in the early 1990s: forecasting an economy on the basis of current statistics is like driving a car with the front and side windows blackened and just a rear view mirror to see where the car is going. Furthermore, forecasts are limited, since they rely on assumptions about policies that may need to change owing to sudden events or revised statistics. There are also problems relating to time-lags, since it often takes years for a specific monetary or fiscal instrument to fully work through an economic system. To continue the analogy of driving a car: the brake and accelerator pedals may only take effect some time after they are applied!

The important point is the message conveyed by the forecast; the trend does not have to be 100% accurate. Forecasting models are no different from any other economic model in that they attempt to simplify reality. In the case of the economy, it is a complex reality and a forecasting model only measures and monitors the key variables. Understanding half of the picture, however, is better than not seeing any of it at all.

Forecasting Property Markets

The collection of official statistics in the UK is based on a history and consensus of conventions, many of which have been agreed internationally. For example, the various statistical series of macroeconomic data referred to above have been comprehensively measured since the Second World War.

In contrast, the collection of property data is still a relatively young science. As the *Estates Gazette* commented in September 2005: property research as we know it is not yet 30 years old. In fact, as was pointed out in Chapter 1, specific information relating to property is nowhere near as comprehensive; indeed, data relating to commercial property, rents and capital returns and the like is reliant on confidential private records. Some of these spill over into the public domain via the weekly 'Finance' section in the *Estates Gazette*, where banks and agents, such as HSBC, Jones Lang LaSalle (JLL), CB Richard Ellis (CBRE) Savills, and Cushman & Wakefield, etc., make their records freely available. But much is retained as confidential.

Fortunately, the main agency collecting this data makes some of it available to others at a price. But apart from the Investment Property Databank (IPD) records, surveyors are often reliant on in-house research and anecdotal stories. In 1993, the Governor of the Bank of England actually remarked that he was surprised at the relative lack of consistent comprehensive data on the property markets and the lack of research into the functioning of that market. Fifteen years later the financial crisis that no one saw coming was partly due to this lack of data, and the problem is currently being addressed; for instance, Figure 8.9

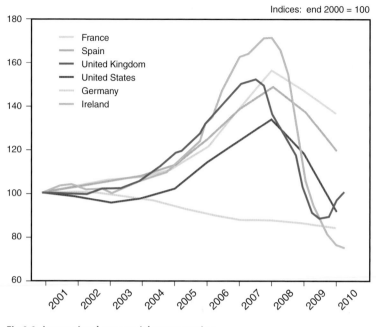

Indices: end 2000 = 100

France
Spain
United Kingdom
United States
Germany
Ireland

Fig 8.9 International commercial property prices

Source: Financial Stability Report, June 2010.

is sourced from a Bank of England publication and based on IPD data and other calculations.

It is often alleged that there is a relationship between changes in property values and indicators of inflation. The empirical evidence certainly suggests that there is some kind of cause or effect relationship, as property prices in both the commercial and residential markets correlate with the headline rate inflation. The problem that we want you to consider is the line of causation; that is, do property values lead to inflation or is it inflation that drives up property prices? To restate the question in more formal terms: do property values represent leading or lagging indicators of inflationary pressure in the economy?

If you follow the research suggestion you will discover that the data record is somewhat mixed. Residential property values and inflation data are easy to source and there does seem to be a close relationship between the two; and presumably that is why the government and the Bank of England are so sensitive to its well-being. In fact, you may remember that we pointed out above that the monetary policy committee studies the housing market as part of its monthly data research. It regards sharp rises in residential property prices not only as a sign of inflationary pressures in the economy, but also as a direct cause of such pressure; in short, a leading indicator.

However, much less is heard about commercial property prices; the sources of data are not as comprehensive and the indices are not regularly produced, so there is no evidence that commercial property plays a causative role in the inflationary process. For example, what does the data shown in Figure 8.9 tell us?

The effects of the commercial property sector on general inflation could work through two channels. First, the decrease in commercial property prices, although not featuring directly in the retail price index, will ultimately impact on retail prices through their effects on business costs. Lengthy periods of fixed rent review, however, mean that decreases in rents would not occur until long after the original deflationary impulse occurs. In this respect, it is best to think of commercial property values as lagging economic activity rather being a key driver of it.

Second, there is the long-term impact on wealth that follows on from decreased capital values of commercial property. A substantial proportion (approximately 60%) of the commercial property sector is owned by investment institutions, so the effect of lower capital values is reflected in loan to value ratios, negative equity and loan defaults. In other words, a poor investment performance of institutional funds will ultimately pay out less in pension funds and life insurance to their clients. These effects will be distributed over long periods into the future and will not be instantly visible to the beneficiaries, let alone realisable by them. The evidence, therefore, suggests that the impact of commercial property values on consumer prices and the wealth of society are more than likely to be experienced in the long term.

The residential sector, therefore, appears to be a confident leading indicator of inflationary pressure, while commercial property values tend to lag behind the trend; furthermore, it is too complex to confidently use as an official lagging indicator.

Aside from the complexities of certain statistical relationships, there is another problem that is commonly attributed to all types of economic forecasting, namely the dilemma of always having to look backwards to look forward. In other words, if statistics allow us to be confident of what has happened in the past, can they through extrapolation enable us to forecast the future with equal confidence? The accepted answer is that statistics alone are not enough. Experience, intuition and other qualitative information are equally important, especially as things change. As emphasised above, no two cycles are the same; history does not repeat itself. Any serious property forecast, therefore, combines both statistical analysis and judgmental, reflective personal knowledge of the marketplace.

Chapter Summary **8.6**

- The nature of business fluctuations are characterised by periods of expansion, boom, contraction and recession (*see* Figure 8.7).
- The measurement data used to investigate the nature of business fluctuations centres on leading, lagging and coincident indicators.
- Leading indicators are of particular significance in macroeconomic forecasting as they change six to twelve months ahead of the main business trend.
- Models used for forecasting the economy and policy evaluation are based on computer programs linking endogenous and exogenous variables.
- Forecasting trends in the property sector as a whole is relatively less developed as a science; for example, there is not the same comprehensive range of forecasts for the property sector as there is for the economy as a whole.
- Forecasting involves completing a picture using as much existing data as possible and combining this analysis with anecdotal evidence to arrive at an overall view. It could be attempted for a single property, a specific sector of the property market or, more commonly, for the economy as a whole.

Tutorial 4

☑ **CHECK POINT**

By this point in the text you should be able to:

✓ Understand commentary in the press and media relating to macroeconomic objectives and policy.

✓ Recognise some of the tensions that are caused by the fiscal and monetary stance adopted by government. Indeed it might be useful to examine some government expenditure and revenue tables, such as those produced to accompany the annual government Budget and/or the Comprehensive Spending Review. Details of both are available from the Treasury website: *www.hm-treasury.gov.uk*

✓ Begin to appreciate the nature of business fluctuations and the economic forecasting of property and construction markets.

✓ Recognise some of the resource implications of economic growth such as the problems of incompatibility between government objectives, and appreciate the increasing importance of the sustainable development debate that is furthered in the next chapter.

Introduction to Tutorial 4

Summer and autumn of 2010 produced a plethora of case study material relating to macroeconomic management as the newly formed coalition Government took drastic measures to reduce the national debt and move the economy on to a more even keel over a four year cycle by 2015. To encourage you to discuss these events and the subsequent impacts, the emergency Budget of June 2010 and the Comprehensive Spending Review (CSR) announced in the following October form a basis to this tutorial. A short exercise relating to the budget is set up in the following reading and the material for the CSR exercise forms part of the online resources that are available to registered users of the text.

The following reading is based on the Treasury Budget press notice released on 22 June 2010. This forms the basis of the commentary expressed by the media and examples are drawn from the broad sheets *(The Times, The Guardian, The Independent and Daily Telegraph and The Economist)*. It is important to note that press comments are not written by academics, but journalists. In other words, they are expected to make quick and astute observations; but their ultimate aim is to serve the interests of the newspaper and make a profit by attracting readers and advertising revenue. In short, the mass media process prevents coverage that is too lengthy or rigorously reviewed before publication.

When you read the edited extract below try and identify the facts from the opinions being stated.

Tutorial Reading

Cutting the Deficit

The emergency budget of June 2010 was designed to cut the budget deficit and balance the economy. Consequently, the chancellor announced that the spending of government departments will be cut by a quarter in the next four years. As emphasised in the Broad sheets at the time: 'libraries and children's homes would be closed or cut, and major roads left unrepaired. The housing market would be hit by a dearth of new affordable homes because of a 25% reduction in the housing budget'. This implied that 250,000 fewer affordable homes would be built over the next decade.

Alongside these cuts, taxes would rise. To be specific, the Government will increase the standard rate of Value Added Tax (VAT) to 20% from 4 January 2011. Capital gains tax will rise from 18 to 28% for those liable to income tax at the higher and additional rates. The 10% rate for entrepreneurial business activities will be extended from the first £2 million to the first £5 million of qualifying gains made over a lifetime; but it is also a chance to strike out from shore and introduce a new carbon tax. Properly designed, such a tax could not just raise revenue but also help to cut greenhouse-gas emissions and encourage investment in alternative energy sources. However, it should be borne in mind that both carbon tax and VAT hikes will hit the poor harder than the rich.

To sum up using *The Economist*'s commentary: 'The fiscal deficit that George Osborne, the chancellor of the exchequer, must tackle is not just the biggest in Britain's post-war history; on forecasts by the IMF in May, getting the public finances back on track is a truly tough assignment... [So it will be necessary for] it to take the radical road, bin previous plans and its own election pledges, and offer up a fiscal system designed for the future, not dictated by the past... The crisis has forced people to focus on the state and what it should provide – free, for a fee or not at all – and in the nick of time'.

Tutorial Questions

1. To demonstrate some understanding of the distinction between rhetoric and fact and the selective and partial process involved in journalism; identify what you would expect the *Estates Gazette* to focus on from the Budget of June 2010 and why.
2. The journalist working on behalf of *The Economist* clearly has no doubt which road should be taken. Explain the direction and discuss the preference adopted by their line of argument.
3. Can you identify the *current* percentage of GDP that is made up by public spending and can you trust the source?

The Sustainable Development Agenda

9

Aims and Objectives

This concluding chapter brings together many of the themes that have been introduced in the text and by the end of it you should understand:

- The history, and pace, of the sustainable development agenda
- The role of markets and government in securing sustainable development
- The significance of sustainability in relation to construction and property
- The barriers to change created by the fragmented nature of the sector

Congratulations on reaching the final chapter. At several points along the way you will have noticed observations relating to the role of property and the problematic nature of securing sustainable development. In this chapter, we revisit some of the central economic concepts in order to examine the barriers and opportunities of successfully promoting sustainable development.

Although the academic community seems to enjoy debating the definitions of sustainable development, it is not a politically contentious idea, and the agenda has support from most governments across the world.

Definition

In simple terms, sustainable development is about securing a better quality of life for everyone, now and for generations to come.

The problem with the sustainable development agenda lies in actually making it happen. The gap between political rhetoric and action needs to be resolved and much of this boils down to effective use of an economic analysis to change the way the built environment is designed, built and managed. This chapter examines the effectiveness of market behaviour and the role of governments to successfully integrate the property and construction sectors to support sustainable development. We conclude by suggesting that property and construction need to be envisaged as one cohesive sector, encompassing the whole supply chain – from conception to demolition – if sustainable development is to happen!

The Role of Markets

As described in Chapters 2 to 5, most modern governments allow the market to allocate resources – in preference to direct government intervention. This means that, increasingly, the difficult questions of allocating the world's resources are left to the private actions of individuals and companies. In fact, in the UK during the past 30 years the public sector has been significantly 'rolled back'; and the economy is now more reliant on the private sector to allocate resources – and in an increasing number of cases global markets exist. Nationalised industries and government services have been privatised, and traditional public sector activities have become more market sensitive, through new procurement models such as public private partnerships and private finance initiatives (some indicative statistics were given on page 71). To some extent, this review of the transition between sectors should remind us of the spectrum of economic systems, which was introduced in Chapter 2. Also, it may be worth considering a modified version of Figure 2.1, which is shown in Figure 9.1.

The spectrum identifies some of the tensions that exist between government policy and market-driven actions. Such tensions seem particularly evident in the government's desire to secure sustainable development. At the heart of the problem lies the overuse of scarce resources and there is some debate about the efficiency of the market mechanism; especially as many environmental goods and services have no obvious market.

As explained in Chapter 6 in the section on market failure, when we consume a good we usually ignore the environmental costs that are incurred in the decision. For example, people seem to be more concerned about the price of petrol than the environmental damage caused by driving. As the concept of externalities highlighted, we don't tend to pay the full price of the environmental damage we cause. Indeed, for most of the 20th century, governments have been reluctant to make us pay the full cost because they were worried about losing votes. Nowadays, however, governments are starting to employ policies relating to the environment in order to gain political advantage. But green taxes are hard to implement and still only form a relatively small amount of the government's total revenue (e.g. in 2008/2009 the three specific green taxes – discussed in Chapter 6, Market-based Instruments (page 86) – contributed no more than 1% to the government income that year).

To counter the argument of market failure, economists emphasise that much greater resource efficiency is achievable through market forces than public sector administration (and the concept of x-inefficiency described in Chapter 5 on page 72 supports this argument).

A similar line of thought that grabbed people's imagination in the late-1990s was the suggestion that resource productivity could be increased by at least a factor of four, so long as market incentives allowed firms to develop a competitive

Fig. 9.1 The public–private sector spectrum

advantage. (Students who want to pursue this optimistic idea should refer to the reference for Weizsäcker *et al.* (1998) in the Further Reading section at the end of the book.) *Factor Four: Doubling Wealth, Halving Resource Use* demonstrated that a quadrupling of resource productivity was technically possible and the book included 50 examples. Twenty were related to energy productivity in various contexts, from refrigerators to hypercars; a further 20 were concerned with material productivity, ranging from residential water efficiency to timber-framed building. And there were 10 examples of transport productivity, spanning the benefits of videoconferencing and locally produced goods. Encouragingly, in the context of sustainable development and property, more than half of the 50 examples were relevant to the markets for green buildings and infrastructure. The type of examples referred to are listed in Table 9.1.

Table 9.1 Quadrupling resource productivity examples

Harvesting sources of renewable energy
Utilising passive ventilation instead of air-conditioning
Marking use of low-emissivity glazing
Retrofitting houses and offices with energy-efficient systems
Encouraging conservation instead of demolition
Using thermoplastic bonding agents instead of concrete

A good current example of halving resource use is the internet and the way it has significantly revolutionised the pattern of office work. There are now many resource saving developments, such as hot-desking, hotelling, teleworking, as well as a plethora of ideas associated with the 'virtual office'. In fact, it has been estimated that across Europe 49% of the workforce use eWork to some degree. This development reduces the amount of time spent within the boundaries of the formal office; and more importantly, in this context, leads to a saving on travel time and related carbon dioxide emissions. Tim Dixon's edited work on the *Real Estate and the New Economy* considers the impact of information and communication technology (ICT) on the shape and form of future retail and office space (full bibliographic details are listed in the further reading section at the end of the book.)

According to Weizsäcker *et al.* (1998), and to some of the authors contributing to Dixon's work, the constraints and barriers to achieving gains in resource productivity are not technological but institutional: in other words, inertia and cultural barriers are regarded as underlying problems. This line of argument emphasises that simply reforming the construction and property markets to introduce more sustainable processes is as much a challenge to our personal values as to our political and economic systems.

Another part of the problem was explored in the section on economic growth in Chapter 8. Here we acknowledged that there was an international consensus of opinion regarding economic development as something positive. This was interpreted as being better off tomorrow (in material terms) than we are today, and this objective adds to the tensions of securing sustainability.

In a traditional economic text the benefit of market efficiency is justified by the way it can lead to increases in gross national income and these are used to indicate an increase in the standard of living; in other words, people's conventional wisdom measures living standards in terms of the quantity of goods and services that can be purchased in the marketplace. There are, however, subtle, but significant, differences between the terms 'standard of living', 'quality of life' and 'sustainable development'.

To proceed with the crux of this chapter we need to clarify the use of the key terms. Sometimes sustainability is used solely to refer to concerns surrounding

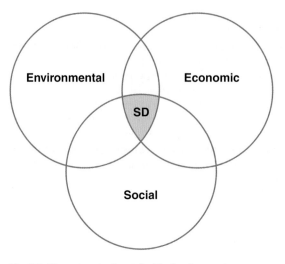

Fig. 9.2 Three strands of sustainable development

the natural environment; at other times, it seems to have a broader connotation, including two other integral strands – sustainable communities and sustainable businesses. The narrow environmental focus is perhaps understandable for historical reasons but, in discussing property, it is important to recognise that sustainability is formed of three constituent parts – the community, business and the environment – and this is the focus of the chapter.

Sustainable Development

It would be a misjudgement to conceive of one strand of the sustainable development agenda without considering the others – especially if the agenda is to become more than a theoretical construct. For example, it is impossible to make an environmental decision without there being social and economic implications and vice versa. The Venn diagram in Figure 9.2 shows the three distinct strands that need to be combined to secure sustainable development.

As such, the starting point is to confirm that **sustainable development** embraces the themes of environmental, social and economic accountability – often known as the triple bottom line. Sustainability can be achieved by minimising negative impacts and maximising benefits. The best way of doing this is to look for solutions that solve more than one problem at a time. These solutions are known as 'win-win-win', as they simultaneously secure economic, social and environmental benefits. Win-win solutions and triple bottom lines are an ideal way of thinking about sustainability as they emphasise the need to integrate social, environmental and economic issues. As highlighted in Figure 9.2, it is impossible to make an environmental economic or social decision without there being repercussions on the other two elements.

It is because of the breadth of the concept that there is some confusion over the precise definition; and more than 70 possibilities exist. One of the most comprehensive definitions comes from the International Council of Local Environmental Initiatives (ICLEI), but the most well-known definition of sustainable development comes from the Bruntland report (these two definitions are stated in Table 9.2).

It is perhaps easier to clarify the definition by starting at the other extreme and setting out features of 'unsustainability'. Unsustainable development is

Table 9.2 Two definitions of sustainable development

1. Development that needs the needs of the present without compromising the ability of future generations to meet their own needs (WCED, 1987)
2. Development that delivers basic environmental, social and economic services to all residences of a community without threatening the viability of natural, built and social systems (ICLEI, 1996)

Table 9.3 What makes sustainable development different?

Unsustainable development	Sustainable development
Aims to raise the standard of living, based solely on monetary measurements of gross domestic product.	Aims to improve the general quality of life, including non-monetary factors to do with the environment and community.
Treats the economy, society and the environment as three separate issues.	Sees economic, social and environmental issues as interlinked.
Focuses on improving things in the short term. Leaves issues to do with the future up to those who will live in it.	Looks at the needs of future generations as well as people today, seeks to avoid future problems by taking precautions today.
Treats the environment as a luxury to be protected if we can afford it.	Takes account of the environment and its capacity to support human activity.

associated with ozone depletion, poor sanitation, extinction of species and habitat, social conflict, toxic pollution and resource depletion etc. In fact, the sustainability movement emerged as a response to these problems as it stems from concerns about the future capacity of the planet's life-support systems. In Table 9.3, we contrast unsustainable development with modern ideas of sustainable development.

To draw a distinction between these contrasting approaches, it is common for environmental economists to present two models. One, an open system, which pays no respects to the limits imposed by the environment; and two, a closed system in which the environment physically contains and sustains the economy. Some economists refer to the traditional view of the open system as an 'empty world' model to contrast with the 'full world' model that is the modern closed system.

Figure 9.3a represents the empty world model – as the economic subsystem is small relative to the size of the ecosystem. It depicts the past, when the world was empty of people and artificial capital, but full of natural capital. In contrast, Figure 9.3b portrays the full world model, describing a situation nearer to today, in which the economic subsystem is very large relative to the ecosystem. This highlights the fact that, unless qualitative changes occur, the ecosystem is going to be pushed beyond its limits. In fact, there are signs that this point is imminent with, for example, global warming, ozone depletion, soil erosion, biodiversity loss, population explosions and resource depletion.

Taking the contrast to its logical conclusion we can envisage two types of economy. An inefficient economy in which all ecosystem services are treated as free goods and used abundantly; and an efficient economic system in which all resources are allocated according to price. This analysis clearly highlights the problems of pursuing unlimited technological growth, and makes a strong case in favour of sustainable development. The gist of this argument is that the world's natural support functions should not be taken for granted; the planet should not be pushed beyond its limits.

(a) Empty world

(b) Full world

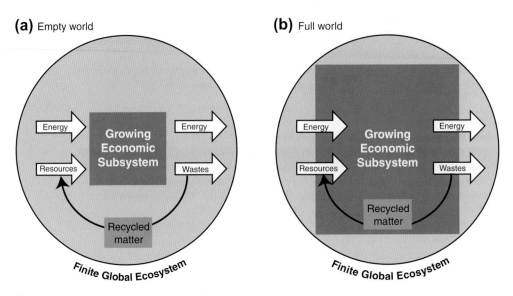

Fig. 9.3

Origins of Sustainable Development

A brief chronology of the development movement shows how the broader concept of sustainability emerged. During the post-war period in the 1950s and 1960s, development was mainly discussed in relation to the less developed countries. Until the 1970s, therefore, development thinking was concerned primarily with economic growth and its distribution.

In the 1970s, environmental concerns of the world's poor, such as a lack of clean water or sanitation, began to take centre stage. In 1973, for example, the United Nations Environment Programme (UNEP) was established to meet demands for an international environmental watchdog. In short, issues relating to the environment and development began to be viewed as interdependent.

The Bruntland Report

The World Commission on Environment and Development was set up by the United Nations in 1983 and produced a report in 1987 entitled *Our Common Future* – though it is more commonly referred to as *The Bruntland Report* after the commission's chair, Dr Gro Harlem Bruntland (Director General of the World Health Organisation). The report, which was eventually translated into 24 languages, explicitly introduced the term 'sustainable development' to the international stage. It identified the environment and economics as key concerns of the future decision-making processes in order to change the quality of growth and meet essential needs. The report prompted political interest in many countries; so the idea is now nearly 20 years old. The challenge to find a way for society to develop in a sustainable manner, however, continues to elude most nations of the world.

Earth Summit 1

In 1992, the United Nations Conference on Environment and Development – the so-called Earth Summit – took place in Rio de Janeiro, Brazil. It was the largest international conference of any kind, with 178 countries represented. This was clearly a sign of the times, as societies felt threatened by the looming problems of resource depletion and environmental degradation. The main document signed at Rio contained 27 principles for sustainable development and an action plan known as Agenda 21. It was here that the three strands – environmental, economic and social – explicitly emerged.

Rio helped to dispel any ideas of achieving environmental objectives without securing the interest and motivation of businesses and communities; and modern policies of sustainable development highlight this interrelationship. However, it can also be argued that there are a number of conflicting tensions that limit the synergy between the three strands. Is it really possible to achieve continuous economic growth and manage emissions and pollution? Are opportunities to enjoy the countryside and its associated biodiversity equally available to all sectors of society? Do the fiscal burdens imposed by market-based instruments cause greater cost to the poor or do they apply fairly to everyone?

In the years following the Rio Earth Summit, individual countries adopted different approaches to tackle these problems. In the UK, for instance, the principles of sustainable development have evolved through several policy statements. The current one, as set out in the *UK Government Sustainable Development Strategy*, published in 2005, identified four priorities:

1. Natural resource protection and environmental enhancement.
2. Sustainable consumption and production, which means achieving more with less.
3. Climate change and energy.
4. Sustainable communities.

Is it Time to Re-think Economic Growth?

There is still room for improvement and, interestingly, a recent government publication regarding the transition to sustainable development raised serious questions about the validity of the economic growth consensus. *Prosperity without Growth* was published by the Sustainable Development Commission (SDC) in March 2009 and within 8 months had been revised and updated by a commercial publisher (the details are listed in the further reading section). The central premise of the book, and report by the same name, is that in advanced economies there is significant evidence to suggest that ever-increasing levels of consumption add little to human happiness. Furthermore, the ecosystems that sustain these economies are collapsing under the impacts of rising consumption. Not surprisingly, this radical line of argument saw the SDC become one of the quangos that was axed in the public spending cuts in 2010, and few political parties really had the nerve to fully adopt the message. However, it makes an interesting read – it builds on work of the environmental economist's introduced in Figure 9.3.

Chapter Summary 9.1

- In the past 30 years there has been a transfer of assets from the public sector to the private sector. As a result, there is an increasing reliance on market forces to resolve questions of resource allocation in most industrial sectors.
- The economic system and the environmental system are inextricably linked, since goods and services cannot be produced or consumed without the use of environmental resources.
- Sustainability embraces three broad themes:
  1. The environment
  2. The community, and
  3. The economy.
- To achieve sustainable outcomes, a more holistic approach needs to be developed, and radical changes considered.

Sustainable Construction

The need to promote sustainable construction has been recognised by several European governments. In fact, in several countries, construction has been explicitly identified as the industrial sector most urgently requiring specific attention in meeting the sustainable development agenda.

In the UK, construction was the first industrial sector to be given its own strategy for sustainability. There are several reasons for this 'accolade'. First, in sustainable development terms, construction is consistently responsible for some of the most profound negative impacts. Examples of the industry's use of large amounts of materials and resources, and its reputation as a huge generator of waste were introduced in Chapter 8. In fact, the construction industry consumes more raw materials than any other industrial sector and is responsible for a significant proportion of Europe's waste stream. In the UK alone, it is estimated that 90 million tonnes of construction and demolition materials end up as waste every year. Waste on such a scale is in a completely different league to other sectors of the UK economy; the amount represents three times the waste generated by UK households and twice as much as the combined total of all other industries.

Second, the construction industry is vitally important to the economy; and the contributions made by it to employment and GDP are quite significant. In Great Britain, the construction industry, in the narrowest sense of the term, employs 1.5 million people across 200,000 companies and the turnover accounts for about 8% of GDP. In Europe, construction employs more than any other industrial sector – accounting for more than 15 million jobs and around 10% of GDP. The industry is not just important economically: it also provides a key to the quality of life as it produces the built environment and puts in place the physical facilities and infrastructure that determine the degree of freedom and flexibility that society may enjoy for anything up to 100 years after construction.

Finally, the most worrying reason that construction has been selected as warranting a special case in the sustainability agenda is because of its perceived lack of change. In nearly every other sector of the economy, technological developments have fuelled several changes to business attitudes. For example, the manufacturing industry has become leaner, cleaner and quicker at all tasks. However, most of the construction process continues to be unsustainable and the industry does not seem likely to make any changes on its own accord.

As Wolstenholme's (2009) review of the construction industry's progress since the highly regarded *Egan Report* of 1998 (see below for details) made clear: construction continues to be characterised by a 'prevalence of old ways of working and confusion about its priorities'. (For Wolstenholme's review, see the Further Reading section at the end of the book.) Of the one thousand construction professionals surveyed to complete the report a significant number complained about 'too much bureaucracy', 'too many targets', a 'tickbox culture' and a tendency for all of this to disadvantage the typical small construction firm who lack the resources to participate in the agenda. In other words, the industry had not changed much in the last decade, or taken up the challenge to become sustainable. Similar sentiments are echoed throughout the world. For example, to paraphrase the opening paragraph of a review of the state of construction in Singapore: the construction industry in many parts of the world has a poor image and it can easily be singled out from the rest of the economy by attitudes, technologies, processes and a culture that are at least half a century old.

The notion of sustainability therefore has a special relevance to construction and a specific agenda is evolving. The first international conference on sustainable construction was held in 1994; and it has subsequently acquired its own definition.

> **Definition**
>
> Sustainable construction is the creation and responsible management of a healthy built environment based on resource-efficient and ecological principles.

The principles of sustainable construction have been taken to mean different things in different countries. In the majority of cases, the policies include economic, environmental and social considerations within their framework and these can be referred to as a 'three-strand policy'. In contrast, there are other countries, such as America and Canada, where the so-called sustainable construction policy only identifies an environmental strand. There are now discussions emerging to bring a separate agenda for sustainable construction to the developing countries where there are significant differences in priorities, skill levels and capacity.

The current interpretation of what sustainable construction involves in the UK is summarised in Table 9.4.

The key ideas that recur in such policies are: to minimise the consumption of fossil fuels (carbon-based energy) and other natural resources, reduce the amount of waste and pollution, and respect the various stakeholders – particularly the users – both now and in the future. It might seem odd to emphasise that an efficient building should support the client's needs, but in Chapter 5 we noted the fragmented, and problematic, nature of the relationships between the client, the developer and the contractor responsible for construction.

Table 9.4 The UK sustainable construction agenda

Reduce adverse impacts on the environment and enhance natural surroundings.
Deliver buildings and structures that provide greater satisfaction, community spirit, and value to all users.
Help to encourage productivity by improving people's working environment.
Take fully into account the impact of construction on the surrounding environment and avoid unnecessary pollution.
Wherever possible, be competitive and profitable: making use of modern methods of construction to improve efficiency.
Respect and treat all stakeholders more fairly.

Chapter Summary 9.2

- Sustainable construction has been singled out by governments to require special attention. This is partly due to its significant contributions to the economy, partly due to the negative impacts that it makes to sustainable development, but mainly because construction is far behind other industrial sectors.
- The key ideas that the policies designed to achieve sustainable construction are comprised of include: reductions in energy, resources, waste and pollution. They are sometimes summarised as the four R's: reduce, recycle, reuse and retrofit.
- Sustainable construction also promotes a respect of all stakeholders – particularly the users – both now and in the future.

Sustainable Property

The intention of this section is to argue that, for a sustainable built environment (and by default sustainable development) to become a reality, it will be necessary to promote more than just policy aimed at the construction stage. The built environment clearly straddles a number of disciplines and it seems ironic that, to date, most related government policy and academic research has primarily focused on the construction of new buildings; to the detriment of existing buildings, and their broader economic, environmental and social impacts. This is why we include a section on sustainable property.

People spend most of their lives inside buildings: either at home – in a flat or house; at work – in an office, shop or industrial setting; or in pursuit of leisure or education – at a cinema, shop, school, university or similar. In fact, we have already indicated the scale of the building stock in Chapters 2 and 3 where Tables 2.1 and 3.4 show that there are more than 2 million commercial buildings and some 26 million homes in the UK. The energy used to heat, cool, light and ventilate these buildings is estimated to account for approximately 50% of the carbon emissions in the UK.

In view of the size and importance of this sector, an argument could be made for widespread replacement of the existing stock with new energy-efficient buildings. However, as pointed out in Chapter 4, a general rule of thumb suggests that new builds represents around 1% of the total stock in any one year. (So it could take at least 100 years to replace the stock.) Even more worrying is the fact that, although the technology exists to design new stock in ways that could reduce the energy consumption by 50% or more, most new builds (about 0.9%) achieve little more than the minimum standards laid down in the building regulations. So, without interventions from governments, it could take 1,000 years to replace the stock with the best energy performance possible at today's standards!

This gloomy portrait confirms the argument that construction and property markets are inefficient. Construction tends to be short-term in outlook; slow to innovate and hesitant to adopt best practice. The market for tenants of property in the commercial sector compounds the problem, as they are subject to long-term leases that have evolved through the post-war years, with large developers supplying a standardised product on a 'let and forget' basis. As suggested in Chapter 5, lease periods are slowly becoming shorter, but the average existing lease length for commercial property still runs on for several years. In the residential sector, market conditions are little better as occupiers have limited control of the quality of the product they occupy. In consequence, by the turn of this century the users of buildings – the real customer of the development process – have become disconnected from the development process.

The separation of interests between the various stakeholders in the built environment is due to the way property markets interrelate. To take an obvious example, the interests of the users are often different from those of the investors that produce the original specification. This makes it difficult for those supplying the products to final users to communicate effectively through market signals. For example, over the years several plans for energy-efficient homes have been shelved as builders have tried to prevent price rises in residential markets characterised by high mortgage rates. This demonstrates the nature of short-termism, and this problem is particularly common when one party pays for the efficiency gains and another party reaps the benefits. In other words, whenever one party develops a property 'on spec' without the actual purchaser, or tenant, being identified. This is easy to see in the commercial sector, in which the priorities of landlords and tenants are frequently regarded as distinct. An often-quoted general rule for traditional commercial buildings is that running costs outstrip capital costs by a ratio of 10:1 over a 25-year period. Regardless of this, far greater emphasis still tends to be placed on the initial capital cost, while demonstrating little respect for the costs incurred by end users. In terms of efficiency, this attitude creates major resource cost implications – indeed, figures suggest that we may be more than 10 times better at wasting resources than using them.

It is in the marketplace that people need to display their credentials, so it is not surprising that property markets have been relatively slower than manufacturing in taking up the challenge of sustainable development. This should not be interpreted to mean that absolutely nothing is happening, it is just rather slow. In relative terms, the most activity has been in the commercial sector, with owner-occupiers beginning to specify bespoke headquarters that reflect their corporate ethos. The level of sustainable activity within the residential sector, however, is not so evident, as the main companies engaged in house building have been slow to see the market potential of adopting an environmentally aware corporate image. In order to understand the nature of the barriers and opportunities, we take each sector separately.

The Commercial Sector

Each year the largest amount of new building work, in value terms, is in the commercial sector. Most of this activity continues to produce a standardised product that tends to be overspecified, fully air-conditioned and energy-guzzling. However, a small proportion – say 20% – of the new additions are able to boast some sustainable features. **Corporate social responsibility** is an increasingly important issue – and businesses and organisations want to reflect their credentials in the types of office that they rent and own. So there appears to be increasingly strong arguments in favour of situating offices in buildings that minimise global and local impacts; reduce energy bills; enable employees to cycle or car share; and to facilitate greater worker productivity.

Productivity

Taking the business case, which forms one of the three strands of sustainability, it is important that office buildings are conducive to economic activity. Yet, in many instances, one hears anecdotal evidence to the contrary. There are even accusations that some office buildings cause employees to suffer headaches, feelings of lethargy, irritability and lack of concentration – and, in some cases, can be responsible for high rates of absenteeism. Even more worrying are the suggestions that the office environment can cause irritation of the eyes, nose, throat and skin. The symptoms usually disappear after a few hours of leaving the related building. This condition is commonly referred to as **sick building syndrome (SBS)** and it clearly leads to an inefficient use of human resources. It is important to remember that, ultimately, buildings are 'machines for working in' and investment in sustainable property should also result in a more efficient working environment.

An interesting example of a highly integrated – healthy – green building is the Rocky Mountain Institute in Western Colorado; as it is claimed that the staff that work in the building are unusually productive, alert and cheerful all day. This high rate of productivity is chiefly attributed to the design of the building, which boasts natural light, indoor air that is not mechanically enhanced; a low air temperature; and even the sound of a waterfall (tuned approximately to the brain's alpha rhythm to be more restful).

Table 9.5 Characteristics of a sustainable commercial property

Make maximum use of natural daylight and ventilation.
Minimise consumption of fossil fuels by use of combined heat and power, and orientation of site to benefit from passive solar energy.
Reduce the use of fresh water by using grey water recycling for landscape irrigation, flushing toilets, etc.
Enable good access to public transport and/or provision for cyclists, such as cycle racks, showers and changing facilities.
Take advantage of effective facilities management to assure a safe, productive, and efficient working environment.
Reuse and refurbish existing buildings and sites.

This is more important than it might at first appear. Occasional sick days mean that employees are being paid but not in return for any productivity. Equally worrying, and damaging to overall productivity, is the situation where employees do attend work but spend a part of each day complaining about their working environment – and ultimately they might even be so fed up that they decide to look for another job. This all adds up to a waste of resources.

The annual cost of absenteeism from the workplace in the UK has been estimated to represent around 1% of GDP each year – that would be approximately £15 billion in current prices. This figure, however, does not fully account for the effects of SBS, which has received little attention from economists. As the following calculation suggests, this is a significant omission.

According to a survey carried out in the late-1980s, involving employees working across 46 office buildings of varied age, type and quality the incidence of SBS is quite widespread. Participants of the survey were asked how much they thought the physical conditions of the office influenced their productivity. The majority thought that their productivity was affected by at least 20%. This is the equivalent of taking one day off in five – and even bearing in mind that worker self-evaluation may be subject to exaggeration – this is still a frighteningly high proportion!

Indeed, in the following worked example we assume a simple reduced SBS figure of 10%; but the outcome is still a significant cost. We begin by assuming that £22,000 is the average office salary, so an organisation employing 1,000 people could be losing in the region of £2.2 million each year. (The calculation is simple: a 10% SBS effect on lost productivity represents £2,200 per employee per year, multiplied by 1,000 gives a potential loss of £2,200,000.) Arguably, these figures are a worst-case scenario, and not everyone is equally affected by SBS – the literature suggests that up to 60% of staff in problem buildings may be affected. It seems more plausible, perhaps, to accept an estimate of £1.1 million per 1,000 employees per year. The more worrying statistic, however, is that the service sector employs more than 15 million people every day in offices. This calculation implies a national cost of SBS in the UK in the region of £16.5 billion, and although the figures might be arguable, they highlight a significant point, namely that certain types of construction result in an inefficient use of resources.

To sum up, a range of features that typify the 'state-of the-art' sustainable commercial property are emerging and the common ones are listed in Table 9.5.

The Residential Sector

The existing stock of houses in the UK exceeds 25 million units. In recent years, much of the new housing stock has been built on greenfield sites that are car-dependent. The majority of these new homes are low-density and inefficient in terms of energy usage. In contrast, recent governments have sought to promote development on brownfield sites that take advantage of good public transport systems, using high-density designs that exceed the minimum expectations for energy efficiency. The government would also prefer to see developments that include some provision of affordable housing. These conflicting priorities highlight the dilemmas that governments face in supporting sustainable development.

To compound the government's frustration, resource-efficient, environmentally friendly housing is by no means 'rocket science' – indeed, technically it can be achieved easily by most volume-housing developers. Take energy efficiency as an example: all that is needed is greater levels of insulation, attention to detail to make sure that all joints are air tight, the positioning of windows to make the most of sunlight, and use of a heat exchange system where air going out preheats the air coming in. The large developers, however, have been reluctant to adopt these energy-efficient measures due to the extra cost (and care) involved. However, as energy becomes relatively more expensive and interest rates fall, the idea of a super-insulated, energy-efficient home should, theoretically, become a more desirable and common product.

The type of building described above is collectively referred to as a 'passive house'; a term used to indicate the small amounts of energy that these buildings require for space heating, and thousands of examples already exist in Scandinavia, Holland, Germany and Austria. In the UK they are still rare, but an exceptional example is the Beddington Zero (fossil) Energy Development (BedZED). This has provided homes to 82 families since July 2002. There are several principles of sustainable housing that underpin the BedZED development. Most of these are easy to replicate and make economic sense. For example, the properties have walls with 300 mm of insulation (three times the typical amount), incorporate triple glazing, utilise heat exchange units and make good use of south-facing conservatories to achieve reductions in energy requirements to a point where there is no need to install central heating. This represents a saving of around £1,500 per home, which makes the expenditure on the increased insulation more acceptable. By reducing the energy requirements by 90% compared to that needed for a typical home which meets UK building regulations standards, it is possible to power the entire BedZED estate with a small combined heat and power unit run on renewable fuel such as woodchip. Another achievement has been the sourcing of most of the materials necessary for the buildings from within 35 miles of the site. The BedZED project also integrates office and leisure facilities, built to the same energy efficient standards, on the same site, thus enabling people to reduce their dependence on cars as they can work, rest and play within the small neighbourhood.

If we take the agenda of sustainability seriously, the development of passive houses similar to those built on the BedZed estate are important. Indeed, the architects of BedZED sometimes boast of achieving Britain's first zero carbon or carbon neutral development.

To sum up, it appears that firms specialising in house building (or other structures) could benefit by differentiating their product in several ways and by demonstrating a greater awareness of the techniques and specifications that support sustainable development. In this way, they could win business in the marketplace by beating their rivals at a new game. As a nation we could then become less dependent on fossil fuels, which would assist the country in moving towards its stated target of cutting emissions by 80% by 2050.

In fact, the Intergovernmental Panel on Climate Change (IPCC) in its 2007 report clearly identified the global stock of buildings as having the biggest potential – of any sector including transport – to cost effectively reduce fossil fuel emissions. In the UK, alone, 30% of building-related carbon emissions is from the residential sector; therefore, the realisation of a low carbon future is largely dependent on the adoption of sustainable property development; and

Table 9.6 Characteristics of a sustainable house

Reduce energy requirements ideally to the point where renewable energy becomes viable.
Reduce mains water consumption by collecting rainwater and recycling grey water.
Maximise the use of local, reclaimed and recycled materials.
Promote public transport, cycle lanes and car pools to create a lifestyle that is less car-dependent.
Design into the estate services to enable on-site composting, home delivery of grocery, and recycling.
Design housing estates in ways that promote community spirit.

for good measure the features that typify a 'state-of the-art' sustainable house are listed in Table 9.6.

Community

The last feature itemised in Table 9.6 is another challenging task, as it requires a co-ordinated approach to delivering public services that work for everyone, including the most disadvantaged.

The term community is interpreted liberally to represent a region, city, town, or village; the emphasis is on tackling issues at the local level. The current *UK sustainable development strategy* places emphasis on sustainable communities and even goes as far as defining it.

> ### Definition
> Sustainable communities are achieved in ways that make good use of natural resources, promote a neighbourhood spirit and care for the environment.

It is considered important, as inevitably the quality of life is underpinned by strong employment opportunities, good access to services, and attractive and safe surroundings. These are often determined at the local level and there is government recognition that people want to live in communities that are safe, inclusive, well-planned, built and run. This not only acknowledges the importance of property, but also highlights the significance of the broader built environment: the spaces in between the buildings; the parks, community centres, playing fields and squares, etc., that form a kind of social glue that pulls an area together to give it character. (Hence planning is another discipline that contributes significantly to the sustainable development agenda.)

Conclusion

Property clearly encompasses a number of sustainable development issues and some of the main ones are captured in Table 9.7. The table summarises the breadth of opportunity for the property sector to contribute to a sustainable future.

The main barrier to these opportunities rests with the multitude of firms involved in the sector, the local nature of their activity, and the lengthy supply chain involved in the process that takes us from the beginning of the development pipeline described in Chapter 5 to the final stage of use and occupation. The problem of fragmentation is examined further at the close of the chapter.

But what does sustainable property mean? The phrase has not been elaborated by government, but on the basis of what has been described it is easy to define.

> ### Definition
> Sustainable property seeks to maximise positive contributions to business, the community and the environment by focusing on the whole life of the building and its various possible uses.

Table 9.7 Property and the sustainable development agenda

Triple bottom line	Scope for property to contribute to sustainability
Environment	Reduction of waste, climate change, and problems of biodiversity. Enhancement of open space. Promotion of energy efficiency.
Economics	Differentiate products; to get into sustainable property. Integrate markets. Maximize productivity and secure high employment.
Social	Provide identity, shelter and safety. Can conserve heritage. Create a sense of place and community. Assure equity.

Indeed, various examples now exist and it might be useful to explore your campus and its surrounding area to identify some instances and take a closer look and find out what a sustainable property looks (and feels) like.

In practical terms, sustainable property (and construction) can be reduced to four important messages for the way the industry should work:

1. Buildings projects should become more cost effective to produce and run, because they have been constructed with less and yield more.

2. Property should contribute positively to the environment, using materials and systems that are easily replenished during its life cycle.

3. Commercial and residential property should help to encourage productivity and community respectively; by improving the local and working, environments and being sufficiently flexible to adapt for future use. In short, property should enhance the neighbourhood and be designed with longevity and resource efficiency in mind.

4. Developers, contractors and clients should, wherever possible, create mutual standards of respect for all the people and communities involved with the project.

An agenda addressing sustainable property, therefore, would take into consideration the design, development, construction, use, management, maintenance, refurbishment and demolition of all buildings.

Chapter Summary 9.3

- Encouraging the creation of property with appropriate characteristics (as listed in Tables 9.5 and 9.6) is important to the success of the sustainable development agenda.

- Inherent to sustainable property are several common characteristics, such as: minimising dependence on fossil fuels, enabling the use of grey water, limiting the need for car use, and promoting economic activity and a sense of community.

- Property developers should differentiate their product by moving towards sustainable specifications, and opportunities to achieve this are slowly emerging in the commercial and residential sectors.

- Thinking long term instead of short term makes an important contribution towards achieving greater resource efficiency in the built environment. For example, the running cost in a traditional commercial building outstrips the capital costs by a ratio of at least 10:1.

- An important consideration of any economic activity is to consider the end user. For instance, the internal design of an office building should be conducive to work.

The Role of Governments

In the UK, during the post-war period, there has been a steady stream of reports commissioned to focus attention on the construction sector. To the extent that some commentators have suggested that the industry suffers from 'initiative overload', 'too much bureaucracy' and too many 'government targets' (for those who wish to know more *see* Wolstenholme, 2009, as he provides an overview of several of the reports).

In this section we have chosen to only review the handful of *government* reports that have been published during the last decade, since they all recognise a need to promote ideas to support a sustainable industry. Indeed, all of the reports published since 2000 explicitly refer to the urgency required in securing sustainable construction. In these reports the government appears to find it easy to identify the barriers that need to be removed for an efficient and sustainable industry to emerge.

Our review begins in 1998 with the publication of *The Egan Report*. This stressed that construction should be viewed as a much more integrated process paying more attention to the needs of the end user; Egan even suggested that completed projects should be assessed for customer satisfaction and the knowledge gained fed back into the industry. The idea of developing a performance benchmark is important as badly designed buildings fail to meet the needs of the end users, and investment into quality design and construction could result in a more efficient working environment and lower running costs.

The Egan Report (1998) also noted that one of the most striking things about the construction industry is the excessive number of small firms. It argues that this fragmentation inhibits the opportunities for efficient working and leads the industry to underachieve. The report also stressed the advantages of partnering, and the need to eliminate waste and to investigate the ideas of 'lean thinking'. In many ways, Egan paved the way for the sustainable construction agenda.

The first strategy written to explicitly commence sustainable construction was published in 2000 under the auspices of the Department of the Environment, Transport and the Regions (DETR). This was subsequently revised: firstly, by the Department of Trade and Industry (DTI) in 2006; and secondly, by the Department for Business Enterprise and Regulatory Reform in 2008. (The shift of government responsibility for the agenda is typical of the way responsibility for the broad remit of construction has been regarded as a movable feast across Westminster; as it has been divided by different governments in different ways.)

The 2008 *Strategy for Sustainable Construction* set specific actions and targets to be met by the industry during the next decade. In short, it divided the agenda for sustainable construction into two sections: 'ends' and 'means'. The 'ends' relate directly to sustainability targets such as climate change, material selection, waste reduction and biodiversity. The 'means' identify the processes such as innovation, procurement, regulation and design that could be adopted to help secure the targets. In other words, the construction industry was encouraged to achieve clear environmental targets by adopting processes that would reduce the environmental impact of buildings and infrastructure.

As indicated in the previous sections, the benefits that can flow from a more efficient and sustainable construction industry are potentially immense. But, as we have also stressed, construction alone will not secure sustainable development.

In all of these official reports the government's role as a major client is acknowledged. *The Fairclough Report* (2002) went as far as identifying four roles for the government to play:

- As a regulator with regard to aspects such as building and planning regulations.
- As a policy maker for issues that directly affect, but go wider than the industry, such as energy efficiency, waste management and climate change.
- As a sponsor to support research and development and articulate a vision for the future.
- As a major client.

It is in its role as a client that the government can make the greatest progress in implementing the sustainability agenda. As *The Fairclough Report* (2002) pointed out, governments have responsibility for a large variety of public buildings and infrastructure, such as schools and colleges, hospitals and health centres, military installations, prisons, courts and roads; plus specialised buildings, such as offices and accommodation. But, just as we have argued that one sector alone cannot implement sustainable construction, nor can it be an agenda just for government!

The shifting of government responsibility for the agenda, and the ways that the various departments oversee different aspects such as planning, conservation and levies, etc., introduces a further level of fragmentation to the overall problem. To some extent this problem was acknowledged by the Business and Enterprise Committee when they published a specific inquiry into the UK construction industry in 2008. Their report, *Construction Matters*, outlined a need for more effective Government leadership both at the strategic level and as a client. Interestingly, it also drew attention to the fact that the responsibility for sustainable construction is fragmented across government departments and highlighted that no individual in the civil service has overarching responsibility for its day-to-day delivery. The main outcome of this report, therefore, was to confirm the need for a permanent senior civil servant to act as the main point of contact between government and the industry and to make sure that sustainable construction is adopted across Whitehall and beyond. Accordingly, the first Chief Construction Adviser (a role equivalent to the chief scientific adviser) was appointed in November 2009.

Chapter Summary **9.4**

- **The government has published many initiatives; five examples are shown in Table 9.8.**
- **The construction process is complex, and this is exacerbated by the diverse and fragmented nature of the construction industry.**
- **There are four roles that government plays in supporting construction: as a regulator, policy maker, sponsor and major client.**
- **Neither the government nor the construction industry alone can be held responsible for the success or failure of sustainable development.**

Fragmentation

As the reports have suggested, the relations between the various parties contributing to property development lead to poor performance and the root of this problem lies in the sector's fragmented structure. In 2002, The Sustainable Construction Task Group pointed out that: the extent to which the property industry moves towards greater levels of sustainability lies squarely in the hands of the executives and directors of the UK's property developers and property management companies. The Sustainable

Table 9.8　Government Reports, 1998 to 2008

1988	The Egan Report
	Rethinking Construction
2000	The DETR Report
	A Strategy for more Sustainable Construction
2002	The Fairclough Report
	Rethinking Construction Innovation and Research
2008	The BERR Report
	Strategy for Sustainable Construction
2008	The Business and Enterprise Committee
	Construction Matters

Construction Task Group (formed in 1998) produced a number of reports based on several joint initiatives; interestingly, this specific one did not include the Royal Institution of Chartered Surveyors (RICS). (The RICS was also not a member of the official (government) Sustainable *Building* Task Group, which was formed in December 2003.)

The kind of rhetoric that apportions the blame to one sector is arguable as it fails to acknowledge the relationships that exist across these sectors. No one specific sector should be allowed to carry all the blame for the failings of the broad property sector. The challenge of engaging the sector as a whole in a common vision of any nature is really difficult. This is further compounded by the lack of joined-up thinking across the various related government departments.

The point is that builders tend to simply carry out the instructions of their clients, such as developers, architects, and occupants. Developers are often restricted by the conditions imposed by investors or banks. Architects are constrained by planners and the users of buildings have their own specific requirements. As such, an important opportunity lies in the integration of the fragmented sectors.

Loose and Tight Couplings

A property project inevitably involves the assembly of a range of materials and services from a broad range of sources. In turn, each of the material inputs is subjected to different types of processing according to their particular use on a specific project. Assembling the materials are teams of subcontractors gathered for the sole purpose of completing the project. As a result, the labour force is often more than one stage removed from the agreement made between the client and the developer. The analogy we employed in Chapter 5 compared the process to film production to emphasise that each project involves a different team; and as a result each building can be regarded as 'unique'. It is this diverse and fragmented nature of the industry that constrains the opportunities to improve performance, learn from experience and introduce innovation.

In the specialised literature dealing with construction economics this problem is analysed using the so-called model of a **loosely coupled system**.

In loosely coupled systems the left hand frequently does not know what the right hand is doing. A good example of loosely coupled activities is the contrast between the manufacture of building materials and the way these materials are used on-site. In fact, one of the hurdles to overcome if sustainable development is to become a reality involves closing the gap between traditional,

Definition

Loosely coupled activities have few variables in common as the units involved in the production process function relatively independently of each other.

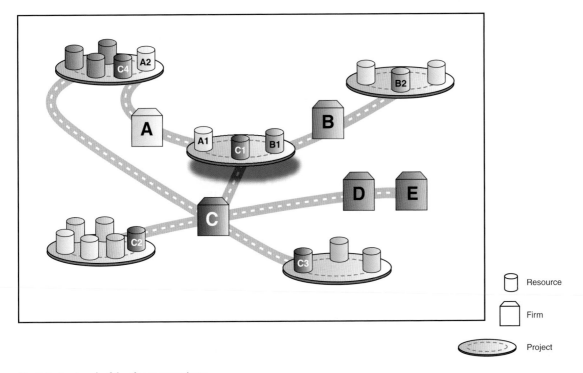

Fig. 9.4 A network of development projects

project-based approaches to more integrated approaches to building involving on-site installation of purpose-made components. The concept of loosely coupled systems builds on the problems of imperfect information that were raised as forms of market failure in Chapter 6.

A property development project can be thought of as a network of firms that are drawn together to complete a specific set of operations on-site. For example, the construction process is mainly about co-ordinating specialised tasks, loose couplings can occur across a number of relationships: among individuals, between subcontractors, at the organisational level, and between developers, financers and clients. The problems generated by these loose couplings is compounded in the property sector as the activity is inevitably carried out at a specific and localised site where different teams have been brought together to complete a unique project. In other words, each project involves a temporary network of firms coming together for the sole purposes of the specific development. At the same time, the firms are possibly involved in other projects in which they are expected to co-ordinate their activities and resources with a completely different set of other firms. For example, in Figure 9.4, firm C needs to consider at least three couplings.

1. Co-ordination with other firms involved in its individual projects – represented by the projects employing resources C1, C2, C3 and C4.
2. Co-ordination with the firms involved in its supply chain; for example, firms D and E.
3. As individual property development projects exist within a broader, more loosely connected, permanent network, firm C needs to co-ordinate with associated firms A and B on activities and resources that lie beyond the scope of each individual project.

In contrast to property development and construction, the manufacturing industry tends to be typified by **tightly coupled systems**. Manufacturing usually involves fewer independent elements and a greater level of co-ordination from a centralised management team. This encourages the use of standardised procedures, uniform product quality, improved management and economies of scale. Long-term relationships, formed in doing the same task with the same team, also encourage product development and learning. It can be argued that it is the difficulties of creating the tight couplings enjoyed by manufacturing that lie at the heart of the problems faced by construction and property, where a lack of integration and innovation cause serious constraints.

An interesting example that illustrated the complexity of the construction industry – and the way it shies away from the use of standardised components – was cited in *The Egan Report* (1998) where Egan referred to the rather startling fact that, while the average car contains about 3,000 components, the standard house has about 40,000 parts! Even with the subsequent momentum of the sustainability movement and its emphasis on the benefits of **offsite production**, construction continues to spend less than 10% on large standardised prefabricated assemblies.

In the UK and elsewhere in Europe, there is still a mindset that tends to fragment the responsibility for sustainable development. Property and construction firms argue that they can only adopt holistic approaches if clients ask for them, developers imply that there is no demand for sustainability, and investors are hesitant to fund risky new ventures. The so-called 'circle of blame' that perpetuates the existing traditional approach to construction was presented in Chapter 7 (see Figure 7.6, on page 115).

> ### Chapter Summary **9.5**
>
> - Construction and property sectors are characterised by a low level of inter-firm connection, which means that the same team seldom works together on more than one project.
> - In the UK and elsewhere in Europe, there is a tendency for property development and construction to be of a fragmented nature.
> - The tightening of the relationships between firms is essential if sustainability is to be taken seriously in the world of property and construction.

Concluding Remarks

Property plays a critical role in determining the nature, function and appearance of towns and the countryside in which we live and work. However, the industry as a whole suffers from inertia and any pressures to change, take an inordinate amount of time; especially as agents in the property sector are often sceptical of government pressure or simply conservative in their manner. For example, sustainable development issues have been in existence since the late 1980s; yet the property industry is still responsible for about half the carbon dioxide emissions, and clearly more thought needs to go into the design, development and construction of buildings. As Sir Crispin Tickell, a former government adviser on sustainable development, perceptively commented in 2006: the property industry still does not play its part in sustainability and deal with the failings encompassed in the design of buildings; provision of infrastructure; development on brownfield sites; and planning issues, and consequently in 20 years time we will be in a bigger mess than we are in at the moment!

In fact, it was not until 2009 that the Royal Institute of Chartered Surveyors (RICS) actually created a specific post – Head of Sustainability – to bring together various initiatives and promote the sustainability of land, property and construction. With the creation of this new role the RICS made explicit its intentions to co-ordinate and encourage its members to address the themes of climate change, waste and materials, water and biodiversity, and sustainable communities.

To achieve a shared vision, clear goals and an industry-wide strategy is becoming an increasingly urgent need that requires a high level of communication between the participating organisations and professional Institutions – such as the Royal Institute of British Architects and the Royal Town Planning Institute. This explains, to some extent, why such a great deal of promise is held in the new forms of partnership that were discussed in Chapter 5 (see pages 00-00). Partnering, whether formalised through arrangements such as PFI or simply achieved by informal relationships, can improve the integrated view and increase value for money. For example, the Dutch have successfully bridged the gap between organisations in the house building sector. Several multidisciplinary teams have been activated early in a housing project to brainstorm how they may contribute to the sustainable process. This tightening of the relationship between firms has encouraged new areas of competence in the field of sustainability and allowed them to work more efficiently than firms not yet included in the network. The strength of this type of network is the team building that emerges across disciplines, as it creates links between developers, architects, contractors and tenants.

Similarly, in *Getting the big picture right*, a recent publication by CABE (the Commission for Architecture and the Built Environment, *see* reference list for details), professionals across the built environment sector were encouraged to work together to explore the most socially sustainable and environmentally sensitive ways to accommodate urban growth during the next decade. The 2010 publication brought together advice and best practice from Holland, Switzerland, Germany, France, South Korea, America and the UK to assure the participation of people in shaping the places that they use for work and leisure, squaring up to the environmental challenges of increasing biodiversity, generating low carbon energy, and generally achieving 'more with less'. The recurrent message throughout this short document was to 'get the big picture right' requires cross-boundary action, interdisciplinary modes of thought and genuine commitment.

The sustainable development agenda has made, and is continuing to make, the industry think about a broader range of strategies; and it is possible to see some players within the property market take up opportunities. Clearly, more work needs to be done to integrate inputs and outputs in a holistic and schematic manner. It is important, therefore, that in the near future all property and construction firms, and not only the brave few seeking to gain a competitive advantage, heed the government messages. Students of this introductory text should recognise the value of breaking the mould and adopting the new values that could carry this forward.

The slow rate of replacement of building stock and the slow integration of sustainable standards into the thinking of property owners, investors, builders, and users make it imperative that some of the budding chartered surveyors reading this text overcome the inertia that is rife in the industry and begin to appreciate the bigger picture. It will, no doubt, take time but it should start to pick up momentum during the professional lifetime of students studying this text!

Chapter Summary 9.6

- The potential contribution that the property sector can make to the sustainable development agenda is immense.
- The problem to be resolved is overcoming the fragmented approach of the various stakeholders in the sector; as the bigger picture needs to be grasped.
- The sheer scale of the property market could enable a huge potential contribution to emerge during the working lives of the forthcoming generation of property professionals.

Tutorial 5

✓ CHECK POINT

By this point in the text you should be able to:

✓ Appreciate that an economics textbook does not set out to provide definite answers, but to introduce students to a way of thinking. For example, in the last chapter we brought together various ideas relating to the agenda of sustainable development, but we were not able to conclude when, or if, it would be achieved.

✓ Begin to understand the magnitude and complexity of the fragmented business interests involved in the built environment, and recognise that both construction and property have vital roles to play in delivering many of the objectives relating to sustainable development.

✓ Analyse the nature of societal problems that will occur both in the present and in the future.

✓ Understand the nature of economic markets and the role that government intervention plays in property and construction sectors.

✓ Appreciate that this text is simply an introduction to the subject area and you would be expected to read more before graduating. Some Readings to follow up are detailed on page 000.

Introduction to tutorial 5

An important objective of this text has been to raise awareness of questions relating to sustainability, and in the concluding chapter we took a detailed look at sustainable development. We tried to clarify that the needs of future generations should not be compromised by the short-term views of those working in property markets today. As an example, the following extract is one of the many that appear in the *Estates Gazette* relating to sustainable development. (The EGi archive holds more than 65 feature items on the topic, published from 2000 to 2010; and more than half of them were published in the last five years.) The specific article chosen reports on a survey – *Hitting the Green Wall…and Beyond* – conducted by three organisations committed to green developments, namely British Property Federation, Taylor Wessing and Spada. The complete report is 60 pages and the details are listed in the Further Reading section.

Sustainability is a topical debate at the moment and it prompts questions at the APC interview (a part of the Assessment of Professional Competence undertaken before becoming a chartered surveyor), so it should be useful to take the opportunity to study the extract in Reading 5.

Tutorial Reading 5: Zero-Carbon ambitions…

The coalition government is decidedly green, in both its mix of Conservative blue and Liberal Democrat yellow and its pledge to become the UK's most eco-friendly administration.

Ministers are lobbying the EU to raise the target for cuts in emissions across member countries from 20 to 30 by 2020. Cameron is also sticking to the Labour government's target for all new homes to be zero-carbon by 2016 and for all commercial buildings to be zero-carbon by 2019.

And a new report, *Hitting the Green Wall…and Beyond* – published by the British Property Federation, law firm Taylor Wessing and consultancy Spada – shows that the property industry, one of the largest emitters of CO_2, is increasingly taking note of sustainability issues, even if, for the most part, it still thinks that government targets are unrealistic.

The report, based on the opinions of 800 property owners, developers, occupiers, advisers and contractors, found that, despite the recession, a clear majority of them (69%) still considered sustainability to be important.

Tutorial 5

Durable commitment

'This indicates remarkable resilience in an industry that has borne the brunt of a major recession', notes the report, 'suggesting that commitment to the sustainability agenda is real and durable – rather than lip-service paid when economic times are good'.

It found that almost 40% of developers rated sustainability as highly important. They were followed by advisers (33%), occupiers (22%) and investors (18%). This finding was also reflected in the fact that 71% of firms had sustainability agendas in place.

Stringent regulation, combined with social and customer pressure, is likely to drive the further development of sustainability strategies among investors and occupiers, says the report.

However, it warns that there is a need for more evidence that investment in such strategies, and the setting and meeting of targets, can be of real commercial value. 'Investment in these strategies now may be a leap of faith', states the report, 'but failure to future-proof a business so as to meet the sustainability challenge will in time become a significant commercial risk...'.

While more than half of developers ask for or provide information relating to sustainability when buying or selling buildings, 47% of investors and 45.5% of occupiers fail to do so.

Helen Garthwaite, UK head of construction and engineering at Taylor Wessing, reckons that the Carbon Reduction Commitment which, from 2011 will rank companies according to their carbon emissions, will become a key tool in influencing investors and occupiers.

Green incentives

'We will see the tax regime changing and more incentives to promote green behaviour coming into play', says Garthwaite. 'But government hasn't got a lot of money to play with. It will look at mechanisms that are cash-neutral, or use tax to push companies down the change route'.

And perhaps just a little push is all that is needed for momentum to gather. While the last sustainability report by Taylor Wessing and Spada, published in 2008, revealed that 36% of the UK development industry had no awareness of green contract provisions, this time almost 60% of respondents had used a green agreement.

The report goes on to say that, of the 40% of respondents who had not used a green lease or building contract, half said they would consider doing so.

Despite this, an overwhelming majority of the property industry (73.4%) still believes that the government's carbon reduction targets for commercial property are unrealistic (see below). This rises to 76% for residential targets.

The report concludes: 'An inconsistent approach to regulation, or the setting of targets that are perceived as unachievable, is likely to impact negatively on the delivery of the sustainability agenda'.

BPF chief executive Liz Peace says: 'With an industry that is sceptical about carbon-reduction targets, closer collaboration between government and the industry is essential if these are to be met'.

Source: adapted from, 'Zero-carbon ambitions not yet as green as money', Patrick Clift, *Estates Gazette* 12 June 2010, page 49.

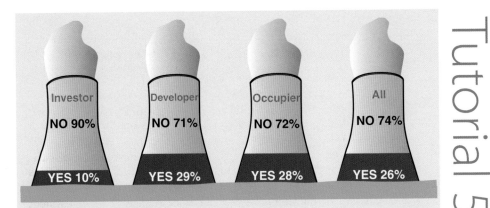

Burning issue or burnt finger?

Is it realistic for the government to plan for all new commercial property to be zero-carbon by 2019?

Tutorial Questions

1. Drawing from the survey data reported in *Hitting the Green Wall…and Beyond* revisit the idea of the *circle of blame* outlined in Figure 7.6, and identify which party is still dragging its feet.
2. The government has several policy initiatives to drive change across the private sector. Write a paragraph describing one of the current ideas relating to sustainability and compare your answer to others in your group.
3. The 800 respondents reported on in the article represent a sample from 7,000 that were e-mailed between 14 October and 10 November 2009. Think broadly about the implication of this data and review the argument about firms differentiating their products and the general pace of change.

Tutorial 5

Glossary

A

affordable housing An adequate standard of housing that is cheaper than equivalents generally available in the local market. Examples include subsidised rented housing, subsidised low-cost home ownership including shared ownership, and in some market situations cheap housing for sale. It is an aim of local planning policy to assure the provision of appropriate quantities of housing in this category.

aggregate demand (AD) All planned expenditures for the entire economy summed together.

aggregate supply (AS) All planned production for the entire economy summed together.

allocative efficiency The use of resources that generate the highest possible value of output as determined in the market economy by consumers; also referred to as economic efficiency.

asset Anything of value that is owned.

asymmetric information A situation where two parties to an economic transaction have unequal knowledge of the risks involved in making that transaction.

average fixed costs Total fixed costs divided by the number of units produced.

average total costs Total costs divided by the number of units produced.

average variable costs Total variable costs divided by the number of units produced.

B

balance of payments A summary of monetary transactions with overseas nations. It is compiled as an account of inflows and outflows recording visible and invisible trade, investment earnings, transfers, and financial assets.

barriers to entry Conditions in the marketplace that make it either impossible or difficult for firms to enter an existing industry and offer competition to existing producers or suppliers. Examples of these conditions include government restrictions and legislation.

base rate The rate of interest that UK financial intermediaries use as a reference for all other interest rates for lending and receiving deposits. For example, large financial intermediaries will borrow from one another at interest rates close to the base rate.

base year A year chosen as the point of reference for comparison to other years.

benefits in kind The government provides certain goods and services, free at the point of delivery, such as health care, education and libraries. They contrast with the various benefits in cash which provide income to buy goods or services.

biocapacity The total usable biological production capacity in a given year of a productive area, for example, within a specific country. It can be expressed in global hectares.

bioproductivity This is equal to the biological production per hectare per year.

boom A period of time during which overall business activity is rising at a more rapid rate than its long-term trend.

Building Cost and Information Service (BCIS) A service set up by the Royal Institution of Chartered Surveyors in 1962 to facilitate the exchange of detailed construction costs. The information is taken from a wide range of differing contracts and traders. The BCIS publishes various indices and data is revised on a quarterly basis.

building regulations A government code of practice that specifies the type and minimum quality of materials to be used in a building. These regulations are legally enforced by district councils via the building controls officer.

Building Research Establishment (BRE) A set of government laboratories based in Garston, Watford. The BRE researches developments concerning the control of fire, energy and the environment across all types of construction.

building societies A group of financial institutions that specialise in providing long-term loans for house purchase (i.e. mortgages).

business cycles see **business fluctuations**.

business fluctuations A type of cycle found in overall economic activity, evidenced by changes in the long-term trends of national income, employment and prices; sometimes referred to as a business cycle.

C

capital All manufactured resources, including buildings, equipment, machines and improvements to land.

capital consumption see **depreciation**, which is another name for the same concept.

capital gains tax This is paid when a profit is made by selling an asset; the tax is imposed on the gain between the purchase price of an asset and its sale price, not on the total sum received.

capital goods Equipment used in the production of other goods, examples include cranes, factories and foundries.

capital value The monetary worth of an asset; the price it could be purchased for.

cartel Any arrangement made by a number of independent producers to co-ordinate their buying or selling decisions. The members of a cartel agree, in effect, to operate as if they were a monopoly. See also **collusion**.

central bank The official institution of a country which guarantees the liquidity of that nation's banking system. In some cases, the central bank monitors and supervises commercial banks on the government's behalf. It normally acts as banker to the banks and other nationally important institutions. It is usually owned by the government and manages the national debt, exchange rates and the issuing of currency. With the birth of the euro in 1999, the monetary policies of 11 respective central banks were delegated to the European central bank in Frankfurt.

Central Statistical Office (CSO) A government office responsible for statistical services up until 1996.

centrally planned model A theoretical system in which the government controls the factors of production and makes all decisions about their use and about the distribution of income. This system is often associated with communism and is sometimes referred to as a pure command system.

ceteris paribus The assumption that all other things are held equal, or constant, except those under study.

circular flow model A model of the flows of resources, goods and services, and the corresponding payments for them in the economy.

claimant unemployment This is a record of the number of people claiming unemployment-related benefits on one particular day each month.

cobweb theorem A model that tries to explain why cyclical fluctuations in output and prices occur in the property and agricultural sectors.

coincident indicators Economic statistics that are used by economic forecasters to track movements in the economy. For example, changes in output and the stock levels of raw material confirm that an economy is changing.

collusion An agreement, written or unwritten, between producers to determine prices, share out markets and/or set production levels.

commercial bank A privately owned profit-seeking institution, sometimes referred to as a joint stock bank to highlight the fact that it has shareholders. High street banks, such as NatWest, HSBC and Barclays, are examples of commercial banks.

community infrastructure levy A type of tax that allows local authorities to charge developers a tariff to contribute towards infrastructure requirements.

Competition Commission This is an independent government agency established by an act of parliament in 1998. (It replaced the Monopolies and Mergers Commission – MMC.) It conducts inquiries into mergers, markets and the major regulated industries.

complementary goods Two goods are considered complementary if both are used together. The more you buy of one, the more you buy of the other – and vice versa. For example, bricks and cement are complementary goods.

Confederation of British Industry (CBI) Founded in 1965 to represent the interests of British firms. Membership consists of thousands of companies, plus hundreds of trade associations and employers' federations. Its main aim is to express views to government.

consumer (or consumption) goods Goods that are used directly by households to generate satisfaction; in contrast to capital goods.

consumer price index (CPI) A monthly measure of the overall cost of goods and services purchased by the average household. Since January 2004 it has been the official target used by the UK government to monitor inflation. The CPI is similar to the Retail Prices Index (RPI), but there are differences in coverage and methodology.

consumer sovereignty The concept implies that the consumer is 'king'. In other words, it is the consumer who ultimately determines which goods and services will be produced in the economy.

corporate social responsibility Contribution of businesses to sustainable development, achieved by taking into account their economic, social and environmental impacts in the way they operate.

cost-benefit analysis (CBA) This is a way of appraising a proposed development. It involves taking into account the external costs and benefits as well as the conventional private costs and benefits. This is done by estimating monetary values for aspects such as health, time, leisure and pollution.

cost-push inflation A rise in price level associated with a rise in production costs, e.g. the price of raw materials.

cover price This describes a situation where a bidder agrees (colludes) with a competitor when placing a tender for work to distort the market by quoting a price that is intended to be too high to win the contract. As a result the tendering authority, such as a local council or other client, is left with a false impression of the level of competition and this may result in it paying a higher price than is necessary.

credit crunch A situation that emerged in the financial markets in 2007 in which lenders began to raise the cost of borrowing and restrict the supply of loans.

cyclical indicators Economic statistics that are used by economic forecasters to analyse the state of the economy.

See entries for leading, lagging and coincident indicators.

D

deflation This is a persistent fall in the general price level of goods and services – the opposite to inflation.

demand function A symbolised representation of the relationship between the quantity demanded of a good and its various determinants. It looks like an algebraic equation but it is actually just shorthand notation.

demand-pull inflation An increase in price level caused by total demand exceeding the current level of supply.

demand schedule A series showing various possible prices and the quantities demanded at each price. In other words, a schedule showing the rate of planned purchase per time period at different prices.

depression The term given to a serious and prolonged economic slump; the most famous example being the great depression of the 1930s. In modern terms it could be described as an extended recession.

deregulation A term popularised since 1979 to describe a situation in any industry where statutory barriers to competition are liberalised or removed.

design and build An all-embracing agreement whereby a contractor agrees to undertake building, engineering work, design and cost estimating as part of a package for a client.

developer's profit The amount which covers the risk element between start and completion of a project plus an element of profit on the venture. A developer's profit has two elements: the return for

undertaking a project and a compensation for the risk involved.

direct policy A phrase used to distinguish direct government intervention from broader macroeconomic policies. Direct policy tends to be of a legislative nature.

direct relationship A relationship between two variables that is positive, such that an increase in one is associated with an increase in the other, and a decrease in one is associated with a decrease in the other.

diseconomies of scale When increases in output lead to increases in long-run average costs.

disinflation A term coined in the early 1980s to describe the trend of a fall in the rate of inflation.

E

ecological deficit The amount by which the ecological footprint of a population exceeds the biocapacity of the population's territory.

ecological footprint A national accounting tool to enable a government to estimate the resource consumption and waste assimilation requirements of a specific geographical territory.

ecological reserve Biocapacity in a territory that is not used for consumption by the population of that territory.

economic goods Any good or service that is scarce.

economic growth An increase in an economy's real level of output over time; normally measured by the rate of change of national income from one year to the next.

economic system The institutional means through which resources are used to satisfy human want.

economically active A statistical category that refers to the population who are either in employment or unemployed.

economically inactive People who are neither in employment nor unemployed. These include those who want a job but have not been seeking work in the last four weeks, those who want a job and are seeking work but not available to start, and those who do not want a job.

economics A social science studying the way in which individuals and societies choose among the alternative uses of scarce resources to satisfy wants.

economies of scale When increases in output lead to decreases in long-run average costs.

effective demand Demand that involves desire and ability to pay. In other words, it is the demand that can be measured by actual spending.

efficiency see **allocative efficiency** and **productive efficiency**.

embodied energy The energy used to create property, such as the extraction of raw material, the manufacture and process of components and the need to transport them to site.

endogenous variables These are economic factors that affect other aspects of a theory or model from within. For example, the level of unemployment will determine the amount of income tax collected.

Energy Performance Certificate (EPC) An official document that shows how energy efficient a property is as a building, in terms of its fabric and its services (i.e. heating, cooling, hot water, ventilation and lighting). The rating is stated on an A-G scale, and is similar to the colour coded labels that are provided with domestic appliances such as refrigerators and washing machines.

enterprise culture A term used since 1979 to describe a hard-working, efficient society driven forward by the profit motive in freely competitive markets.

entrepreneur A factor of production involving human resources that perform the functions of raising capital, organising, managing, assembling other factors of production and making basic business decisions. The entrepreneur is a risk-taker.

equilibrium A situation in which the plans of buyers and sellers exactly coincide so that there is neither excess supply nor excess demand.

equilibrium price The price that clears the market, at which there is no excess quantity demanded or supplied; also known as the market-clearing price.

equity see **horizontal equity** and **vertical equity**.

equity withdrawal In property parlance, the term equity can be used to represent the owner's fund. For example, if you buy a £100,000 house of which £60,000 is borrowed 'potentially' you may be able to release the £40,000 that you own; hence the phrase equity withdrawal.

excludability see **principle of exclusion**.

exogenous variables These are economic factors that impinge upon a theory or model from the outside, e.g. the weather. They are sometimes referred to as autonomous variables; and they contrast with endogenous variables.

expenditure approach A way of measuring economic activity (see **gross domestic product**) by adding up the values of all spending on final goods and services.

externalities The benefits or costs that are experienced by parties other than the immediate seller and buyer in a transaction. Also known as external costs or benefits.

F

factor markets In this market, households are the sellers; they sell resources such as labour, land, capital and entrepreneurial ability. Businesses are the buyers of these resources to generate output (see Figure 8.1).

factors of production Often grouped under four headings. See **resources**.

Financial Services Authority (FSA) An organisation responsible for regulating and supervising all financial intermediaries in the UK.

fiscal policy A combination of government spending and taxation used to achieve macroeconomic management.

fixed costs The costs that do not vary with output. Fixed costs include such things as rent on a building and the price of machinery. These costs are fixed for a certain period of time; in the long run they are variable.

free enterprise A system in which private business firms are able to obtain resources, to organise those resources and to sell the finished product in any way they choose.

free goods Any good or service that is available in quantities larger than are desired at a zero price.

free market model A theoretical economic system in which individuals privately own productive resources and can use these resources in whatever manner they choose. Other terms for this type of system are a 'pure market' or 'pure capitalist economy'.

free rider Individuals who do not pay for the goods and services that they consume.

full repairing and insuring lease (FRI lease) Rental terms under which the tenant bears most of the running and maintenance cost. Institutional investors favour these leases.

G

global hectare is 1 hectare (2.47 acres) of biologically productive space. In the 21st century the biosphere had approximately 11. 3 billion hectares of biologically productive area; this corresponds to roughly one-quarter of the planet's surface.

golden rule A fiscal objective that constrains government only to borrow to finance investment not to fund current spending.

government failure The concept that government policy intervention may not necessarily improve economic efficiency.

government intervention Measures undertaken by the state to achieve goals not guaranteed by the market system.

gross domestic product (GDP) The most common measurement of a nation's income generated from resources within its own boundaries – the monetary value of its output of goods and services.

gross national income (GNI) A measurement of a country's wealth. It represents the total output of goods and services produced by the country in a year, in terms of residence of the owners of productive resources. In other words, it is GDP plus the net value of overseas assets.

H

harmonised index of consumer prices (HICP) A standard measure of consumer price inflation that allows comparison between EU countries. The series commenced in January 1996 and became the official target of government policy in 2004. It is usually referred to as the consumer price index.

headline inflation rate The change in the Retail Price Index that is announced in the UK government's monthly press release. It contrasts to the official rate of inflation, which is based on the consumer price index.

Henry George theorem An idea proposed by an American economist named Henry George that dates to 1880. He advocated that all public funds should be raised from a single tax on land.

hereditament A legal term used to distinguish a property asset that can be valued as a separate item for inheritance or business rate purposes. Broadly speaking, these are buildings or premises within buildings.

horizontal equity The concept that all people should be treated identically; an idea that informs policy directed towards equal opportunities.

human capital Investment in education and training that enhances the productivity of individuals.

I

ILO measure The International Labour Organisation measure of unemployment; see next entry.

ILO unemployment rate A measure of unemployment produced by the International Labour Organisation. It defines unemployment as people who are without work yet actively seeking employment. Data is gathered through labour force surveys.

income approach A way of measuring gross domestic product by adding up all factor rewards – that is, the sum of wages, interest, rent and profits.

index numbers A way of expressing the relative change of a variable between one period of time and another, selected as the 'base year'. For example, the base year index number is set at 100 and the value of the variable in subsequent years is expressed above or below 100 according to its percentage deviation from the base.

inferior good A good of which the consumer purchases less as income increases. Goods of this nature are exceptions to the general rule.

inflation A sustained rise in prices, which is officially measured by the consumer price index.

inheritance tax Makes a compulsory transfer of funds from an individual estate to the government at the time of death, it only applies, however, if the taxable value of the estate on death is over a certain amount (for example, this amount was £325,000 in the tax year 2009–2010).

institutional model This is a kind of Darwinian approach to economics that emphasises how changes to the political, social, legal, financial and professional framework effect the nature of markets over time.

interest rates These are the payments made as the cost of obtaining credit, or the rewards paid to owners of capital.

International Monetary Fund (IMF) An organisation set up to monitor the world's financial system. It was established in 1944 to supervise the newly established fixed exchange rate system. Since this collapsed in 1971–1973 it has become more involved with the macroeconomic policies of member countries.

inverse relationship A relationship between two variables in which an increase in one variable is associated with a decrease in the other, and vice versa

investment Spending by businesses on things like machines and buildings, which can be used to produce goods and services in the future.

Investment Property Databank (IPD) The name of a UK company devoted to the objective analysis of property. The index is based on a large sample of the total commercial property market.

investor-developer A property company that retains completed schemes as part of its own asset portfolio.

J

joint-stock bank see **commercial bank**.

K

Keynesian economics A branch of economics based on the ideas of John Maynard Keynes. It is characterised by a belief in government intervention to correct the sluggish nature of labour markets. Keynes' ideas formed a central part of economic and government thinking for 30 years following the Second World War.

L

labour The human resource involved in production; in other words, the contributions of people who work.

lagging indicators Economic statistics (such as unemployment and investment) that change approximately 12 months after a change in overall activity.

land The factor of production that is virtually fixed in quantity. In the economic sense, it includes both the physical space and natural resources, such as coal, oil and water, natural vegetation and climate.

law of demand Quantity demanded and price are inversely related – more is bought at a lower price; less at a higher price (other things being equal). Also known as the *theory of demand*.

law of diminishing (marginal) returns States that after some point, successive increases in a variable factor of production, such as labour, added to fixed factors of production, will result in less than a proportional increase in output.

law of increasing costs States that in order to get additional units of a good, society must sacrifice ever-increasing amounts of other goods. It is also referred to as the law of increasing opportunity costs.

law of supply The relationship between price and quantity supplied (other things remaining equal) is a direct one. For example, as price increases so does the quantity supplied.

leading indicators Economic statistics (such as retail sales and consumer credit) that change approximately six months in advance of gross domestic product and are used to predict changes in the economic cycle.

liabilities The legal claims for payment that can be made on an institution or company. In short, the amount owing to others.

liquidity This describes the ease with which an asset can be used to meet liabilities. Cash is the most liquid asset.

long run Time period in which all factors of production can be varied.

loosely coupled system Every industrial activity is, to some extent, interdependent with a number of other activities; that is, they are coupled in some way. Some of the couplings are 'tight' while others are 'loose'. Construction and property development are typified as loosely coupled activities as the firms involved in each sector operate fairly independently of others.

low inflation A term used to describe a trend of annual price increases below 5%.

M

macroeconomics The study of economy-wide phenomena, such as total consumer expenditure.

macroeconomic objectives Targets relating to the whole economy, such as employment, price stability and the balance of payments.

market An abstract concept concerning all the arrangements that individuals have for exchanging with one another. Thus, we can speak of the labour market, the car market, the commercial property market, the housing market, the building materials market, the credit market and so on.

market-based instruments These involve various incentive systems designed to operate through the price mechanism to encourage environmentally friendly behaviour. Examples include carbon taxes, the climate change levy and landfill tax.

market-clearing price see **equilibrium price**.

market economy An economy in which prices are used to signal the value of resources to firms and households.

market failure A situation in which the free forces of supply and demand lead to either an under- or over-allocation of resources to a specific economic activity.

market mechanism see **market economy** and/or **price mechanism**.

market structures The characteristics of a market that determine the behaviour of participating firms, such as the number of buyers and sellers, and the ease of entry into (and exit from) a market.

market supply schedule A set of numbers showing the quantity supplied at various prices by the firms comprising the industry. The horizontal summation at each price suggests the market supply.

maximum price legislation A price ceiling set by a government agency that identifies a level in a specific market beyond which prices must not rise.

menu costs Just as a restaurant has to print a new menu when it changes the price of its food, other firms also face a potential outlay each time they revise contracts due to inflation.

merit good A good that has been deemed socially desirable by politicians. If left to the private market these goods may be under consumed.

microeconomics Study of the economic behaviour of individual households and firms and how prices of goods and services are determined.

MITR see **mortgage interest tax relief**.

mixed economy An economic system in which the decision about how resources should be used is made partly by the private sector and partly by the government.

models Simplified representations of the real world used to make predictions and to provide greater clarity to economic explanations.

monetary policy A policy, usually implemented by the central bank, to control inflation rates by influencing aggregate demand through changes in interest rates.

monetary policy committee (MPC) A Bank of England committee, established in 1997, to set interest rates independently of HM Treasury, in order to achieve the UK government's predetermined target rate of inflation.

money supply A generic term used to denote the amount of 'money' in circulation, which has many definitions; some include different types of bank deposits.

monopoly A market structure where a single supplier dominates the market.

mortgage interest tax relief (MITR) A government subsidy paid to mortgage holders, that dates back to 1805 when allowances were permitted on various forms of loan interest. It is no longer in operation in the UK.

multiplier The number by which an initial injection into an economy must be multiplied to find the eventual change in national income.

N

national accounts An annual record of an economy's performance.

national income A generic term for all that is produced, earned and spent in a country during one year. Strictly speaking, it is defined as GNI minus capital depreciation.

national income accounting A measurement system used to estimate gross domestic product (GDP) and gross national income.

national insurance contributions (NICs) A type of tax that entitles one to social security benefits and a retirement pension. The amount of contribution depends on how much you earn and whether you're employed or self-employed.

nationalised industries These are government owned and run industrial sectors, in the sense that the products are sold through the market and priced accordingly; examples of such industries vary from time to time and country to country.

negative equity This describes a situation in which the value of someone's home has fallen below the value of their mortgage; approximately one million people were in this position during 1993.

neutral equilibrium A theoretical concept closely associated with a two-sector economy where the established levels of activity persist forever, since there are no pressures for change.

new economy A term coined in the late 1990s to describe a way of restructuring economies through the use of information technology.

normal goods Goods for which demand increases as income increases; by definition this includes most products and services.

normal profit The minimum rate of profit necessary to ensure that a sufficient number of people will be prepared to undertake risks and organise production. In more formal terms, it is the normal rate of return on investment which differs from industry to industry.

O

OFCOM see **Office of communications**.

Office of communications The office that regulates the activities of those involved in communications; it has responsibilities across television, radio, telecommunications and wireless services.

Office of Fair Trading This government agency was established in 1973. Since then it has acquired the acronym OFT. Its purpose is to protect consumer interests.

Office of Gas and Electricity Markets This office is funded by the energy companies who are licensed to run the gas and electricity infrastructure. Their first priority is to protect the consumers' interests by promoting effective competition.

Office of National Statistics (ONS) The government agency responsible for compiling and distributing official statistics on the UK's economy, demography and society at a national and local level.

Office of Water Services (OFWAT) The government's water services authority responsible for regulating sewerage and water in England and Wales.

official rate of inflation In most industrialised countries, the target, or, typically, the mid-point of a target range, for consumer price inflation is between

1% and 2.5%. In the UK, the current official target rate of inflation is 2%, as measured by the consumer price index.

offshoring A process where certain functions of a company are moved overseas where they can perform at a lower cost.

offsite production The production of a whole section of a building, such as a bathroom pod or shop fitting that is brought to site from a factory. This has the potential to improve standards and efficiency in construction as it reduces defects, improves safety and increases productivity.

OFGEM see **Office of Gas and Electricity Markets**.

OFWAT see **Office of Water Services**.

oligopoly A situation in which a large part of the market is supplied by a small number of firms. The firms may behave as if they are interdependent.

opportunity cost The highest-valued alternative that has to be sacrificed to obtain something else.

output approach A way of measuring gross domestic product by adding up the value of the output produced by each sector of the economy.

outsourcing The provision of business services and accommodation by third parties in exchange for rent and income.

P

particulars delivered (PD forms) These are official instruments used to administer any transfer or sale of land or property. The relevant 'particulars' of the transaction must be 'delivered' to the HMRC Stamp Duty Office and Land Registry within 30 days of the transfer.

partnering A broadly defined term to describe a situation in which two or more organisations work openly together (over one or several projects) to improve performance by agreeing mutual objectives and ways for resolving any disputes.

per capita A Latin phrase meaning per head of the population.

perfect competition A theoretical model in which the decisions of buyers and sellers have no effect on market price.

perfectly competitive firm A firm that is such a small part of the total industry picture that it cannot affect the price of the product it sells.

perfectly elastic A supply or demand curve characterised by a reduction in quantity to zero when there is the slightest increase or decrease in price. Producers and consumers are 100% responsive to any change of price. This concept is associated with firms in perfect competition.

perfectly inelastic The characteristic of a supply or demand curve for which quantity supplied remains constant, no matter what happens to price. Producers and consumers are completely unresponsive to price changes.

planning gain A trade-off arrangement between a local authority and developer, formalised in a section 106 agreement, that permits a developer to build in return for funding or organising some community benefit(s). A common example involves the provision of social housing as an integral part of a proposal to develop a new housing scheme.

planning regulations Each local authority has a set of plans on how its area will develop and a committee responsible for deciding what is allowed to be built and where. The terms of reference are determined by centrally produced planning policy statements and guidance.

polluter pays principle A strategy based on market incentives to assure that those who pollute are encouraged to reduce the costs that fall on society. The principle was succinctly set out in 1987 by the Secretary of State for the Environment: 'The polluter must bear the cost of pollution'.

post-occupancy survey These involve questioning tenants about experiences relating to their property's performance. The survey is carried out after the tenants have been resident for a short period of time.

price elasticity A measurement of the responsiveness of the quantity demanded/supplied to a range in unit price.

price elasticity of supply A measurement of the responsiveness of the quantity produced for the market due to a change in price.

price index The cost of today's basket of goods expressed as a percentage of the cost of the same basket during a base year.

price-inelastic demand When a change in price results in a less than proportionate change in demand.

price mechanism Prices are used as a signalling system between firms and households concerning the use of resources. Where the price mechanism operates there is a market economy, consequently the terms 'price' and 'market' are interchangeable.

price system An economic system in which (relative) prices are constantly changing to reflect changes in supply and demand for different commodities. The prices of commodities are signals to everyone within the system about which are relatively expensive and which are relatively cheap.

price-taker A key characteristic of a perfectly competitive firm. A price-taker is a firm that must take the price of its product as given from those that it competes with.

principal-agent A concept used to highlight market failure caused by a conflict of interests between the consumer (buyer or tenant) of a good or service, and the supplier (the agent), such as a developer or property owner.

principle of exclusion This means that anyone who does not pay will not be allowed to benefit from consuming a particular good or service.

principle of rivalry The principle that private goods cannot be shared. If person A uses a private good, then that prevents the possibility of person B using that good. Persons A and B cannot eat the same apple simultaneously.

private commercial A category used to consider privately funded commercial developments such as shops, offices and leisure facilities.

private finance initiative (PFI) A form of procurement devised to encourage private investment in public sector projects. PFI consortiums are typically responsible for the construction, finance and management of a facility and thereby provide support services for a period of years following construction.

private goods A product that can only be consumed by one individual at a time. Private goods are subject to the principle of exclusion.

private industrial A category used for considering the construction of privately funded developments like factories and warehouses. Since the privatisation of public utilities such as gas, water, electricity, the significance of this category has increased.

privatisation In very general terms, this involves the transfer of assets from the public sector to the private sector.

procurement A generic term used by professionals within the built environment to describe the general process of obtaining, acquiring or securing some property or land.

productive efficiency The utilisation of the cheapest production technique for any given output rate; no inputs are wilfully wasted. Also known as 'technical' efficiency.

profit The income generated by selling something for a higher price than was paid for it. In production, the income generated is the difference between total revenues received from consumers who purchase the goods and the total cost of producing those goods.

progressive income tax A tax system in which, as one earns more income, a higher percentage of the additional income is taxed.

project partnering An arrangement between the main contractor and the client working together on a single project. It is designed to encourage contractors to consider the long-term operational success of a project.

Public choice theory A relatively new concept to mainstream economics, that seeks to explain how government policy is selected.

public goods Goods and services that can be consumed by everybody in society, or nobody at all. In technical language, for goods in this category the principles of exclusion and rivalry do not apply.

public private partnership (PPP) This is a specific type of contractual arrangement between the public sector and private sector firms. These give the private sector a greater role in financing, building and maintaining public sector facilities, although the government retains a stake in the PPP company.

public (non-residential) An accounting category used to consider the construction of roads, prisons and schools etc. In short, public sector works other than housing.

public sector The simplest definition is to include all forms of ownership by central and local government.

public sector net cash requirement (PSNCR) This is a measure of the public sector's short-term financing requirement. It covers the combined funding requirement of both central and local government. The concept was previously known as the public sector borrowing requirement (PSBR).

Q

quantitative easing The purchase of financial assets by a central bank with the expressed objective to increase the supply of money in the economy, and ease conditions in credit markets.

quasi-public goods Goods or services which by their nature could be made available for purchase by individuals, but the state finds it administratively, more convenient to provide them (e.g. roads).

R

Real Estate Investment Trusts (REITs) A property fund based on tax incentives designed to improve the flow of funds into commercial and residential property. Several models exist around the world, the longest standing being in the US and Australia. The UK government introduced them in January 2007.

real rate of interest The rate of interest obtained by subtracting the rate of inflation from the nominal rate of interest.

real value Measurement of economic values after adjustments have been made for inflation; also referred to as real terms.

recession A period of time during which the rate of growth of business activity is consistently less than its long-term trend, or is negative. If it is unduly prolonged, a recession may become referred to as an economic depression.

recovery The phase of a business cycle when output begins to rise towards the long-term trend.

registered social landlords A group of private organisations that manage approximately two million homes for tenants on lower incomes with support from the government. Examples of organisations on the register include charitable companies, housing associations and co-ownership societies.

rent controls A law which imposes a price ceiling on rents charged for private rented accommodation. First introduced in 1915, the initial intention was to protect tenants from unscrupulous landlords; subsequently, however, rent controls distorted the housing market (see Figure 6.3 on page 93).

rental value The periodic return (monthly/yearly) that a property might reasonably be expected to command in the open market at a given time.

repo rate The interest rate at which the Bank of England lends on a short-term basis to the UK banking sector.

resource allocation The assignment of resources to their various uses. More specifically, it means determining what will be produced, how it will be produced, who will produce it and for whom it will be produced.

resources Inputs used in the production of the goods and services; commonly categorised as land, labour, capital and entrepreneur (see separate dictionary entries for details). Factors of production are another way to refer to resources.

retail price index (RPI) A statistical measure of the change in the prices of goods and services bought for the purpose of consumption by the vast majority of households in the UK.

Right to Buy (RTB) Government legislation that was passed in 1980 to allow council tenants of two or three years' standing the legal power to acquire their houses at a discount of the market value.

Royal Institute of British Architects (RIBA) The principal professional body in the UK concerned with architecture; established in 1834.

Royal Institution of Chartered Surveyors (RICS) The main UK professional body concerned with surveying in its various guises; founded in 1868.

S

sale and leaseback The splitting up of a trading company into an operating company and a property company; the so-called 'opco-propco' structure.

satellite accounts An extension to the national accounting system used to describe areas or activities not dealt with by the core economic accounts.

scarcity A reference to the fact that at any point in time there exists only a finite amount of resources in relation to the infinite amount of 'wants' that people have for goods and services.

seasonally adjusted A process of estimating regularly occurring effects caused by weather and holidays and removing them from the data.

serviced office A commercial property where the landlord provides a complete range of services such as furniture, cleaning, IT, reception and secretarial support, etc.

short run The time period in which a firm cannot alter its current size of plant.

sick building syndrome Defined by the World Health Organisation as a general feeling of malaise caused by working in certain modern buildings. No definite causes have yet been identified, but reference to mechanically ventilated buildings do seem to be prevalent in the literature reporting this syndrome.

social housing Dwellings provided for households in 'need' by Local Authorities and Registered Social Landlords. It is usually rented, but may be owned on a shared basis, in all cases the provision is below market cost; the difference being made up by government subsidy.

social price The total price when all costs and benefits have been considered, i.e. when the private costs and benefits are added to the external costs and benefits.

stable equilibrium A situation in which, if there is a shock that disturbs the existing relationship between the forces of supply and demand, there will normally be self-corrective forces that automatically cause the disequilibrium to be remedied.

strategic partnering An agreement between a contractor and client to work together on a series of construction projects in order to promote continuous improvement.

substitute goods Two goods are considered substitutes when one can be used in place of the other. A change in the price of one, therefore, causes a shift in demand for the other. For example, if the price of butter goes up, the demand for margarine will rise; if the price of butter goes down, the demand for margarine will decrease.

supply curve The graphic representation of the supply schedule; a line showing the supply schedule, which slopes upwards (has a positive slope).

supply-side economics This generally refers to government attempts at creating incentives for individuals and firms to increase productivity; i.e., it is concerned with the level of aggregate supply.

sustainable development In general terms, this represents progress that balances social, environmental and economic concerns. As a consequence there are several specific definitions for the two that are most widely quoted, see Table 9.2 (page 153).

sustainable investment rule A fiscal rule stating that public sector net debt as a proportion of GDP should be held over the economic cycle at a stable level – say, below 40% of GDP.

T

tax bracket A specified interval of income to which a specific and unique marginal tax rate is applied.

tax burden The distribution of tax incidence within society.

third party Persons who are external to negotiations and activities between buyers and sellers. For example, if person A buys a car with no brakes and then runs person B over, person B becomes a third party to the deal struck between person A and the seller of the car.

tightly coupled systems An industry typified by close relationships and high levels of co-ordination between producers. For example, manufacturing displays many tightly coupled systems. In contrast property development is characterised by loosely coupled systems.

total costs All costs of a firm combined. For example, rent, payments to workers, interest on borrowed money, rates and material costs.

total expenditure The total monetary value of all the final goods and services bought in an economy during the year.

total income The total amount earned by the nation's resources (factors). National income, therefore, includes wages, rent, interest payments and profits; received respectively, by workers, landowners, providers of capital and entrepreneurs.

total output The total value of all the final goods and services produced in the economy during the year.

trade balance the difference between the value of goods and services one country sells to other countries and the value of the goods and services it buys from other countries.

trader-developer A property company that disposes completed schemes (often to institutional fund holders) in order to raise collateral for the next development.

transaction costs All of the costs associated with exchanging; such as the costs of finding out price, quality, service record and durability, and the cost of enforcing any contract.

transition economies A term popularised in 1989 (following the fall of the Berlin Wall) to refer to economies of Eastern Europe and the former Soviet Union that were moving from a centrally planned to a market system. The term, however, can be used less strictly to refer to any economy changing its system of resource allocation.

U

upwards-only rent review This is a standard clause of a commercial property lease. It permits the landlord to raise the rent at set intervals. For example, the traditional lease ran for 25 years with upward reviews every five years.

V

variable costs Costs that vary with the rate of production; they include wages paid to workers, the costs of materials etc.

vendor A seller of land and property.

vertical equity A concept used to achieve social justice or fairness by providing benefits targeted at people with specific needs; this idea supports means-tested benefits and taxing the rich more heavily than the poor.

X

x-inefficiency The organisational slack that emerges when a sector (or firm) is not in a competitive market-place. It can result in relatively high unit costs.

References to Further Reading

British Property Federation, Taylor Wessing and Spada (2010) *Hitting the Green Wall…and Beyond: How is the UK development industry building sustainable foundations?* Taylor Wessing: London

CABE (2010) *Getting the Big Picture Right: A guide to large scale urban design.* Commission for Architecture and the Built Environment: London

Dixon, T. (ed.) (2005) *Real Estate and the New Economy.* Blackwell publishing: Oxford

Egan, J. (1998) *Rethinking Construction.* Report of the Construction Task Force to the Deputy Prime Minister, John Prescott, on the scope for improving the quality and efficiency of UK construction, Construction Task Force

Guy, S. and Henneberry, J. (ed.) (2002) *Development and Developers: perspectives on property.* Blackwell Publishing: Oxford

Harris, R. (2005) *Property and the Office Economy.* Estates Gazette Books: London

IPCC (2007) *Fourth Assessment Report.* Cambridge University Press (Chapter 6 is about commercial and residential buildings. Each Chapter is available as a download.)

Jackson, T. (2009) *Prosperity without Growth: Economics for a Finite Planet.* Earthscan: London

Kaletsky, A. (2010) *Capitalism 4.0: The birth of a new economy.* Bloomsbury Publishing: London

Malpass, P. and Rowlands, R. (eds) (2010) *Housing, Markets and Policy.* Routledge: London and New York

Weizsäcker, E., Lovins, A. and Lovins, H. (1998) *Factor Four: Doubling Wealth, Halving Resource Use.* Earthscan: London

Wolstenholme, A. (2009) *Never Waste a Good Crisis: A Review of Progress since Rethinking Construction and Thoughts for Our Future.* Constructing Excellence: London

Outline Answers

Tutorial Reading 1

Answers to Tutorial Questions on Page 36.

1. **From the above extracts, select examples that can be used to fully explain any two of the economic concepts introduced so far.**

   There are more than 20 emboldened terms in Chapters 1 and 2 that could be explored. Using examples drawn from the four extracts, the easiest to exemplify are the following: government planning (intervention); opportunity cost; market mechanism; scarcity, investment and/or resource allocation due to price signals; supply and demand; etc.

2. **Using economic ideas summarise the recurrent themes of all four extracts.**

   Each extract describes the state of the market. These can be summarised in various ways, such as: the different rents stated per square foot across office and retail and/or comparing and contrasting retail rents across shopping centres; opportunity costs; the fact that the decisions are reliant on Flagship tenants; and the idea of the mixed-economy could be used to good effect.

Tutorial Reading 2

Answers to Tutorial Questions on Page 63.

1. **Can the free market be left to allocate housing?**

   The answer should not simply be 'no'. At the very least after reading Chapters 2, 3 and 4, some review of the different forms of housing tenure would be expected; there needs to be some acknowledgement that the housing market comprises at least four sectors. The owner-occupied sector is largely market-determined. Financial restrictions to entry, however, necessitate government intervention to provide for those in need of social housing.

2. **Using supply and demand analysis explain and discuss the function of price signals in housing markets.**

   In theory, 'price' signals changes in supply and demand. In any property market, these signals are sluggish as there is a marked time-lag between the planning and delivery of the finished product. This could effectively be discussed using a supply and demand diagram similar to the one in Figure 4.4 (some reference to the inelastic nature of supply should be alluded to). If the supply of social housing decreases, then theoretically the market rent should increase. However, if there are fewer subsidies there is a chance that the increase might not be possible. It all depends if the landlords have previously over-priced the product on the basis of the high rate of housing benefit paid by the government.

3. **The article suggests that social housing providers will need to adapt to changes in market conditions if they are to continue acquiring sources of funding in the future. State two examples of the changes that are envisaged in the market for social housing.**

As stated in the article, in future the emphasis for social housing provision will become more reliant on private sector funds and less reliant on the tax payer. Several possibilities are outlined in the article, such as: (1) encouraging housing associations to issue bonds as a means of raising capital; (2) promoting shared equity schemes where the tenant partly rents and partly buys (the proportions and arrangement being decided in conjunction with a developer and/or housing association); and (3) introducing greater flexibility to encourage new providers into the market by allowing companies to become 'for profit registered social housing providers'.

4. **In what ways would the answers change if commercial property became the point of focus to questions 1 and 2?**

The commercial market is driven by profit-seeking enterprises. As a result, most of the property in the sector is allocated without government intervention. The answer to questions 1 and 2 would, therefore, involve fewer qualifying remarks.

Tutorial Reading 3

Answers to Tutorial Questions on Page 100.

1. **Comparisons are often drawn between the automotive and offshore oil industries. Identify at least two reasons for the comparison.**

There are several possible reasons for the comparisons being made, such as these sectors have: effective supply chain management/integrated processes/employ modern methods of production/use partnerships/ accept change, etc.

2. **Various forms of government intervention mean that much of the demand for construction output is derived from the public sector: (a) Identify the two most obvious examples, and (b) broadly interpreted what percentage of total construction demand is currently derived from the public sector.**

    (a) PFI and regulated industries

    (b) Wolstenholme (2009) estimated that widely interpreted the public sector accounts for up to 40% of total construction demand. Cut backs may have reduced this slightly – but you should be able to make an up to date estimate using data from the *Construction Statistics Annual*.

3. **What would you recommend to the government to increase the pace of change in the construction industry?**

This answer could go off in several directions but we anticipate the idea that: the government could lead by example, or the market should be left to its own devices. Finally, it might be worth noting that this question is also the subject matter of Chapters 6 to 9.

Tutorial Reading 4

Answers to Tutorial Questions on Page 147.

1. **Identify what you would expect the *Estates Gazette* to focus on from the Budget of June 2010 and why.**

The *Estates Gazette* would address those aspects that would be of interest to its readership, namely: the changes to capital gains tax, cuts to social housing, and the new private sector opportunities that might open up following the public sector cut backs.

In fact a search of the *Estates Gazette* archive **reveals** the following items:

- *Budget 2010: Industry concerns focus on VAT and CGT rises* – 22 June 2010
- *Some gains, more pain ahead* – 26 June 2010 (an editorial discussing the Budget, in particular how it provided the opportunity to deal with the UK's woes; but left an awful lot of issues unresolved).
- *Emergency Budget: views from the auction room* – 26 June 2010.
- *The Budget and World Cup exit leave us with very little to cheer* – 3 July 2010 (this drew an analogy between the National psyche deflated by World Cup defeat and Housebuilders playing down fears resulting from proposed Budget cuts).

2. **Explain and discuss the line of argument adopted by The Economist.**

   The article seems to suggest that the British government should commit itself to a radical overhaul of the British budget; to tear up the election pledges and start from scratch.

   It suggests that the Chancellor of the Exchequer, George Osborne, will need serious cuts in government spending and also tax raises (such as VAT and carbon tax) if the country's fiscal deficit is to reduce to a manageable level. For a more explicit idea of *The Economist* argument search the archive in an academic library or website for: *The Economist*; 19–25 June 2010, Vol. 395, Issue 8687. Specifically *see* the leader article *This Won't Hurt (much)* – on page 11 – and the three page briefing with the fuller details entitled *Pick your Poison* (on pp 29–31).

3. **Can you identify the *current* percentage of GDP that is made up by public spending and can you trust the source?**

   For this answer to be correct you would need to look up official government data, the answer that you are looking for will be around 40 to 50%. Some data is presented in the web material that accompanies this text; it is derived from the Comprehensive Spending Review announced in October 2010.

Tutorial Reading 5

Answers to Tutorial Questions on Page 172.

1. **Drawing from the survey data reported in *Hitting the Green Wall...and Beyond* revisit the idea of the *circle of blame* outlined in Figure 7.6, and identify which party is still dragging its feet.**

   Investors are the weak link as they appear to be the least interested in sustainability (18% compared to developers 40%) and 47% of investors fail to ask about it when property is transacting.

2. **The government has several policy initiatives to drive change across the private sector. Write a paragraph describing one of the current ideas relating to sustainability and compare your answer to others in your group.**

   For example, notes could be made relating to:

   - Carbon reduction commitments
   - Tax incentives or other market-based instruments
   - Regulations
   - Targets

3. **The 800 respondents reported on in the article represent a sample from 7,000 that were e-mailed between 14 October and 10 November 2009. Think broadly about the implication of this data and review the argument about firms differentiating their products and the general pace of change.**

    800/7,000 represents a response rate of slightly more than 10% – which is quite acceptable for an e-mail based survey. However, the worrying thing is the relative few who have genuinely begun to differentiate their product. In other words, beware of surveys from agents who are trying to differentiate their products exaggerating the pace of change. It is clearly a slow gradual change, with a few firms genuinely participating.

Index